BREEDER'S GUIDE TO

MARE, FOAL & STALLION CARE

BREEDER'S GUIDE TO
MARE, FOAL & STALLION CARE

Christine M. Schweizer, DVM

Christina S. Cable, DVM

E. L. Squires, PhD

*the*HORSE HEALTH CARE LIBRARY

ECLIPSE PRESS

Lexington, Kentucky

Library of Congress Control Number: 2006928603

ISBN-13: 978-1-58150-143-8
ISBN-10: 1-58150-143-9

Printed in the United States
First Edition: 2006

Distributed to the trade by
National Book Network
4501 Forbes Blvd., Suite 200, Lanham, MD 20706
1.800.462.6420

Contents

Contents *(continued)*

FOAL CARE

STALLION CARE

Introduction

For anyone involved with breeding horses, the safe delivery and maintenance of a healthy foal are the ultimate goals. Although nature can interfere with this objective, good management practices increase the chances of success. Good management involves both the mare and the stallion and begins well in advance of conception.

Breeder's Guide to Mare, Foal & Stallion Care provides novice and experienced breeders alike easy-to-understand and necessary information to maximize the reproductive health of their mares and stallions and to ensure the well-being of their foals. It contains the latest information from the authorities in their respective fields.

In the section about the broodmare, Christine Schweizer, DVM, addresses the problems and questions she frequently encounters in her thriving broodmare practice. She provides an overview of the breeding process, explaining the broodmare's anatomy and reproductive cycles, behaviors, and health considerations. Schweizer also discusses diagnosing a pregnancy, conception challenges, expectations of a normal pregnancy and foaling, recognizing pregnancy abnormalities, and knowing when to seek a veterinarian's help. Dealing with high-risk pregnancies and late-term complications, as well as the challenges of infertility, also is covered.

Veterinarian Christina Cable shares her extensive knowledge of foals, starting with creating an optimal environment for mother and foal to bond and explaining the care and monitoring of the newborn. She discusses what owners should expect in the first weeks and months of their foals' lives and what steps they can take to keep their foals healthy. Cable also provides information on handling foal rejection and the challenges posed by orphan foals and twins. Neonatal problems such as foal diarrhea, pneumonia, and septicemia are discussed as are flexural and angular limb deformities and what to do about them.

Equine reproductive expert E.L. Squires provides an overview of reproduction in the stallion. This includes information on the anatomy and physiology of the stallion, as well as details on proper care and management such as feeding, exercise, and housing. Squires discusses teaching the stallion how to breed and what factors can affect reproductive performance. With the increasing popularity of artificial insemination, Squires provides current information on collecting, storing, and transporting cooled and frozen semen.

Pertinent photographs, a glossary, and an index provide additional resources for the reader.

This book brings together all the pieces that go into a soundly managed breeding program and thoroughly explains how humans can best work in conjunction with the natural cycles and physiology of mares and stallions to produce healthy foals.

BROODMARE
CARE

by Christine M. Schweizer,
DVM, Diplomate ACT

The Open Mare

The broodmare is at once one of the most delightful and most frustrating creatures a horse owner or veterinarian may encounter. The mare's reproductive cycle and behavior are such that even though a given mare usually follows the basic reproductive script of her species, she often will put her own individual spin on events. She might be perfectly normal; she just doesn't choose to be average. Mares will differ in intensity of behavioral signs of receptivity, reproductive tract changes, and size of ovarian follicles just before ovulation. To make matters worse, mares also will vary these findings depending on whether it is early or late in a breeding season. Fortunately, however, most mares are consistent in their "reproductive expression" on an individual basis and will tend to repeat behaviors and findings cycle to cycle. It is extremely important, therefore, to maintain accurate records and observe mares closely.

Mares' ovulations are notoriously difficult to predict exactly, and average pregnancy rates per cycle bred are in the neighborhood of 65 percent to 75 percent. Mares also experience a high percentage of early embryonic loss. It is therefore advantageous for mare managers to stack the deck in their favor to breed a mare successfully. This is especially true when assisted reproductive techniques such as artificial insemination with extended, chilled semen and frozen equine semen are being applied. Good management is vital to successful breeding of mares, and careful observation and accurate, complete records are necessary components of any breeding program.

Anatomy of the Mare's Reproductive Tract

The mare's reproductive tract is made up of internal and external structures. The mare has two kidney-shaped ovaries (a left one and a right one), each with a distinct ovulation fossa where the surface indents. All of a mare's ovulations (rupture of an ovarian follicle with simultaneous release of a fertilizable egg [or oocyte]) occur through these fossae. This differs from those domestic species that ovulate from any point on the surface of their ovaries. The mare's oviducts (uterine tubes) attach at the site of the ovulation fossa and receive the ovulated oocyte. The oviducts are the site of fertilization, and each oviduct connects to the uterus at the tip of each uterine horn, through a papilla. This papilla is called the tubo-uterine junction.

The equine uterus is shaped like a capital "T." The left and right uterine horns form the crossbar, and the uterine body forms the base. The point where the base of each uterine horn meets the apex of the uterine body is called the bifurcation. The uterine body ends at the mare's cervix. The role of the uterus is to help transport sperm to the site of fertilization (the oviducts) and to nourish and support the developing foal throughout the mare's pregnancy. The ovaries, oviducts, and uterus are suspended on either side within the mare's pelvis by the left and right broad ligaments. The broad ligaments therefore are supportive tissues to the reproductive tract. The ovarian and uterine blood-supplying vessels run through these ligaments.

The cervix serves as one of three barriers between the outside world and the uterine lumen. It is a straight, tubular structure, about the length and width of an average person's index finger. It is composed of an internal uterine opening (or os); a body; and an external, vaginal os. The cervix connects the uterus to the vagina, and during pregnancy it is tightly closed, forming a barrier seal. During foaling the cervix must dilate fully so the foal can pass from the uterus into the birth canal. The front (or cranial) end of the vagina begins at the external cervical os and the back of the vagina (or caudal vagina) ends at the vestibular-vaginal junction — the second barrier between the outside world and the uterine lumen. When fully extended, the equine vagina is about 12 inches long in the average 1,000 to 1,200-pound mare, and runs horizontally along the pelvic floor. The vagina has the dual role of being the copulatory organ and the birth canal. The vestibule connects the vagina to the vulva. The vestibular-vaginal junction forms a sphincter of tissue at about the level of the rear (or caudal) brim of

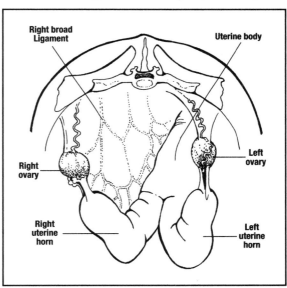

The mare's reproductive tract

the pelvis, and it is the location of the hymen when one is present. In a mare with good pelvic and perineal conformation, the vestibule slopes upward from the vulva to the vagina at about a 60-degree angle, and the vestibular-vaginal sphincter forms a tight seal between the vestibular and vaginal lumens. Just behind this sphincter, the urethra exits through the floor of the vestibule. The mare's clitoris also is in the floor of the vestibule just within the bottom commissure of the vulvar lips.

The mare's vulva is just below the anus and is made up of two labia, or lips. These lips form the third and final seal between the uterine lumen and the outside world. Mares with good perineal conformation have a vulva that is upright and in a vertical line with the anus. Two-thirds or more of the vulva should be below the floor of the pelvis, and the lips should meet evenly and tightly to close the vulva effectively. Any deviation so that the vulva is pulled above the floor of the pelvis and sloped forward predisposes the mare to aspirating air and fecal contamination into her vagina (windsucking or pneumovagina). Any growths (melanomas are especially common in the perineal tissues of gray mares) or injuries with resultant scarring that interferes with the lips of the vulva meeting properly also could predispose a mare to windsucking.

The Reproductive Cycle of the Mare

The mare's reproductive, or estrous, cycle lasts an average of 21 days. A follicle is a fluid-filled structure on the mare's ovary that contains the oocyte. Mares develop waves of multiple follicles once or twice in a 21-day period. One or two of these follicles will mature and become dominant and ovulatory. Those follicles that do not go on to ovulate regress and atrophy (or become atretic), and eventually disappear. In general, follicular development on the ovary is stimulated by the release of follicle-stimulating hormone (FSH) by the pituitary. The mare will develop and ovulate a mature follicle between 35 and 50 mm in diameter on average. The cells lining the follicle produce the steroid hormone estrogen, which is responsible for causing all the behavioral and tubular tract (uterus and cervix) changes we associate with a mare in heat (receptivity to a stallion; open, soft cervix; soft, edematous uterus). The follicular phase, or estrus, typically lasts five to seven days and ends with an ovulation.

When a mare ovulates and the oocyte passes through the ovulation fossa and into the ovident, the follicular fluid is lost and the follicle collapses. Rupture of the follicular membrane causes bleeding, and the ovulated follicle fills with blood and forms a corpus hemorrhagicum, or CH, a structure that lives only 24 hours. The cells that formerly lined the follicle begin to change (luteinize), multiply, and reorganize under the influence of a second pituitary hormone, luteinizing hormone (LH), to form a corpus luteum (CL). The initial rise in LH is also the trigger that stimulates ovulation in the first place. As the cells of the former ovarian follicle luteinize, they stop producing estrogen and begin to produce another steroid hormone, progesterone. Progesterone causes the mare to become unreceptive to the stallion, tightens and closes the mare's cervix, and stimulates the uterus to provide an environment supportive to a developing embryo. The ovarian primary CL is responsible for maintaining the early equine pregnancy, and it also prevents the development of another ovulatory follicle. It takes four to six days after ovulation for the CL to mature fully and produce high levels (more than 5 nanograms per milliliter) of progesterone. The period during which the CL is initially forming is called metestrus. The CL has a life span of about 14 days in the non-pregnant mare. This luteal phase that is dominated by progesterone is called diestrus. If a pregnancy is not present by 14 days after ovulation, the lining of the uterus, the endometrium, produces the hormone prostaglandin. Prostaglandin destroys (or lyses) the CL and terminates progesterone production, allowing a dominant follicle to form from the current wave of follicles. The period between the termination of the CL and clear development of a dominant, ovulatory follicle is called proestrus. Day 1 of the 21-day cycle is considered the first day after ovulation. The non-pregnant mare's next ovulation usually occurs 21 days later, and the cycle repeats itself.

The tubular portion of the mare's reproductive tract, the uterus and cervix, changes in response to the different ovarian steroid hormones. During estrus, estrogen is the dominant hormone. Under its influence, the uterus becomes soft and limp. The folds of the endometrial lining become filled with edema and become prominent on palpation and on ultrasound examination of the uterus. This endometrial edema is particularly pronounced during proestrus and early estrus, and it is markedly less pronounced in many mares on the day they will ovulate. The cervix also is highly responsive to the follicular estrogen from the dominant follicle(s). During estrus the cervix softens and becomes edematous. As the cervix softens, the lumen of the cervix becomes increasingly open. The stallion is thought to ejaculate through the open cervix, depositing his semen directly into the mare's uterus. The mucosa of the mare's vagina also pinkens because of the increased blood flow to the tract during estrus, and the walls are moist with clear, lubricating mucus. The vulva of many estrous mares will likewise soften and lengthen under the effects of estrogen. Overall, the mare in heat has a tract that is open and inviting to facilitate the deposition and transport of semen. When a mare is in diestrus, the opposite is true.

During diestrus, progesterone from the CL dominates. The role of progesterone is to safeguard and facilitate the development of an embryo, as evidenced by changes in the tubular tract. The uterus becomes toned and tubular, and there is no edema. Uterine tone is thought to be important for making contractions that move the embryo through the uterine lumen, a process thought to be critical to maternal recognition of pregnancy. The cervix becomes firm and tightly closed. The vagina becomes dry and pale, and the vulva becomes shortened and tight as compared to those of an estrous mare. Taken all together, the tract of the diestrous mare basically hangs a Do Not Disturb sign and the cervix maintains a tight barrier to keep intruders out.

The mare's behavior also reflects her cyclic changes. Under the influence of estrogen, she becomes increasingly receptive to a stallion's romantic overtures. When presented to a stallion, she will stand still, move her tail to the side, urinate and/or flash her clitoris in and out of her vulva (winking), squat and posture with her hind

AT A GLANCE

- A mare's reproductive cycle lasts about 21 days.

- The behavior of mares in heat can include "winking" and frequent urination. Estrous mares also can act restless.

- In the wild the breeding season occurs during spring and summer in response to daylight.

- Maiden mares, mares with foals by their side, and mares that have received anabolic steroids might fail to show estrous behavior.

end, and allow the stallion to mount and penetrate her vulva. The behavior of estrous mares' squatting, winking, and urinating frequently is sometimes referred to as horsing. Mares typically become restless during estrus and may walk the fence line, whinny, and call to other horses, trying to seek out a mate. Many mares will stand as close as their stall or fence will allow to a stallion that might be as far away as another barn or paddock, and posture and try to get his attention. If there are no stallions around, a mare might tease to a gelding or mare, or even to a person. Early on in proestrus and early estrus the mare could demonstrate lukewarm receptivity, but the intensity of the signs usually increases so that the mare is red-hot receptive within two to three days of her ovulation and could remain receptive 24 to 48 hours after ovulation. In general, mares are most receptive during the 24 hours surrounding ovulation. These shifts in intensity can be subtle, and it is important to pay attention to what the mare is saying. Most mares will demonstrate signs of heat for five to seven days although some show signs for shorter or longer periods. It is therefore difficult to predict by behavior alone when a mare will ovulate. Retrospectively, ovulation can be assumed to have occurred 24 to 48 hours before the mare began "teasing out."

Under the influence of progesterone, the mare is motivated to reject a stallion's advances. This makes sense because an established pregnancy would be jeopardized and likely aborted if a pregnant mare were bred by a stallion (or inseminator!). If approached by a stallion, the mare's body language usually conveys her lack of enthusiasm for his propositioning, and frequently the "No!" will be violently enforced should the stallion persist. The mare will refuse to stand still, swish her tail, pin her ears, and possibly squeal and kick at the stallion. It is little wonder that stallions experienced at pasture breeding usually approach mares with caution. Some mares are not as vehement in their response as others (i.e., their idea of saying "no" could just be not saying "yes"), but even those mares that stand quietly for the teaser during diestrus usually will refuse to allow themselves to be mounted. Mares will remain unreceptive until their next estrous period. That means it will be 14 to 18 days after an ovulation before an open mare begins showing signs of heat — once the progesterone from the lysed CL is gone from her system and estrogen released from the new ovulatory follicle is rising.

Seasonality of the Equine Reproductive Cycle

Mares are seasonally polyestrous, long day breeders. In simple terms this means mares have multiple, repeating 21-day estrous cycles in response to increasing day length, and therefore have a well-defined breeding season limited to the spring and summer. In the Northern Hemisphere, mares will cycle from March or April through September or October. The peak of the equine breeding season occurs in May, June, and July. The winter months — November, December, January, and February — are marked by a period of anestrus (inactivity of the mare's ovaries and tract). Between the cycling and non-cycling periods are the spring and fall transitional periods.

The winter anestrous period is marked by a deep quiescence of the mare's ovaries and reproductive tract that mirrors the sleeping, snow-filled landscape around her. The ovaries become shrunken and small with little to no follicular activity. There is no progesterone and not much estrogen in her system, and thus the mare's uterus becomes thin, slack, and atonic with no signs of edema. The uterus of the anestrous mare is, therefore, often a challenge to palpate. The cervix likewise becomes inactive,

Winter is an anestrous period for mares

and though it has palpable tone, it will vary from closed to mildly open. The appearance of the cervix, in contrast to that of the estrous cervix, will be pale and non-edematous. Anestrous mares frequently will be indifferent to a teaser and might even permit themselves to be mounted. There is no progesterone to tell them "no," but there is no estrogen to tell them "yes" either, so they will be passive.

In the Northern Hemisphere, the shortest day of the year is the winter solstice, on or about December 21. From this day through the next calendar year, the day length gradually increases. The increasing photoperiod stimulates the mare's pituitary gland (via the pineal gland and hypothalamus) to begin producing FSH, which in turn begins to stimulate the development of ovarian follicular activity. This spring transition from anestrus to normal cyclic activity is marked by the development of numerous large follicles that rise and regress without ovulating in a repeated, overlapping fashion. Typically, during this period, mares will demonstrate irregular and/or prolonged heat periods under the influence of all this follicular activity. (Some mares have been known to display continuous

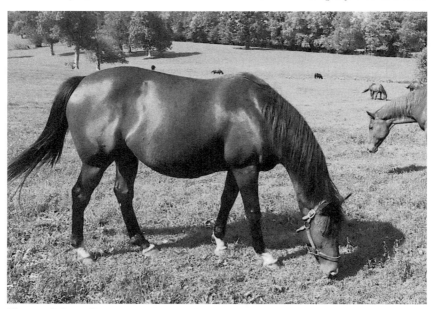

The peak breeding season occurs in late spring and early summer

behavioral estrus for six straight weeks during the spring transitional period.) Eventually, the mare recruits an ovulatory follicle, and the transitional period ends with the first ovulation of the spring. Many mares accomplish this first ovulation by or shortly after the spring equinox, on or about March 21. After this first ovulation, the normal mare falls into her 21-day cyclic pattern for the remainder of the physiological breeding season, or until she becomes pregnant.

The normal events of the mare's estrous cycle have already been discussed; however, some generalized detailing of the patterns observed during the physiological breeding season is worth mentioning. In general, the initial heat periods during the early part of the spring tend to be longer (i.e., seven to nine days) and mares tend to ovulate larger follicles (i.e., 55 to 60 mm follicles in the average Thoroughbred or Warmblood mare) than they do later in the season. By May, June, and July, heat periods are usually five to seven days long and mares are ovulating 40 to 50 mm follicles on average. The tendency for multiple ovulations during a single heat period also increases as the season progresses. Toward the end of the breeding season, heat periods can become abbreviated (i.e., three days or so), and mares sometimes ovulate small (30 to 35 mm) follicles.

The longest day of the year is the summer solstice, on or about June 21. After that, the day length begins to decrease, and by the time the fall equinox has been reached, on or about September 21, some mares are entering fall transition in preparation for shutting down for the winter. Fall transition is marked by the development of one to three large follicles during the final heat period of the season that hang and fail to go on to ovulate. Often these follicles become hemmorhagic after reaching peak diameter and staying that size for a couple of days (a change that is readily identifiable on ultrasound examination). These follicles do not luteinize but rather gradually regress and disappear as the tract settles into anestrus. Occasionally, mares will repeatedly bring up one or more additional anovulatory follicles, and heat periods might appear prolonged or irregular before they settle down for the winter. By late October to early

November, the majority of mares have entered fall transition, and by December most of them are in anestrus. A small percentage of mares appears to continue to cycle throughout the winter.

Cyclic Abnormalities

Mares that fail to show behavioral estrus during the physiological breeding season require investigation. They might be pregnant. Many mares presented to a veterinarian for infertility are found to be pregnant on rectal palpation and ultrasound examination. Any mare with an unknown or uncertain breeding history or one that has had known or potential exposure to a stallion (even a yearling colt!), that fails to cycle behaviorally, should be closely examined by a veterinarian before more invasive diagnostic procedures that would disrupt an existing pregnancy (i.e., uterine culture, cytology, or biopsy) are performed. Some mares cycle normally but fail to give any outward indication of their heats. Maiden mares (mares that have never been bred), protective mares with foals at their sides, or mares that have received anabolic steroids commonly fail to show behavioral estrus when presented to a teaser even though they are cycling normally and are in heat (i.e., have a breedable, ovulatory follicle and no CL). Observe these mares carefully to pick up on subtle changes in behavior and external signs.

Maidens sometimes fail to show heat to a teaser because they are fearful and unsure of the situation. These mares often will show heat to other mares, however, and if they are handled with care and patience and are not allowed to have a bad experience, they usually will start teasing well to a stallion after one or two cycles. Mares with foals at their sides (especially newborn or very young foals) often are more interested in protecting their babies from the teaser than demonstrating what their estrogen is telling them. However, these mares will frequently lift their tails, urinate, wink, and break down into a still, squatting, stance in their stalls, if they hear the sounds of a stallion teasing another mare a perceived safe distance away. It behooves the mare manager to have someone stand and watch such mares while someone else is teasing other horses. Presenting the mare to the teaser away from her foal or with the foal safely restrained within her line of vision but away from the stallion sometimes works, and in some cases careful application of a twitch to restrain the mare will turn her attention to the sexual business at hand.

Performance mares that have been exposed to anabolic steroids also will sometimes be cycling normally but will not be receptive to teasing. These mares need time to allow the effects of the steroids to wear off (sometimes they never do) before they will demonstrate normal estrous behavior. It is ideal to turn out mares coming from a training/competition situation (once they have settled in) and allow them several months to unwind and become accustomed to the daily rhythms, sights, and sounds of stud farm life before being thrown into the hustle of the breeding season.

Mares that cycle normally but fail to demonstrate it behaviorally can be successfully bred, but they require more intensive breeding management and veterinary monitoring (i.e., every other day or, ideally, daily rectal palpation and ultrasound, and vaginal speculum examinations, etc., to identify and monitor their estrous periods). In breeds that permit it, artificial insemination might be the only way to safely achieve a breeding with mares that violently resist being live covered by a stallion.

Very old mares that fail to show heat might truly be no longer cycling. There is some reported evidence of a growing number of mares older than 25 that experience

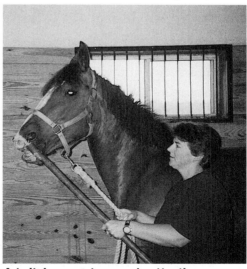

A twitch can get a mare's attention

reproductive senescence (menopause) much the same as women do. Our ability to care effectively for equine senior citizens through better diets and health care has led to an increase in the geriatric equine population in the past few years, and it is likely this population will continue to grow. Mares with abnormal chromosomal numbers usually fail to cycle altogether. Because their genetic programming has gone astray, ovarian function is absent or abnormal, and their reproductive organs are frequently atrophied. These mares might demonstrate a variety of behaviors and a variety of abnormalities in their reproductive tract. The most common genetic abnormality is the presence of only a single X chromosome so that their karyotype is XO rather than XX. These mares are identical to women who have Turner's Syndrome. These mares are typically very passive (and will sometimes even allow themselves to be bred by a stallion much as occasional anestrous mares will do), but they will not demonstrate overt estrous signs.

Variations from the 21-day estrous cycle length also are observed frequently in mares during the normal spring/summer breeding season. Increased number of days between ovulations (increased interestrous interval) and decreased number of days between ovulations (short cycling) occur as a result in the prolongation or abbreviation (respectively) of the life span of the mare's CL (i.e., the diestrous period). Prolonged diestrus (or pseudopregnancy) in the horse is defined as maintenance of the CL beyond 15 days after ovulation in a nonpregnant mare. Retention of a CL might occur in as many as 15 percent to 20 percent of all estrous cycles, but the reasons remain sketchy. Occasionally, a mare will experience a prolonged diestrous period because she has a diestrous ovulation more than eight to 10 days after the initial ovulation in spite of the negative feedback on the pituitary LH from the already existent CL. This second CL is too young (less than six days old) to respond and be lysed by uterine prostaglandin when prostaglandin is produced by the uterine endometrium 14 days after the first ovulation. There is, therefore, an overlap in progesterone production from the two waxing and waning CLs, so the mare remains in diestrus and the second CL is retained. Early embryonic loss after maternal recognition of pregnancy also could result in retention of a CL. Uterine production of prostaglandin is blocked by the presence of the pregnancy so the CL is maintained, and the CL then persists after the embryo is lost.

Mares that have extreme endometrial damage (usually from long-standing or severe infections, from a chronic uterine foreign body, or from exposure of the uterine lining to harsh substances) might no longer be able to produce prostaglandin in sufficient quantities to effectively lyse a CL and will, therefore, retain a CL following an ovulation. These mares are particularly at risk of developing a pyometra (a dilated, fluid- and pus-filled uterus with a closed cervix and an active CL on an ovary) if any organisms or established infections are in the uterus at the time of ovulation. Also, many mares retain their CL on any given cycle with no ready explanation as to why. Prolonged diestrus in an open mare is readily treated by lysing the offending CL with a shot of prostaglandin administered by a veterinarian after careful examination to ensure that the mare is not pregnant. It is important to identify this condition as early as possible, not only because of the risk of established uterine infections in some mares but also because the retained CL can persist for as many as 60 days if left untreated. Valuable time during the limited breeding season can be lost waiting for such a mare to return to estrus on her own.

Mares that short cycle have the opposite of pseudopregnancy. They have a premature release of prostaglandin from their endometrium (i.e., fewer than 14 days after ovulation). The mare's endometrium prematurely produces the prostaglandin in response to uterine irritation and inflammation (endometritis). The most common cause of endometritis is uterine infection, but it might also be incited by chronic endometrial exposure to urine (vaginal urine poolers) or air (windsuckers), or the presence of a foreign body. (The chronic presence of a uterine foreign body results in a mare repeatedly short cycling until enough damage has been done that the endometrium

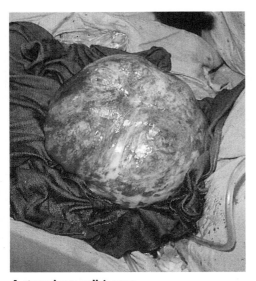

A granulosa cell tumor

can no longer produce prostaglandin and then a pyometra could result). Mares that have a history of short cycling need to be examined closely to determine the source of the inflammation. Occasionally a mare will short cycle for no discernible reason, but this is the exception. During estrus the mare's uterine defense systems are more active (i.e., uterine clearance of accumulated fluid and cells is heightened; the cervix is open so uterine drainage can occur; white blood cell defenses are more active; progesterone during diestrus suppresses neutrophil [WBC] function, etc.), and so an early return to estrus, or short cycling, can be viewed as nature's way of helping a mare help herself clear a uterine infection. Mares that have a history of short cycling need to be examined closely to determine the source of inflammation. Occasionally a mare will short cycle for no discernible reason, but this is an exception.

Ovarian Tumors

The most commonly encountered ovarian tumor in the mare, the granulosa-theca cell tumor (GCT) also will cause behavioral and apparent cyclic abnormalities in an affected mare. The GCT is a biologically active tumor that produces varying amounts of all the hormones normally produced by the cells lining the ovarian follicle, the granulosa and theca cells. Hormones produced include estrogen, progesterone, testosterone, and inhibin. Inhibin is a protein hormone produced by the ovulatory follicle that negatively feeds back on the pituitary to decrease FSH production. Mares might outwardly exhibit behavioral signs of prolonged estrus (nymphomania) or intermittent estrus, anestrus, or stallion-like behavior, depending on the amount and ratio of the steroid hormones being produced by the ovarian tumor.

When palpated by a veterinarian during a rectal examination, the GCT usually presents as an enlarged ovary that has no discernible ovulation fossa. The opposite ovary usually will be small and quiescent (hormone production by the GCT suppresses pituitary stimulation of the ovaries, so the unaffected side is usually in an effective anestrous state). Rarely does the mare continue to cycle normally off of the unaffected ovary once a GCT has formed. On ultrasound examination, the tumor will classically have a multi-follicular/cystic appearance with many small and/or large follicular structures. The unaffected ovary will be small and devoid of significant active structures (i.e., no follicles or CLs). Diagnosis is made based on the mare's clinical signs and the classical findings of an enlarged cystic ovary on one side and an inactive ovary on the other. Occasionally it will be difficult to assess definitively by physical exam findings alone whether a GCT is the source of the problem (these tumors could start out small and in the early stages the opposite ovary might still be cycling normally), and hormonal assays might help to diagnose the problem definitively. Elevated testosterone and inhibin levels are considered to be diagnostic for GCT (although the lack of elevated levels of these two hormones does not rule out the problem). In cases where it is unclear, time usually will tell as these tumors tend to grow and can become quite large. Fortunately, they are usually slow to metastasize, although that has been reported to occur. Granulosa cell tumors have been reported in young and old mares alike as well as in pregnant and non-pregnant mares.

Treatment is the surgical removal of the affected ovary. The non-affected ovary should recover and begin to cycle normally again within 12 months after the surgery. (The longer the GCT has been active, the longer it takes to recover function on the remaining ovary. Also, if surgery is performed in September, the mare could wait until the following breeding season to begin cycling again.) GCTs usually affect only one ovary but can occur in both or recur later in the originally unaffected ovary.

Pre-Breeding Management of the Mare

Before You Begin Breeding Your Mare

It is of paramount importance that any mare intended for breeding be in optimal health before the beginning of the breeding season. The mare should have her Coggins test updated, as well as annual vaccinations such as Eastern and Western encephalitis, tetanus, rabies, and Potomac horse fever. It is probably a good idea to give the mare a booster against rhinopneumonitis and influenza before the beginning of the season as well. If the mare is going to be bred to a stallion positive for equine viral arteritis (EVA) and the mare does not have a protective titer against the disease, she also will require an EVA vaccination before being exposed to that stallion's semen. Owners of mares being bred with frozen semen also might wish to vaccinate previously unexposed mares for EVA as a precaution. Fecal examinations should be performed, and any parasite infestations corrected under a veterinarian's supervision. Ideally, mares already on a regular deworming schedule using anthelmintics should have their treatment coordinated with the first breeding cycle so that anthelmintics (even those considered safe for administration during pregnancy) will not be required during the first 60 days of pregnancy. The mare's feet should be trimmed and cared for on a regular basis as prescribed by a farrier and veterinarian. A potential broodmare's feet and legs need to be carefully evaluated before breeding to determine whether she can support the added weight of pregnancy without undue pain or stress. Likewise, if the mare has a chronic medical condition such as laminitis, Cushing's disease, or heaves, a critical and honest evaluation must be made as to whether the mare is capable of carrying a pregnancy to term and whether it is fair to ask her to try.

Dental maintenance also should be addressed before the breeding season. A veterinarian who is knowledgeable about equine dentistry should perform a thorough examination and correct any problems and perform the annual floating so that the mare can make the most of her diet and not have to undergo the stress of dental procedures during pregnancy.

The mare's overall body condition should be evaluated to ensure that she is neither too thin nor too overweight when it is time to breed her because both conditions sometimes hamper a mare's ability to settle. In addition, her coat and eyes should have a bright, healthy appearance and expression. A potential broodmare's age also needs to be considered carefully. The optimum period of fertility for a mare seems to be between the ages of six and 11, and, correspondingly, foal birth weights also appear to be optimal when a mare is between seven and 11 years of age. That is not to say an older mare cannot successfully conceive, carry her pregnancy to term, have a

Some performance mares need time to unwind

healthy foal successfully, and raise that foal to be in a good and appropriately grown condition at weaning. Many older mares do this just fine. In general, however, a mare's overall fertility decreases after she is 12 years old while her risk of pregnancy-related complications also increases. In general, the older girls will require especially careful management both at home and in the breeding shed to reproduce successfully.

AT A GLANCE

◆ Mares should be current on vaccinations before being bred.

◆ Mares being bred to EVA-positive stallions need to be vaccinated.

◆ Regular deworming and foot care are important.

◆ Age and physical condition should be considered before breeding a mare.

◆ Health and reproductive records should be maintained.

When a young mare (less than four to six years of age) is being considered for breeding, it is prudent to choose one that is physically mature enough to handle the demands of pregnancy and lactation without compromising her own or her potential foal's well being and to feed her appropriately to meet her growth and pregnancy needs.

Lastly, a comment on mares that are in athletic training or have recently retired. Some experts agree that a mare performs her best reproductively when she is allowed time to settle into the reproductive rhythms of her body and to become comfortable in her environment. Many athletic mares need time to unwind from their peak training condition, undergo withdrawal from anabolic steroids they might have received, and get reaccustomed to being out with other mares and competing in a herd situation before they will become pregnant and stay that way. With some mares, this can take months. In an ideal universe the decision about whether to breed a performance mare is reached the fall before the breeding season. This way, the mare can take the fall and winter off to begin making these adjustments, and she can be teased and managed in the beginning of the breeding season (as opposed to the frantic and hectic middle and end months). This allows the extra time, patience, and handling a maiden mare will require while she is learning and adjusting to her new role in life. Events, however, don't always turn out as planned, and whether due to injury, lackluster performance, opportunity, or human capriciousness, mares often are asked to change from a performer to a broodmare overnight. It will require diligent management and observation for them to be bred successfully in a timely fashion. For some mares, no matter how well they are managed, time and persistence ultimately will be required.

A number of clinicians have noted that some mares recently out of training have the best chance of conceiving if bred on their very first estrus upon arrival from the training center (some as they actually come off the van!). If this first opportunity after training is missed, it usually takes the mares valuable time before they get into the swing of things and cycle and breed appropriately. A critical point to remember is that the more the mare is asked to alter her natural way of doing things, the less likely she is to succeed, which ultimately will require more intensive breeding management.

Record-keeping

The importance of accurate, detailed health and reproductive records when breeding and foaling mares cannot be overemphasized. The human memory is unreliable. Good record-keeping is vital to successful broodmare (and stallion!) management. Breeding records come in a variety of formats and technologies, ranging from a well-marked wall calendar and individual mare cards in a notebook to elaborate computer systems. It makes little difference what system is used, provided that the system contains all the information required, recorded in a clear fashion. Information needs to be readily accessible and retrievable. Records by their nature are useless if they are not well maintained, and the more complicated, time consuming, and inaccessible the system is, the less likely it is to be maintained.

Each mare needs to have a running health record that details her vaccinations, deworming schedule, hoof maintenance, dental maintenance, chronic medications, and any health problems (what they are/were, when they occurred, what diagnostics were performed, what treatments were administered, and what the outcomes were). Notes that also mention and detail individual mare's preferences, sensitivities, stable vices, and social skills also can be useful, especially if more than one person routinely cares for the horse or if the regular caretaker is unavailable for any reason.

Specific reproductive records for a given mare should be maintained season to season because mares tend to repeat foaling patterns. Initiate a record for each mare at the start of each season. Record such general information as the year, the mare's registered name, her age, owner, owner's address and telephone numbers and previous pertinent reproductive history. The latter would include number of foals, foaling complications, breeding injuries, tendency to urine pool, previous abortions and their identified cause if known, and previous uterine biopsy scores. Also, record her status at the beginning of the current breeding season: maiden, open, barren, or foaling. A maiden mare is a non-pregnant mare that has never been bred. An open mare is a non-pregnant mare that previously has produced a foal but was not bred during the previous breeding season. A barren mare is a non-pregnant mare that was bred during the previous breeding season and either failed to establish a pregnancy or lost the pregnancy at some point during the gestation either through embryonic resorbtion or fetal abortion. A foaling mare is a pregnant mare that will foal sometime during the upcoming breeding season. For foaling mares, highlight the last known breeding and ovulation dates as well as the estimated due date based on 340 plus/minus 10 days. Foaling mares should be further classified as maiden (having her first foal) or multiparous. If a mare has had previous foals (she is multiparous), record her previous gestation lengths as well as any neonatal complications. For foaling mares, record the name of the sire of the expected foal. It is important to record a mare's status as it reflects possible management differences a given mare might require during the upcoming breeding season. For example, unless the mare is old or has a history of a certain problem, it is not anticipated that an open mare will be difficult to breed. On the other hand, a barren mare might require investigative work and a breeding soundness examination as well as more intensive monitoring and minimal contamination breeding techniques. A maiden mare, meanwhile, might require more time for patient handling.

To complete the general portion of an individual mare's reproductive record for a given breeding season, report the following: the name of the stallion to which she will be bred, his owner/manager, the address/phone numbers, the breeding of breeding (natural cover or artificial insemination [fresh, extended cooled and shipped, or frozen]), the stallion's collection or cover schedules, and availability of semen transport (same day air or overnight express). It also helps to know if the stallion produces long-lived, fertile sperm to determine whether shipped semen will impregnate the mare. Detailed records of each estrous cycle during the season a mare is monitored and/or bred are critical for effective management, and these records commence with the first reproductive-related event of that particular mare's season. For all non-pregnant mares, it could begin as innocently as recording the date in November or December that the mares are put under lights and subsequent daily teasing activity leading up to and through the spring transitional period. (Mares typically will be up and cycling 60 to 90 days after the initiation of the artificially extended daily photoperiod.)

For foaling mares, make daily notations on mammary gland and teat development, relaxation and softening of tailhead and croup tissues, behavioral changes, and milk electrolyte values. Also, report the date she foaled, the difficulty of the delivery, and any post-foaling complications. Additionally, report the details of her first postpartum reproductive examination seven days after foaling and the progress of the foal heat. Records of daily events should include how the mare teased and what the results of any examination were, such as the size and consistency of structures (follicles or corpora lutea) palpated and/or ultrasounded on each ovary; the palpable tone and quality of the uterus and cervix; the visual vaginal and cervical findings on a speculum examination; and the presence of uterine edema or fluid on an ultrasound examination. Records should include important details such as ovulations, breedings, uterine culture and cytology results, and treatments on the days they occurred. It is useful to have a record-keeping system that allows the manager or veterinarian to detail this daily information while providing a monthly overview of the mare. The days the mare spent in behavioral estrus, ovulation dates, breeding dates, diestrous length, manipulative treatments such as prostaglandin and human chorionic gonadotropin and pregnancy status are laid out in a calendar fashion to provide a ready feel for a given mare's patterns and calculation of inter estrous intervals, days in behavioral estrus, and early pregnancy examinations.

Some veterinary practices use a double-sided card with 21-day periods laid out per month in a calendar fashion for an entire six-plus month period in the spring and early summer on one side. The other side contains individual lines with columns to record detailed teasing, palpation/ultrasound findings, treatments, and observations for a given date. These cards are maintained in a notebook the examiner takes to the barn to record details about teasing and examination so the overall record for a given mare can be checked and reviewed at that time and management decisions made. Each record is reviewed again at the end of each day, and breeding management plans and schedules are made for the following day. Reviewing every mare's records every day ensures that very little is lost through the cracks. Having a visualized overview of what a mare has done and is doing helps the manager and veterinarian anticipate what she should be doing next and highlights possible problems. (For example, say a mare was bred on March 31 and had an identified ovulation on April 1. A quick glance has the manager anticipating that the mare should tease out by April 3 and should be ready for her first pregnancy ultrasound examination on April 14. If the mare is carrying a pregnancy, it likely will be identified on that date. If the mare is open, the mare manager would anticipate that she should begin teasing back in by April 18 or 19. Should this mare deviate from this expected pattern, a red flag should go up, and the mare should be examined more closely.)

A variety of scoring and symbol systems are used to describe and categorize things such as type and quality of ovarian structures, uterine tone, teasing, and intensity. Each one can be as individual as the person using it. As an example, in one system the designation of "m20f" under the daily column for findings on a mare's left ovary means multiple 20 mm follicles were on that ovary. In other farms' record systems, the term "clustered" under a left ovary column refers to the same thing. Some practitioners and farms score follicles on a number or a letter scale such that a " ripe 3" follicle on one farm may refer to a 45 mm follicle that seems ready to ovulate, while another might use a straight diameter millimeter scale to record the follicle or perhaps designate such a follicle as being a "Grade A." The lack of an industry-wide form of record-keeping can cause confusion when a mare moves from one management system to the next, so it is important to be able to read and interpret your own records, as well to communicate their meaning clearly to others who might be involved with the breeding of your mare.

Teasing

I n the natural state, a stallion and mare interact continuously. This interaction allows the stallion to identify easily (by behavior, scent, persistence) when a mare is ready to permit breeding, and he follows through accordingly. The intensity of a mare's receptivity is linked closely to her ovulation. As a result, the fertility of wild horses is typically higher on a per-cycle basis than that of domestic mares. It is important to recognize that the more removed the mare is from the wild state of affairs, the more the mare's handlers must work. Humans determine when the mare is optimally ready to be bred. Teasing mares on a routine basis provides invaluable information about the mare's current cycle status and helps us determine how close the estrous mare might be to ovulating. Teasing is an important and highly recommended breeding management tool that should not be overlooked or disregarded unless a farm cannot accommodate the maintenance and handling of a teaser male.

The teaser is an integral part of any breeding management team. His job description, if printed, likely would read, "must be courtly, and a good conversationalist, attentive and tractable, sexy and persistent, but always a gentleman." A teaser can be either a stallion or a gelding that demonstrates good libido (many geldings still have plenty of will!). He needs to be talkative, but not a screamer that might unduly frighten a shy mare. He must be persistent and stimulatory to a mare. He should nuzzle, sniff, nudge, and nip at the mare but never be vicious or savage. It is equally important that he be easy to handle and obedient so that he will back away from a mare when directed to do so. It is also helpful if he has a good measure of sense and self preservation to help him when he encounters mares that would just as soon kill him as look at him. A teaser can be any breed or size, although some mare managers prefer to work with pony stallions. A teaser should be free of communicable diseases, have a negative Coggins, be up to date on his vaccinations, and receive regular health and maintenance care just like any other horse. A good teaser is worth his weight in gold and more than earns his oats and keep on any breeding farm.

Equally vital to a successful teasing program is a highly observant individual who can accurately interpret the behavioral interactions and displays of the teaser and the mare being teased. It is important that the same person observe the daily teasing sessions of each mare on the farm so that subtle nuances and shifts in a mare's behavior as she progresses through her cycle are more likely to be noticed. This individual may be the farm manager or another member of the farm personnel. The "tease man" must be exquisitely in tune with the reproductive behaviors of mares, and he or she must know each and every mare's individual behavior patterns well enough to interpret correctly what she is saying. As previously mentioned, the maintenance of complete and accurate records is vital. Some mares are obvious in their behavior. They are blatantly "in" from the first day they are in estrus. They stand, break down and urinate, and wink the instant they come into contact with the teaser, and have to be pulled away from him when the session is completed. And they are blatantly "out" when they are in diestrus, such that they immediately pin their ears, swish their tail, move about at the first nicker of the teaser, and begin letting fly with their hind legs if the teaser so much as breathes on them. These mares can be like clockwork, teasing in for five to seven days and then teasing "out" for 16 to 18 days. These mares make it all look easy. Then you have the shy mares that routinely resist a stallion's advances even when they are approaching ovulation but finally break down with a little patience and persistence on the part of the handlers and teasers. This mare's gradual receptivity could subtly intensify on the day of ovulation but not so much that the average observer off the street might notice. The extreme is the mare whose idea of receptivity is striking out with her front and rear feet, then perhaps standing still for a moment or two while the teaser cautiously sniffs her over. She routinely will submit only to this minor extent on the day she is ovulating.

AT A GLANCE

◆ The intensity of a mare's response to a stallion or teaser is linked closely to her ovulation.

◆ Teasing is an important part of breeding management and should be part of a farm's daily routine.

◆ There are various ways to tease, including presenting an individual mare to a teaser in a controlled setting.

Good records and having someone who can read each mare accurately are the only way of identifying behavioral estrus in these more difficult mares. The information and interpretation that an experienced and knowledgeable tease man provides to an examining veterinarian are invaluable in helping that veterinarian identify where a given mare might be in her overall cycle on a particular day, predicting how close she is to ovulation and determining the best time to breed her.

There are various ways of teasing mares. One method is placing a teaser in a small fenced paddock in the middle of a larger pasture containing a group of mares, then watching to see which mares come visiting. One problem with this system is that a dominant mare in estrus may not permit a subordinate estrous mare to approach the teaser, and you run the risk of missing the estrous mares. There also is the problem of accurately identifying mares from a distance as well as having to sit on the fence all day watching (a pleasant way to occupy one's day, perhaps, but too inefficient for many management situations). Therefore, many farms prefer to present mares individually to the teaser in a controlled situation. This could take the form of placing the teaser and mare in large adjacent box stalls divided by a solid half wall and sliding window divider that can be opened so the two can interact freely with the half wall between them. Another approach involves placing the stallion in a "tease box" where he is loose and free to extend his head and neck over a half wall to touch and sniff mares led up to him individually. Conversely, the teaser may be led to a mare's individual stall, where the two can interact through the doorway either by backing the mare part way out for the stallion to examine her hindquarters (brave teaser!) or by merely letting the stallion talk to the mare from outside the stall. Finally, the mare and the teaser can be led individually to opposite sides of a tease wall where they can interact while remaining in hand. No matter what system is used, safety for both the horses and the handlers should be a paramount consideration.

Sex is exciting. The teaser and the mare both will get a little wound up by this experience, and even when a mare is in red-hot standing heat she can squeal and strike out at the stallion to convey to him that he should mind his manners. Likewise, the teaser can strike out in retaliation or anxiety. Mares that are not in estrus are prone to displaying their displeasure by kicking out with their hind feet. For this reason, it is highly recommended to have a solid padded or wooden wall between the horses to ensure

Teasing is an important part of breeding management

their safety. (There is also the added benefit of having a barricade of sorts between the teaser and the mare just in case the teaser stallion decides he would like to be the main performer for a change and not just the warm up act.) While it might be tempting to tease over already existing fences or gates, it is not a good idea because it is easy for one of the horses to entangle a leg should they kick or strike out. Likewise, it is not safe for the teaser to have to approach the hind end of a mare that has been backed through her stall door.

Handlers need to be calm, professional, observant, and cautious. When horses are being teased in hand, the handler needs to be in control without interfering and at the same time remain out of harm's way. The handler should never allow himself to be directly in front of or behind either horse. Probably the best place to stand to be relatively safe from both teeth and hooves and retain control is off to the left side at the level of the horse's shoulder. The handler should hold the shank so that each horse remains in control but has some freedom to interact. Too much slack raises the risk of the handler or the horses becoming entangled.

Anyone who undertakes the responsibility of handling a mare or stallion in a teasing or breeding situation needs to be the consummate horseman and well experienced handling horses in all types of frightening situations. The breeding shed is no place for egos and bravado. It is extremely important for everyone's safety (man and beast) that handlers in these situations be well trained and competent. Novices just becoming initiated to the equine breeding routines and activities need to learn under the tutelage of an experienced horseman. Too much can go wrong too quickly and with dire consequences.

Teasing mares should be part of the daily routine on any breeding farm, large or small. During the breeding season, open mares should be teased regularly. Mares in estrus should be teased daily through their heats to monitor the intensity of their signs and to double check that the mare teases out as expected. Mares thought to be in diestrus and/or early pregnancy (less than 40 days) should still be teased at

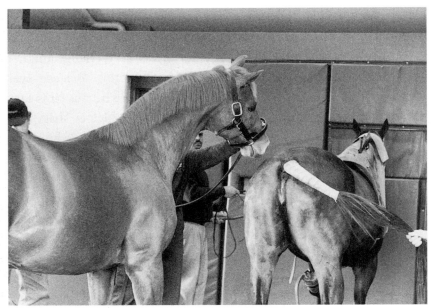

Handlers need to be professional

least two to three times a week so short-cycling, possibly infected mares and mares that lose their pregnancies and unexpectedly return to estrus are not missed. Mare managers need to pay careful attention during the 14 to 18 days following an ovulation and to tease the mares again so as not to miss the beginning of the next estrous period.

Mares that have been diagnosed as open (not pregnant) following an initial pregnancy ultrasound examination at 14 days and then fail to return to estrus warrant a second ultrasound examination. It is possible that she is pregnant and the embryo was overlooked at the initial exam because it was a little small for its gestational age or because the mare conceived on a second undetected ovulation a couple of days after the first ovulation (some stallions do produce extremely long-lived sperm). Likewise, it sometimes is difficult to determine accurately the early pregnancy status of mares that have numerous endometrial cysts. Again, failure to return to estrus could indicate that the veterinarian's optimism is about to be rewarded by the detection of an enlarging embryo nestled amongst the cysts.

(Cysts don't grow nor do they develop heart beats, so serial examinations are helpful and indicated.) Remember, too, that some pregnant mares can demonstrate mild signs of heat around 18 to 20 days; mares showing lukewarm signs definitely warrant a second look by a veterinarian before they are sent back to the breeding shed. It could also be that a mare that fails to tease back in at this time is truly not pregnant but has retained her CL and requires a shot of prostaglandin to get her back on the right track. A second timely examination by a veterinarian will save valuable time. Mares that have been given prostaglandin to bring them back into heat also warrant close daily teasing so as not to miss the start of the ensuing estrous period. Late winter anestrus and spring transitional mares also should be teased biweekly so as to get a handle on their progress. As always, keep good records.

As useful and important as it is to be able to tease regularly any mare intended for breeding, it is unfortunately not always possible. Some owners who breed their mares at home by artificial insemination do not have access to a teaser. Other farms, for various reasons, simply do not wish to have a teaser around. In still other instances, some mares simply do not display overt signs of behavioral estrus even though they are cycling normally (maiden mares, performance mares, mares with very young foals, etc., as previously discussed). In these instances more intensive observation of mares is required to detect subtle signs such as vulvar lengthening, clear and slight mucous vulvar discharge, increased restlessness, and vocalizations that all might indicate the mare is in estrus. Remember also to watch the mares' interactions with each other and with people to detect whether they are demonstrating behavioral estrus. Good record-keeping also can be a critical ally when trying to predict the occurrence of an estrous cycle in protective mares that will not show heat well in the initial weeks following foaling.

Recording the foaling date and then counting ahead 10 days to try to catch the foal heat or counting further ahead 30 days from foaling to predict when the second estrus following foaling (the 30-day heat) should occur can be helpful in determining when a veterinarian should be scheduled to begin examining the mare rectally to facilitate breeding. Remember, too, that the initial veterinary reproductive examination routinely performed seven days after foaling will help predict when the foal heat ovulation might occur.

Reproductive Examinations

B reeding mares is sometimes a humbling experience. Many mares seem to take perverse delight in outsmarting their managers and veterinarians, almost as if to say, "So you think you have it figured out? Watch this!" On average, mares will demonstrate receptivity for five to seven days, and we know they will likely ovulate during the last 24 to 48 hours of the heat. But accurately predicting exactly which day a given mare will ovulate can be difficult, especially if no records exist of her behavior and reproductive tract parameters on previous cycles.

One strategy to combat the unknown is to breed a mare every 48 hours during her heat cycle, beginning on the second day of receptivity, until she is no longer receptive to the stallion. This strategy is based on the knowledge that the average fertile stallion's semen will last in the mare's tract for at least 48 hours and that she will begin teasing out within 24 to 48 hours of ovulation. Therefore, breeding her every 48 hours during her heat increases the likelihood that fertile sperm will be waiting to fertilize the oocyte when the ovulated oocyte arrives in the oviduct. There are drawbacks to this approach, however, especially an increased likelihood of the mare developing a uterine infection. Semen is not sterile, and every breeding introduces contaminants and bacteria as well as sperm into the uterine lumen. Well conformed, healthy, young mares are adept at clearing this contamination in a timely fashion and are less likely to become infected as the result of breeding. Older mares, mares that have anatomical differences that incline them to pneumovagina and/or pooling vaginal urine or uterine fluid, and mares that have cervices that remain somewhat closed and fail to relax completely during estrus have a much more difficult time clearing contamination and are likely to develop an endometritis/uterine infection following breeding. For this latter class of mares, multiple breedings during a heat cycle are contraindicated

With heavily booked stallions (especially in live cover scenarios) it might not be possible for a mare to get in to be bred more than once during a given estrus. Likewise, for logistical reasons, it sometimes is difficult to obtain numerous semen shipments when breeding artificially with shipped semen (it also becomes quite expensive), and frequently the number of available breeding doses is limited when dealing with frozen semen breedings. For these reasons the breeding management goal for each mare is to breed her in front of, and as close to, ovulation as possible to limit the number of breedings necessary.

When the timing is right on the mark (i.e., she is bred less than or equal to 48 hours before her ovulation), she will need to be bred only one time during the cycle, which is the ultimate goal of the breeding management. When breeding based solely on the mare's behavior, one effective strategy for some farms with exceptionally good and careful teasing management is to breed mares on the third day of their behavioral estrus, then once more on the fifth day if they continue to tease strongly. Because most mares ovulate sometime on or between the third and fifth day of estrus, this method can be quite effective for mares that show heat well and reliably. A more intensive breeding management approach is to combine serial teasing of a mare with serial rectal examination of her reproductive tract via direct palpation and ultrasonography. This method provides direct information about the structures on the mare's ovaries as well as the tonal quality of her uterus and cervix. The combination of this information and the mare's teasing behavior considered on multiple, sequential examinations throughout the heat provides a much more accurate picture of how the mare is progressing through her estrus and therefore a more valuable method of predicting her ovulation and the best time to breed her. Mares are crafty enough that it always behooves the examining veterinarian and mare manager to have as much

AT A GLANCE

◆ Serial veterinary examinations can help determine when it is optimum to breed a mare.

◆ During a rectal palpation the vet can feel the ovaries, uterus, and cervix.

◆ With ultrasound, sound waves give a visual image of the reproductive organs.

◆ A speculum can help a vet see cyclical changes to the vagina and cervix.

information as possible on which to base their breeding decisions. It is time and money well spent because it will save both in the long run by decreasing the guess work and increasing the likelihood that the mare will successfully become pregnant on a limited number of attempts.

Rectal Palpation

Rectal palpation of a mare's reproductive tract involves the veterinarian carefully grasping and/or feeling the ovaries, uterus, and cervix through the rectal wall. The veterinarian has to stand adjacent to the hindquarters of the mare and place his or her well-lubricated and gloved hand and arm through the mare's anus and into her rectum. This is a potentially dangerous procedure for both the examiner and the mare, so it is important that proper restraint and good technique are employed to safeguard both participants. It never ceases to amaze me how well mares tolerate this procedure when the examiner takes the time to be gentle and unhurried, but, understandably, even the best-mannered mare may become a little goosey. A set of stocks is ideal for examining mares safely because they limit the mare's ability to swing side to side and forward and back, and afford the examiner some protection in the event the mare decides to kick out. It has been my experience that the majority of mares (even maidens) will readily accept being led into a set of stocks and stand quietly, provided that the mares are handled with a little con-sideration. Not every farm has the luxury of a set of stocks, and in these instances mares may be restrained within a box stall or by backing their hindquarters out partially through the stall doorway. Where a box stall is unavailable, tractable mares sometimes can be palpated effectively when their free side is placed against a wall, again so that their ability to swing side to side is limited. If the mare is not in stocks, I prefer not to place anything behind her while I pal-pate her although some practitioners are more comfortable placing

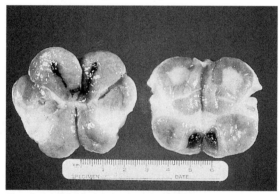

Ovaries with multiple corpus lutea

a bale of straw behind the mare's legs or pal-pating over a low Dutch-type door. (The latter can be danger-ous for the examiner if the half door is too tall. Should the mare suddenly decide to drop and tuck her hindquarters under herself, she will likely cause the examiner to break an arm on the edge of the half door.)

A handler should always stand at the mare's head to soothe, dis-tract and steady her during the examination. A halter and lead shank are obligatory, and many handlers prefer to restrain the mare further with the aid of a twitch. In my experience, many mares (regardless of their breed) do not require a twitch for this procedure as, judging by the mares' reactions, it does not appear to cause them pain or undue discomfort. I usually reserve the twitch for mares that con-tinuously strain during examination or fidget excessively. Having said that, however, many mares are well accustomed to a twitch and relax and stand readily with one applied by a person well-schooled in its proper application (too much unrelenting pressure on a twitch will actually cause horses to "blow up" — quite the opposite of the desired effect). Exceptionally nervous, fractious, or downright combative mares often benefit best with sedation (or "chemical attitude persuasion"). I like to sedate the mare before she can become excited, then work calmly and quietly all the while, trying to make the experience as good as possible. It is important to remember that some horses actually become more inclined to kick under the influence of xylazine, so this drug often is used by veterinarians in combination with butorphenol or acepromazine to keep the mare's feet on the ground. With repeated good experiences, some mares may no longer require sedation to permit examination. Safety, however, should always be of paramount concern, and safeguarded with whatever means are necessary (including not palpating the mare if it cannot be done safely for her or the examiner). Veterinarians have been seriously injured and even killed working on mares, and they are responsible for not only their own safety but that of the animal.

The rectal wall of the horse is a thin and somewhat fragile structure that can be damaged and even torn during an examination. A tear rarely will occur in the hands of a careful, experienced examiner, but the possibility exists if the horse suddenly strains, moves, or jumps around unexpectedly. Rectal tears in horses are very serious. Horses do not deal well with the resultant peritonitis following fecal contamination of their abdomen, and the injury is likely to cause the horse's death due to the subsequent complications. In some instances, horses can recover provided surgical repair and medical treatment are prompt and aggressive, but it is far better to avoid the injury by using appropriate and judicious restraint.

Ultrasound

Ultrasound examination of the mare's reproductive tract uses sound waves to image the reproductive organs. Except for transabdominal imaging of the fetus during mid-to-late gestation, this examination also is performed rectally by introducing the probe into the mare's rectum in the hand of the examiner and systematically scanning the reproductive structures. B-mode (brightness modality), real-time scanners typically are used to image the organs. High frequency sound waves are produced and emitted by a crystal within the probe. These sound waves then pass into the soft tissue structures and are either transmitted through the tissues or reflected back to the probe, depending on the tissue density. The sound waves readily pass through fluid and move through soft tissue densities to varying degrees but are bounced back to the probe by bone and air. The image produced by the reflections of the sound waves reconstructs the reproductive organs in two-dimensional form in varying shades of white, gray, and black. Fluid appears black, soft tissues appear varying shades of gray, and bone and air appear white and cast a shadow over the image so that whatever is behind them cannot be imaged. The image is constructed and changes as the probe is passed over the structures so that the image is the real-time reflection of what is being examined. As this procedure is being performed rectally, all of the precautions pertinent to rectal palpation apply here as well.

The combination of palpation and ultrasound of the reproductive tract is a powerful tool for determining the status of a mare. Follicles are readily identifiable both by palpation and ultrasound on a mare's ovaries. These fluid-filled ovarian structures project above the surface of the ovary proper and palpate much like a blister. Follicles first become identifiable to an experienced veterinarian's fingers when the follicles are 10 to 20 mm in diameter and are readily identifiable when they are at the ovulatory size of 35 to 60 mm. As we have previously discussed, cycling mares typically produce one to two

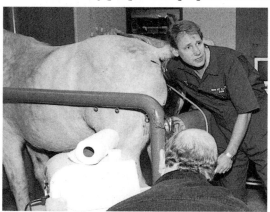

Palpation and ultrasound are powerful tools in determining a mare's status

waves of developing follicles during a given 21-day estrous cycle. From any given wave, a dominant follicle will emerge, and if this follicle's development should coincide with the regression of the previous cycle's corpus luteum (CL) — at approximately 14 to 17 days after ovulation — then that follicle will go on to become the ovulatory follicle for the next estrous period. This dominant follicle (or sometimes two follicles) is readily identifiable among the cohort of follicles because it has the largest diameter in the developing "wave," and frequently can be identified as early as 10 to 14 days into the diestrous period during which it is developing (i.e., four to eight days before the start of the next estrous period). Frequently, the dominant follicle will be 25 to 30 mm in diameter at the beginning of the estrous period. A developing follicle typically will grow 3 to 5 mm in diameter each day. As the follicle approaches ovulation, it has a tendency to soften and become fluctuant, and this change is readily apparent to the palpating veterinarian who has been following the follicle's development.

Likewise, the follicle also will begin to change in shape. The mare's follicles ovulate through the ovulation fossa on the ovary. The follicle maintains a somewhat spherical shape in the ovarian tissue up until the time when it is close to ovulating. As ovulation approaches (within 24 hours or less), the follicle begins to "cone down" toward the ovulation fossa and takes on a pear shape or grows a small comet tail toward the fossa. This change is not palpable; it is only discernible with an ultrasound machine.

One of the best predictors of impending ovulation in a mare is follicular size. In general, a mare will ovulate a follicle 35 to 60 mm in diameter (larger early in the physiological breeding season and smaller later), with the average mare most likely to ovulate a follicle when it is 40 to 50 mm in diameter. An experienced veterinarian can discern and identify these follicular diameters. An ultrasound machine increases the accuracy of these assessments and gives the examiner additional information about the appearance of the follicle. Ultrasound also can readily distinguish when there are two smaller follicles back to back that may palpate like one large follicle, thereby foiling the mare's attempts to fool her examiner. In general, then, when a mare's dominant follicle reaches a diameter of 35 to 40 mm, it is a reasonable guesstimate to say that she is within 24 to 48 hours of ovulation. This prediction can be further modified based on how the follicle looks and feels, how strongly the mare is teasing in, what her uterine and cervical tone feel like, how much uterine edema the mare is displaying, and, just as importantly, what the mare has done during previous ovulations.

Complete, accurate records are a useful reference when a veterinarian and manager are following any mare, especially when dealing with mares that like to ovulate smaller diameter follicles, double ovulate, and/or bring up a 45 to 50 mm follicle and then hang there for 24 to 72 hours before going on to ovulate. For example, if I am dealing with a mare that fooled us by ovulating a 30 to 35 mm follicle on the previous cycle before we could breed her, I am much more likely to get some semen into her early the next time (provided everything else looks all right) when she is showing a 30 mm follicle, in the hopes of catching her at her own game. By contrast, the corpus luteum (CL) is not always readily palpable on the ovary. In the first few hours after ovulation, a palpable crater or depression appears on the ovary where the ovulated follicle had been. Touching this area can be painful for the mare. Occasionally, a mare will react to the palpation of this site by jumping about or even kicking. But most mares will merely tense up as the examiner grasps the ovary, and there will be a discernible, slight quivering in the mare's flank as the ovary is handled. Within 12 to 24 hours of the ovulation, this sensitivity disappears, and the ovulated, collapsed follicle has filled back up to a greater or lesser extent with blood to form a corpus hemorrhagicum (CH). This structure is usually the same size or smaller than the previous follicle but will have a thicker, meaty texture rather than the smooth, tense, fluid feel of the follicle. The hemorrhage into the collapsed follicle can be extensive, and the mare may have a 60 to 90 mm hematoma where the follicle used to be, but this occurs infrequently if at all during the physiological breeding season in most mares. The collapsed, recently ovulated follicle is discernible with an ultrasound machine (especially if the examiner knows there was a large follicle just a few hours before), as a bright, echogenic and lacy CH. As the CH begins to organize and luteinize to form the CL proper, the structure shrinks and consolidates so that it no longer projects above the surface of the ovary and, therefore, becomes increasingly difficult to identify by palpation alone as the mare progresses into her diestrous period. Remember, the mare continues to bring up one or two waves of follicles throughout the entire estrous cycle, and it is quite possible for a mare to have a fairly large follicle (30 mm-plus) along with a CL during her diestrous period. Therefore, a large follicle on an ovary does not guarantee that a mare is in heat. The presence of a large follicle needs to be considered in the totality of all the behavioral and examination findings. An experienced veterinarian often has a pretty good idea if a mare has a CL on an ovary based on palpation alone. Indications include increased uterine and cervical tone and one ovary that is somewhat larger than the other with a larger diameter to one pole but no discernible follicle (this is where information about how the mare is presently teasing is particularly useful). However, examination of the ovaries with an ultrasound or measurement of circulating levels of progesterone in the mare's blood will be necessary to confirm and identify the presence of an active or developing CL. The progesterone assay will in all likelihood require 24 to 72-plus hours before the results are known. Mature CLs, however, might be identified with a high degree of accuracy on the spot with an ultrasound examination.

Under the influence of the steroid hormones (estrogen and progesterone), the mare's uterine and cervical tone and texture undergo dramatic changes from one phase of the estrous cycle to the next. These palpable and imaged changes are valuable pieces of information that the veterinarian uses to fine-tune his or her predictions of when ovulation is likely to occur. During diestrus, the progesterone produced by the mature CL causes the cervix to become tightly closed and the uterus to feel toned and somewhat tubular. These changes are amplified during early pregnancy. During diestrus normally no uterine edema is discernible on ultrasound; the uterine image is a homogenous gray and the horns are distinctly circular on a cross-sectional image. At the end of diestrus in the non-pregnant mare, the CL regresses in response to the uterine release of prostaglandin.

As progesterone levels fall, the mare's tract is free to respond to the increasing levels of estrogen being produced by the developing dominant follicle. The uterine tone loses its tubularity, and the uterus becomes softer and somewhat limp in the veterinarian's hand. During the early estrous period in particular, edema begins to fill the tissues of the endometrium, and the folds become more prominent. On palpation these edematous folds also cause the uterus to feel somewhat thicker and flatter but still soft, and the folds can be discerned on deep palpation of the uterus.

On ultrasound, the edema-filled endometrial folds give the cross-sectional view of the uterine horns a "sliced orange" or "wagon wheel" appearance. As the mare progresses into her estrus and the time of ovulation approaches, the amount of edema in her uterus begins to decrease and the uterus becomes subjectively thinner, but even softer and more draping. This loss of edema is readily identifiable on serial ultrasound examinations, and cross-sectional views of the uterine horns increasingly lose their circularity and begin to conform somewhat to the pressure of the examining probe and flatten. Many mares at this time also will have small amounts (10 mm or less) of trace, clear, free fluid in their uterine lumen that is identifiable on ultrasound examination. Small amounts are normal, and often these mares will also have a slight, clear, thin mucous discharge from their vulva. Large pools of free uterine fluid and/or cloudy fluid, however, indicate that the mare might have an infection and require a closer look and possibly treatment before she is bred. Likewise, aspirated air in the uterine lumen is readily imaged with ultrasound and quickly identifies a mare that had what appeared to be normal perineal conformation when she was in diestrus, but begins to windsuck when her tissues relax during estrus and therefore needs a Caslick's procedure (the vulvar lips are sewn together to protect the mare's reproductive tract). As the mare progresses into and through the heat, the cervix demonstrates a dramatic, palpable change as it shortens and becomes thicker with edema early on in estrus as compared to its diestrous feel. As ovulation draws closer, the edema is lost and the cervix becomes softer and loses its normal palpable shape, becoming flatter and more difficult to discern. This latter finding, taken together with the described pre-ovulatory changes in the uterus and a 40 to 50 mm follicle on an ovary and no discernible CL, is a good indication that this mare needs some semen.

A note of caution and again a reminder to keep good records. These estrous uterine and cervical changes are demonstrated in most mares and will be reliable from cycle to cycle in most cases. But some mares routinely do not demonstrate much uterine edema or do not seem to relax their cervix to the same degree as other mares just before ovulating. Good records will identify those mares that bear particularly close scrutiny during breeding.

Speculum Exam

Lastly, these cyclic changes to the mare's tract (in particular her cervix) can be seen by a veterinarian using a vaginal speculum. The information that can be gathered by "specking" a mare is very useful. This technique is routinely used during early estrus, especially in those instances when palpation alone (without the additional benefit of ultrasound) is being used to manage a mare. The pallor and moistness of the vaginal mucosa shift with the phase of the mare's cycle. During diestrus the mucosa is pale and somewhat dry and tacky (this finding is particularly pronounced when the mare is pregnant). During estrus the mucosa is increasingly a rich, moist pink. Conversely, any mare experiencing any type of vaginal irritation or an infection deeper within the tract will typically have a mucosa that is reddened and angry looking. Accumulations of urine (many mares only pool urine when they are in estrus) or exudate in the floor of the cranial vagina are readily identified as is the presence of fecal material and/or froth that indicate a mare suffering from pneumovagina or a small, previously undetected recto-vaginal fistula. The cervix undergoes a typical visual transformation throughout the cycle following the same previously described palpable pattern. During diestrus the cervix is pale and tightly closed, and the external cervical os projects into the vaginal lumen from the cranial wall of the vagina up off of the vaginal floor. As the mare enters estrus, the cervix pinkens, softens, and begins to relax. The folds of the external cervical os begin to swell with edema, and the cervix takes on the appearance of a moist "rosebud." As ovulation gets closer, the cervix continues to relax until it melts onto the floor of the vagina and is open with mucosal folds draped over the opening.

Again, a veterinarian can identify any abnormal redness or discharges coming from the cervical os (and therefore the uterine lumen) by directly looking at the cervix. Speculum examination also can identify previous foaling injuries to the cervix such as tears and bruising (the former are often easier felt than seen). In normal estrous mares the degree of cervical relaxation seen on speculum examination, taken in conjunction with rectal palpation findings, helps the examining veterinarian more accurately predict how close a given mare is from ovulating. The more information obtained from breeding management and the reproductive examination, the easier it is for a veterinarian and manager to determine the status of a given mare. Stack the deck in your favor as much as possible. Mares defy human prediction a good deal of the time if they are allowed to get away with it. Why guess any more than necessary? Good breeding management is essential to success. Good records and serial (daily or every other day) thorough teasing and veterinary examinations throughout the mare's heat cycle will identify possible problems and make it easier (and less expensive) in the long run to accomplish the goal of a live, healthy foal.

Natural Matings

The optimal goal of closely following a mare's heat period is to time her breeding in advance of and within 24 to 48 hours of ovulation. The objective is to breed her only one time during a single estrus period. The actual breeding of the mare can be accomplished naturally or artificially, depending primarily on the regulations for registering the resulting offspring. Many breed registries now permit the registration of foals resulting from artificial insemination and embryo transfer. Some, such as The Jockey Club registry for Thoroughbreds, only allow the registration of foals from natural matings, or live covers. Many breed organizations that permit artificial breeding impose a strict set of criteria (i.e., they might permit artificial insemination with fresh semen but not frozen or shipped). Therefore, breeders should consult with a given organization in advance of a planned mating so that the breed organization's rules will be followed.

Pasture breeding and hand breeding fall within the context of natural mating. Breeding by artificial insemination (AI) involves 1) using semen that has been freshly collected from the sire; 2) using collected, cooled, and transported semen; 3) or using frozen semen, stored in liquid nitrogen, that is thawed just prior to breeding.

Pasture Breeding

As the term implies, pasture breeding involves natural mating in a pasture and most closely resembles natural behavior in that it leaves estrus detection, timing, and frequency of breeding up to the mare and stallion. When the stallion is fertile, the conception rates are typically quite high (85 percent-plus). Left to their own devices, the estrus mare and stallion interact continually throughout the 24 hours. During the early stages of estrus, mares can be ambivalent or even hostile toward the stallion and typically will not allow themselves to be mounted. As ovulation approaches, however, the mare's receptivity intensifies, and the breeding pair frequently will copulate every few hours around the clock.

Pasture breeding has distinct advantages: There is little need for human interference other than to observe the goings on closely, maintain good records, and conduct regular pregnancy checks to identify pregnancy and to gauge gestational age. This method works well when the players (i.e., the stallion and the mares) are maintained in a stable, compatible group. The potential for injury to the mares and, especially, the stallion in this method is obvious, and for this reason pasture breeding is not typically used with very valuable animals. Nor is this method practical or safe when outside mares are presented for breeding. Reshuffling the group dynamics with the constant introduction and removal of mares creates an unstable environment for all the horses, especially when mares have foals by their sides. Disease transmission between resident and transient horses also poses a concern. For these reasons, many managers prefer to hand mate individuals.

Hand Breeding

Hand breeding involves the mare and stallion being presented and mated to one another in a structured setting where handlers control and direct the actions of the two horses without getting in the way. Hand breeding requires professionalism, good horsemanship, and common sense to avoid injury to horse and human. It also involves monitoring the routines, reactions, and idiosyncrasies of the horses, and taking steps to prevent disease.

In order to be safe, hand breeding a stallion and a mare requires a minimum of three people in the breeding shed. A mare handler is required to hold, calm, support, and restrain the mare as necessary. A stallion handler

> **AT A GLANCE**
>
> ◆ Natural mating, or live cover, includes pasture and hand breeding.
>
> ◆ Due to possible injury, valuable mares and stallions are not typically pasture bred.
>
> ◆ Well-managed breeding sheds can have a crew of up to five people to assist a breeding.

controls and directs the actions of the stallion. This individual should have a good rapport and working relationship with the stallion. The third person acts as a swing man of sorts. He holds up a mare's front leg (usually with a leg strap) to discourage her from kicking as the stallion mounts, or he stands next to the hind end of the mare to assist or steady the horses. The swing man might pull the mare's tail out of the way, help guide the stallion's penis into the mare's vulva, place a steadying hand on the hindquarters to help the mare and stallion maintain their balance and position, and catch a dismount sample of semen as the stallion withdraws from the mare's vulva. He also might position and hold, if needed, a breeding roll — a padded tube attached to a stick handle that is used to prevent lacerations or rupture of the mare's vaginal wall by the stallion's penis during the course of a natural breeding.

Regardless of the number of people involved (many well-managed breeding sheds use five people), each member of the breeding crew must know his or her job and work in concert with the others, relying upon one another's horsemanship and skills to keep everyone safe. The activities within the breeding shed can rapidly erupt into an explosive situation. The breeding crew should comprise experienced individuals who are excellent horsemen and horsewomen.

Beginners should read all they can, but the knowledge and experience needed only can be acquired through firsthand experience under the tutelage of veterans. People just starting out in the breeding business should find a breeding farm that has excellent breeding shed management and seek to apprentice before trying to breed horses on their own. Chances are good that small breeders (those with only a few mares) will not be breeding their mare to their own stallion. The mare instead will go to an outside stallion for breeding, and she will most likely be the responsibility of the stallion's breeding shed management during her visit.

Most well-run breeding sheds handle the mare themselves and only permit the mare owner or agent to watch from a safe observation area. However, even if asked or offered the opportunity to handle your own mare during the cover, the mare owner or agent should only do so if he or she has the experience. If you are green in this area, please be honest with yourself and the stallion's personnel. Do not place yourself, the people around you, and the horses at risk.

A breeding session should be performed efficiently. The environment should be calm, professional, and free of distractions. Breeding horses should never be rushed or frantic but, instead, well-planned to ensure safety and success.

The breeding shed itself should be large enough to allow everyone ample room for escape should the activities go awry. The ceiling should be plenty high so that the stallion does not hit his head on anything while he is on his hind legs. The footing must be secure so the horses do not slip. The floor should be dust free with good drainage and have some degree of cushion so that if a horse falls it is not as likely to be severely injured. A large grass paddock that is safely fenced (a wire fence is not appropriate) is adequate in good weather but a covered enclosure is preferable. Padded

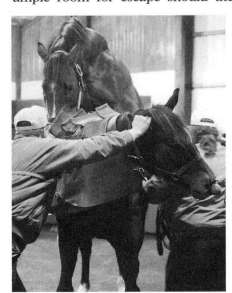

In the breeding shed

walls also are a nice feature.

During a live cover the mare and stallion by definition are in direct contact. Therefore, disease transmission between the two horses is a concern. Equine viral arteritis, contagious equine metritis, and coital exanthema (herpesvirus type III) are all transmitted venereally. The mare's vulva and vagina and the stallion's penis and semen are not sterile, and contamination and transmission of normal flora as well as pathogenic bacteria can occur during coitus. Many stallion managers require that mares have a negative uterine culture prior to breeding to prevent the futile breeding of an infected mare and to protect the stallion from infection from a pathogenic bacteria.

Cleanliness and proper preparation of the mare's and stallion's external genitalia for breeding further reduce the possibility of contaminating the mare's uterus with fecal organisms and penile smegma. The mare's tail is wrapped prior to breeding. This not only aids in cleanliness but also keeps her long tail hairs out of the way during breeding so they don't lacerate the stallion's penis. The mare's hindquarters, perineum, and vulva are washed thoroughly with a mild soap and clean water, taking extra care to make sure that the vulva is free of contaminating dirt and fecal material and that all of the soap is carefully and completely rinsed away (soap is spermicidal!). It is impossible to sterilize the mare prior to breeding, and the use of strong disinfectants is actually contraindicated as repeated use of these substances disrupts the normal flora of the mare's skin and instead promotes the growth and colonization of pathogenic organisms such as *Pseudomonas* and *Klebsiella*. For this reason, the stallion's penis is routinely washed only with clean water before and/or after breeding. Strict cleanliness between horses and the use of disposable tail wraps, bucket liners, wash cotton, and gloves further reduces the likelihood of spreading contamination and organisms between mares as well.

Restraint Devices

Restraint of the mare during a live cover is a practical safety consideration. Most mares in good standing heat will do just that, stand still and allow themselves to be bred. However, even the most willing of mares can become agitated or frightened during the process, and it is imperative that the mare not topple the stallion by moving about while he is mounted or kick out with her hind feet, especially when he is at his most vulnerable (i.e., as he is exposing his belly and genitals to her hind feet as he raises up to mount). In addition, the mare should not have leeway to kick, strike, or run over any of the handlers. For this reason, some mares are restrained using a twitch or a chain shank applied over their nose or their upper gum.

To decrease the severity of a kick or prevent one, some handlers will apply a leg strap to one front leg, lift the leg while the stallion mounts and enters the mare, then release the leg once the stallion is in place so that the mare can stabilize herself and support the weight of the stallion. Breeding hobbles are sometimes used instead of the leg strap, but they should be used with the utmost caution and only on those mares that have been trained to accept them. There is a very real danger of the mare, and even the stallion, becoming tangled up in the hobble ropes if the mare struggles. Many mares react violently to the hobble restraints on their hind legs and panic at the feel of the restricted movement. It is imperative, therefore, that a mare be introduced to the hobbles slowly and patiently well in advance of their use in a breeding situation so that she is completely comfortable wearing and walking in them. The surest way to get into a bad situation is to hustle a maiden mare into a breeding shed, throw on a set of hobbles, then confront her with a lusty stallion (not a good idea!). In an effort to literally soften the blow of a kick, padded booties are placed over the mare's hind hooves. Again, it is imperative to allow the mare a chance to become accustomed to the feel and sound of these boots; otherwise, she is likely to kick like a mule in an effort to get them off and bolt.

In addition to equipment to protect the stallion and handlers from the mare, the mare needs to be protected from the stallion. Many stallions will stabilize themselves on the mare's back by taking hold of her crest or poll with their teeth. Some stallions are overly aggressive with this type of biting and others are downright nasty and like to savage a mare's neck. Not only is this painful for the poor mare (who could blame her for not wanting to stand in such a situation), but such bites can cause severe lacerations. For this reason, many breeding sheds routinely place a heavy canvas or leather cover or shroud over the mare's poll, neck, and withers. These breeding shrouds are attached with straps affixed to her halter and a surcingle that goes

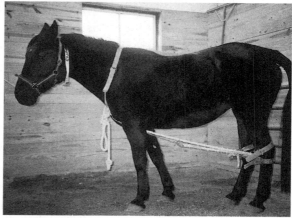

Breeding hobbles

around around her girth. The cover usually will have flaps attached to its surface that the stallion can bite if he so chooses and the mare remains unharmed.

Breeding rolls also are used sometimes to protect mares. Some stallions are extremely well endowed and/or are extremely vigorous upon entering and thrusting within a mare's vagina. Some mares also have somewhat shorter than average vaginal cavities or are proportionately smaller than the stallion's penile length because they are a proportionately smaller horse. In these instances the mare is at real risk for potentially serious injury to her vaginal wall. The stallion could completely rupture the cranial vaginal wall and penetrate her peritoneal cavity, putting the mare at risk of developing peritonitis or of herniating her intestine through the opening. Use of the breeding roll lessens the likelihood of such an injury occurring by preventing the stallion from fully penetrating the mare. The breeding roll is slipped above the stallion's penis and between the hindquarters of the mare and stallion after the stallion has penetrated the mare. In this way the stallion is held a good six to 10 inches out of the mare.

Even with the use of a breeding roll, however, injury is still possible, and any sign of blood in the dismount sample, on the stallion's penis as he withdraws, or in or on the vulva of the mare should be investigated immediately. A mare might only bruise, but on a subsequent cover during the same estrus, she might tear if the injury is left unattended. A breeding stitch is sometimes put into place in the vulva of a mare to protect a Caslicksed vulva from being torn open and apart during coitus.

Many mares that have been Caslicksed still have a large enough vaginal opening to permit penetration and breeding by a stallion. A breeding stitch is a heavy-gauge loop of suture material that is placed at the bottom most aspect of the healed together or stitched together vulvar lips. As the remaining open portion of the ventral vulva is spread apart, the breeding stitch takes up the tension before it is applied to the scar or suture line. By taking up the tension in this fashion, the breeding stitch prevents the Caslick's repair from being stretched and torn open during the course of the cover.

It is imperative that each mare's vulva be thoroughly examined prior to breeding live cover to check for a Caslick's and whether such a mare is open enough to permit breeding or whether she needs her Caslick's partially opened or completely opened prior to the breeding. It is the stallion manager's decision whether to breed a mare with a breeding stitch in place or to remove it and open the mare's Caslick's. The heavy-gauge suture of the stitch can severely damage a stallion's penis if it is in the way, so it is important to assess the situation carefully beforehand. Always check every mare for the presence of a Caslick's repair prior to breeding live cover. Some mares are sutured quite tightly, and this will prevent the stallion from being able to penetrate the mare at all.

Handlers themselves also should don safety equipment. There are some wonderful chest protectors on the market these days, and a strong argument can be made for wearing such devices while breeding horses. Protective headgear should be a mandatory piece of equipment for anyone managing and participating in any part of the breeding shed activities. Whether intentional or accidental, a hoof strike can do a person's skull a lot of damage. There is no reason to risk serious brain injury or death, and it is sheer arrogance and foolishness to ignore the possibility of an accident. By the very nature of the cover the stallion has to be up in the air mounting and in some cases dismounting. Distractions happen; horses get startled. Sometimes they strike out unexpectedly. No matter how experienced you are you can still be at risk, and it only takes a split second.

The basic components of the cover require the stallion to become aroused, achieve an erection, mount the mare in a controlled fashion, achieve intromission, thrust and ejaculate, then dismount. The mare needs to remain cooperative and calm throughout. Specific routines designed to accomplish this in a clean and safe fashion will differ slightly from shed to shed and can vary to suit the individual stallion and mare involved. In some shed routines the stallion is initially presented to the mare and teased in a controlled fashion so that he achieves an erection. He then is turned away from the mare to a designated corner so that his erect penis can be washed and dried prior to the cover. Other sheds only wash the stallion's penis after the dismount. In some instances, mares are too tall for a given stallion to breed without some adjustments. Some mares will stand well as long as no one tries to twitch them; others dance about until the twitch is applied. Mare handling methods in these cases are adjusted as required.

Some stallions need no formal teasing time and enter the shed ready to go. Other stallions require careful teasing and patient handling to become aroused enough to breed the mare. Some stallions have decided preferences for mare color, teasing at the mare's head as opposed to her hindquarters, or having a moving, reactive mare to interact with as opposed to a mare that stands stock still. It is important that the overall routine for a given horse remains consistent. In this manner the horses (the stallions in particular) become comfortable and relaxed within the routine, and the cover can be accomplished efficiently.

During the cover it also becomes necessary to verify that the stallion has indeed ejaculated. If he has not, then the mare obviously has not been bred. It is not unusual for some stallions to require more than one mount to ejaculate (although most stallions can be trained to ejaculate consistently on the first jump provided their individual needs are met). Normal stallions with good libido and no ejaculatory failure problems generally will ejaculate upon entering the mare after approximately seven thrusts. The ejaculation of the sperm is achieved in several distinct pulses or jets of sperm-rich fluid being passed through the penile urethra. As ejaculation occurs, many stallions' tails will jerk up and down. This ejaculatory motion is termed flagging and is readily visible to observers when it occurs. The ejaculatory pulses also can be felt by the handler if he or she is palpating the base of the stallion's penis while the horse is servicing the mare. Many stallions do not mind having their penis handled in this fashion while they are breeding, and some actually find the addition of manual pressure quite stimulatory. Other stallions resent having their penis handled at this moment and are distracted from ejaculating.

Once a stallion ejaculates, he frequently will relax and actually take a few moments just to drape over the back of the mare before dismounting. As the stallion dismounts and withdraws, the end of his penis (the glans) will appear quite enlarged and flared. This "belling" occurs as a result of the erectile bodies within the glans becoming distended by the ejaculatory pulses. Therefore, a penis that is belled out during dismount can be another indication that the stallion has ejaculated. So can demeanor. If he remains calm, relaxed, and even a little drowsy with no further interest in the mare, then he probably has ejaculated. If he remains alert and very interested in the mare, and he returns to an erect state within a couple of moments, then he probably has not.

Lastly, an objective measure of whether the stallion has ejaculated is to collect a sample of the fluid dripping from the stallion's penis as he withdraws from the mare (a dismount sample) and examine it under the microscope for the presence of sperm. The mere presence of fluid is not enough to say the stallion has ejaculated. Many stallions produce a lot of pre-ejaculatory secretions while thrusting, but these do not contain sperm. Only the use of a microscope can ascertain this. It is important to mention that the presence of sperm in the dismount samples only allows the examiner to confirm that the stallion has ejaculated, along with some gross visual observations on the sample itself (i.e., is blood or urine present?). The dismount sample does not allow the examiner to assess the semen's quality. The sperm in the dismount sample merely represents the dregs of the semen deposited, not the overall sperm parameters of the ejaculate.

The bottom line in a live cover is that the mare ultimately has to stand and permit herself to be bred. She must be in estrus and ready to ovulate. Teasing the mare prior to breeding is an integral part of the breeding shed routine. Uncooperative mares that do not tease well should be re-examined rectally by a veterinarian prior to attempting to breed them to be sure that they are truly at the correct point in their cycle. Occasionally mares are presented for breeding that are not very close to ovulation or are not even in estrus. These mares might have not been teased at all but only palpated one time without any follow up and the presence of a large follicle was misinterpreted. (It is difficult to tell sometimes by a single palpation whether a mare is coming in or going out of heat. It is important to follow mares serially and, if needed, use an ultrasound to help make these determinations, especially when the mare is not being teased at home.) Another possibility is that the mare is not teasing well prior to breeding because she is in fact pregnant (approximately 18 to 20 days of gestation), but she has a large follicle and half teases in anyway and so has misled her managers (rectal palpation and visual inspection of the mare's cervix and an ultrasound of the mare's uterus quickly will identify pregnancy). A mare that has recently ovulated (i.e., within the last 12 to 24 hours) might not tease in strongly or at all, and so she will not stand as well when presented. At the opposite end is the mare that is presenting early in her estrus and is more than 24 to 48 hours away from ovulating.

Occasionally a heavily booked stallion cannot service a mare at her ideal time. Instead she has to go in early or not at all. A mare like this might not be at her most receptive. Just to make life interesting, some mares do not tease well when presented for breeding even though the timing is absolutely perfect for their impending ovulation and they should be red-hot receptive. There is that subclass of normally cycling mares that do not demonstrate signs of heat because of poor socialization, prior exposure to anabolic steroids, dominance, or some unknown factor. Maiden mares sometimes are frightened by the new sights, smells, and sounds of their first trip to the breeding shed and will not show heat well. There are also those mares that show heat very well at home, but are uncomfortable away from home and do not tease when they reach the breeding shed. Some mares have a decided stallion preference and will act receptive to one stallion but not another.

Lastly, mares with young foals frequently are too protective to show heat. If the breeding shed is close to the mare's farm, the foals often are left at home under supervision for the one to two hours that the mare will be away. The foal's absence can make it easier on the breeding shed personnel. Without their foals by their sides, many mares are more willing to listen to their estrogen, but some mares have the opposite reaction and are too agitated to cooperate. These ready-but-reluctant mares will require a more patient and

Washing the stallion before breeding

creative approach. Patient and persistent teasing is often all that is necessary to convince an initially frightened mare to break down for a stallion. Obviously such a mare will require careful and considerate handling while being covered, and hopefully the first stallion to breed a maiden mare will be a gentleman and not a rapist.

Some farms train their maiden mares by allowing a teaser stallion to mount them. The teaser stallion wears a breeding apron that covers his penis and thus prevents him from actually breeding the mare. A mare that knows what to expect is not as likely to blow up while being bred for the first time, possibly injuring a valuable stallion or the handlers in the process. Many stallion managers likewise will test jump mares in this fashion immediately prior to their being bred to their valuable stallion if there is any question about the mare's receptivity and her willingness to stand. Some dominant mares initially will try to intimidate a stallion, but then submit once the stallion is mounted. By sending the teaser stallion into the lion's den first, the mare is given the chance to demonstrate she will behave. An experienced jump teaser is usually quite good at taking care of himself and avoiding injury. Ultimately it is the stallion manager's call whether a mare will be covered. If she will not stand, she won't be bred.

The use of restraining devices, such as twitches or foreleg straps, can help recalcitrant mares become more cooperative. It is very important to remember that too much restraint can backfire. Employing these methods must be approached using care and common sense. There is no way a human will win an argument with an 800- to 1,500-pound horse should she choose not to give in. Never allow a situation to escalate to the point where the mare is willing to fight.

Chemical sedation is a last alternative to try on a ready-but-unwilling mare. A fine balance has to be reached between sedating the mare to the point at which she will quietly stand but remain balanced enough to support the weight of the mounted stallion. Only an experienced veterinarian should administer sedation in these instances, and it should be noted that even a sedated mare might wake up in a hurry when mounted. In those breeds that permit its use, the simplest and safest way of breeding a recalcitrant estrus mare is to bypass the natural cover and breed her via artificial insemination.

Artificial Insemination

B reeding with artificial insemination offers a number of advantages. First, it is far safer to collect semen from a trained jump mare (or, even better, an artificial phantom mount) than to undertake a live cover with an unknown mare.

Second, AI eliminates the possibility of the stallion contracting something from contact with the mare. From the mare's health perspective it is without a doubt the cleanest breeding option available if performed correctly. Semen extenders often include an antibiotic, the addition of which can lessen the likelihood of bacterial contamination of the mare's tract through the semen itself. (Remember, however, antibiotics do not protect against viral contamination of the semen.) Also, careful manual insemination results in less overall contamination of the mare's uterus than does natural breeding.

Third, AI increases the breeding efficiency of the stallion as a number of mares can be bred using a single ejaculate. The average number of breeding doses available per ejaculate ranges from five to more than 10.

AI also extends the breeding life of valuable stallions that have musculo-skeletal, neurological, or behavioral problems that prevent them from performing live covers. Lastly, it allows close monitoring of a stallion's semen quality as every ejaculate can (and should) be fully evaluated.

Breeding artificially with transported semen eliminates the need to transport and board mares and their foals away from home and increases a stallion's availability to faraway mares. This way, regional gene pools stay diverse, and mare owners can breed to superior stallions otherwise unavailable to their breeding program.

With the good, however, there is always the bad. Any time man steps in and substitutes for, or changes, natural equine reproductive events, the degree of reproductive management must intensify to ensure success. When you are breeding horses artificially, the semen handling on the stallion's end must be done correctly to safeguard the semen's fertility. In addition, the mare's connections must ensure the mare is in fact in heat and at her optimal readiness to be bred.

Also bear in mind that the longer fresh chilled or frozen semen has to survive outside the stallion's tract before insemination and the more the sperm cells are manipulated, the less fertile the semen becomes. Sperm motility, longevity, and its ability to fertilize an oocyte begin to suffer. To worsen matters, some stallions' semen does not freeze and/or ship well. The bottom line is this: Using AI requires excellent breeding management and organization.

Insemination Technique

The technique for actually inseminating a mare with semen artificially is fairly straightforward. The mare is restrained as needed, ideally in a set of stocks, much the same as she is for rectal palpation. Her tail is wrapped with disposable gauze and her perineum and vulva are thoroughly washed and rinsed free of dirt, fecal material, and soap residues.

Preventing cross contamination between horses is important, so use roll cotton and clean buckets with disposable liners for each use. A mild soap and clean, preferably warm, water work best. Be sure to rinse thoroughly. Once the cleaning is finished, the vulva and perineum are carefully patted dry with a clean paper towel or wrung out cotton (water is spermicidal).

The veterinarian then puts on a sterile sleeve and glove. A long, sterile inseminating rod (pipette or insemination gun, depending on the type of semen being used) is placed in the vet's gloved hand. Sterile, non-spermicidal lubricant is placed on the back of the glove or sleeve. The veterinarian then introduces his or her arm with the pipette through the vulva, into the mare's vestibule, and further inward to the cranial vagina. Once positioned into the cranial vagina, the vet carefully feels for the external os of the mare's

AT A GLANCE

◆ Artificial insemination is safer for horses and their handlers.

◆ Transported semen increases a stallion's availability to mares.

◆ Breeding a mare via AI requires excellent management and organization.

◆ Proper handling of semen during collection, extension, and insemination is vital to the semen's fertility.

cervix. Once the cervix is located, the tip of the inseminating pipette is carefully guided through the mare's cervix until it is just inside the mare's uterus. When the pipette is properly positioned, the semen (either preloaded in a syringe attached to the pipette or in straws loaded into the inseminating gun) is deposited through the pipette into the mare's uterus. The pipette is then withdrawn.

Some veterinarians choose to elevate and stimulate the mare's cervix with their finger for a moment or two before withdrawing their arm with the thought that the semen will run downhill more deeply into the mare's uterus. Others simply withdraw their finger as they withdraw the pipette.

Semen Handling

Given the challenges of preserving viable semen outside the body, extenders are typically mixed with the semen soon after it is collected from the stallion regardless of whether the mare is to be inseminated with fresh semen or chilled transported semen.

The typical semen extender used for fresh and transported semen is a skim milk/glucose-based extender first developed by Dr. Bob Kenney of New Bolton Center at the University of Pennsylvania. It is commonly referred to as Kenney's Extender.

If the semen is to be processed immediately after collection for

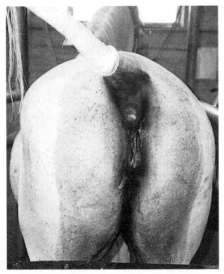

A mare is prepared for insemination...

freezing, it usually will be mixed with a standard semen extender initially, then later spun down in the lab.

After centrifugation, the sperm-rich pellet is removed from the supernatant of seminal plasma and extender, and the sperm is then resuspended in a specialized freezing extender prior to being packaged, cooled down, and frozen in liquid nitrogen.

The purpose of the semen extender is to protect and nourish the sperm cells en route to the mare's uterus. It protects the live sperm cells from cold shock and changes in pH and osmolarity. Extender also protects the live sperm from the deleterious effects of remaining in contact with dead and dying sperm cells within the ejaculate and the seminal plasma for unnaturally prolonged periods of

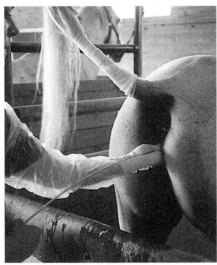

...and the sperm is introduced

time. Various antibiotics or combinations of antibiotics are routinely added to the semen extenders to reduce bacteria in the ejaculated semen and to prevent any further bacterial growth within the extended semen.

Many large breeding operations and veterinarians whose practices work with a large number of stallions often formulate their own supply of semen extender, but it can be purchased commercially, with or without antibiotics.

Conception rates with fertile, fresh semen AI can be as good or sometimes better than hand breeding the same mare and stallion. Standardbred registries, among others, used to permit artificial insemination only when the mare and the stallion were physically present on the same farm at the same time. As a result, many more farms used fresh semen AI at that time. Now many more breed registries permit the use of transported fresh, chilled semen. Even so, fresh semen AI is still heavily used by many farms for breeding resident mares both because of safety and convenience issues, as well as a means of extending the sire power of heavily booked stallions.

With many breed registries easing restrictions in recent years (the Quarter Horse registry, for example), breeding mares artificially with transported fresh, chilled semen has become increasingly commonplace. Many mare owners today are choosing this option to breed their mares without having to leave home. Quite a few mare owners opt to send their mares to local breeding centers for management in those instances in which the intensity of mare monitoring required to breed successfully with shipped semen is not available at home. Conception rates when breeding with transported chilled semen can be just as good as AI with fresh semen, provided the mare and stallion are both fertile and the breeding management and semen handling on both ends are correct.

A number of commercial shipping companies and airlines will overnight containers of extended, chilled semen safely and reliably. Shipping via airlines that offer counter-to-counter same-day service is particularly expeditious if the stallion's and mare's farms are within reasonable driving distances of airports. This same-day air option is of great help when a mare is being bred to a stallion whose semen longevity is not the greatest and the collected semen needs to make it into the mare's uterus with as little delay as possible.

Various container systems designed to cool and maintain semen at the colder storage temperature (4 to 6 degrees Celsius) during transport are available commercially. These containers are designed to maintain optimal conditions for semen preservation during transport but are not truly meant to serve as storage tanks for multiple semen doses for lengthy periods. With the exception of semen that does not ship well, most equine semen, when properly handled and extended, will maintain good motility and fertility after storage at 4 to 6 degrees Celsius for 24 hours, the usual amount of time it takes to collect, ship, and inseminate a dose of semen.

However, the fertility of the chilled extended semen begins to drop after 24 hours, by as much as 50 percent, on average, by 48 hours. It is also not a good idea to store multiple doses of semen in these containers for prolonged periods because temperatures inside fluctuate once they are opened, even briefly, to remove a dose. As a result, the remaining stored semen begins to warm, which decreases its overall longevity and fertility.

There are two types of fresh, chilled semen shipment containers available in the United States: disposable and reusable. The most common reusable system now available is the Equitainer and Equitainer II made by Hamilton-Thorne Research. These durable containers are designed to maintain a set volume of liquid (semen dose(s) and ballast fluid bag) at 4 to 6 degrees Celsius for 48 to 72 hours, using pre-frozen coolant cans and a second insulated semen holding cup in a large plastic thermos. Their large thermos-like design resists fluctuations in outside temperatures, making them fairly good at maintaining the necessary internal storage temperatures, provided the containers are properly assembled and maintained by the user. Another potential benefit of this particular system is that the semen holding cups that fit inside the container can be purchased with lead shielding that protects the semen from X-ray irradiation during airport luggage screening. The disadvantage of this system is the cost.

Disposable containers have the advantages of convenience, lightness (which may decrease shipping costs somewhat), and reasonable cost. A number of different brands use a similar design made up primarily of a Styrofoam-insulated box with cold packs. Some are made to carry the semen dose already prepackaged in a sperm-friendly syringe (some types of generic rubber syringe plungers are spermicidal and should be avoided). The major disadvantage of these systems is that the internal temperature of the package (and therefore the semen) is more susceptible to temperature fluctuations, so the quality of semen shipped during hot or cold weather can be unreliable. These box systems also are not designed to maintain the necessary 4 to 6 degree Celsius internal temperature for much beyond 24 to 48 hours, and the semen can start to warm if delivery is delayed. Under ideal conditions, however, these disposable systems offer a less expensive alternative for successfully shipping fresh, chilled equine semen.

Proper handling of semen during collection, extension, and packaging, as well as before and during insemination into the mare, is vital to the semen's fertility. Shipped semen is routinely packaged as single dose aliquots and double bagged in plastic baby-bottle liner bags or whirl pack bags. These bags are sealed separately using either rubber bands, heat sealing devices, or incorporated twist ties. Equine semen is very susceptible to cold shock damage, so in addition to being clean and dry, all equipment and extender coming into contact with the raw or recently extended semen should be at body temperature (37 degrees Celsius).

Once extended, the semen is cooled gradually to reach storage temperature. Light and air affect stored semen adversely so the semen should be handled efficiently and quickly. The bag holding the packaged semen should contain little or no air. It is important to label, identify, and write down the date the semen was collected and the number of breeding doses contained per package (one dose being the preferred number).

It really helps the inseminating veterinarian if the shipped semen is accompanied by a semen evaluation form that describes the pre-shipment parameters of that ejaculate. These parameters include the number of progressively motile sperm cells packaged per dose, the ratio of extender to semen, the extender used, and what, if any, antibiotics were added to the extender. In this way, the inseminating veterinarian can compare the quality of what was shipped to what was received and contact the stallion manager if any problems are noted with the shipment. Many breeding farms will keep a small portion of each stallion's extended ejaculate to monitor each shipment's longevity, and thus have a backup for comparison if a given shipment has a problem. Carefully assessing and monitoring each ejaculate this way helps keep track of a stallion's performance throughout the breeding season.

A breeding dose containing a minimum of 500 million progressively motile sperm cells at the time of insemination is the accepted minimum number of sperm cells required when using chilled semen to maximize conception rates. It also is an industry standard for shipped semen. There is a gradual loss of viable sperm in extended chilled semen even over the initial 24 hours after collection. (For some stallions, the loss is more rapid.) Therefore, the initial packaged dose of extended semen should contain in excess of 500 million progressively motile cells to ensure the minimum number of motile sperm cells is present when the dose is inseminated into a mare.

The volume of extended semen in a typical insemination dose will range between 30 to 120 ml, although many stallion managers prefer not to exceed 60 ml if at all possible, as larger doses can be awkward to handle.

Recent work has shown that there is not a detrimental amount of semen backflow through the mare's cervix during insemination until a volume of 120 ml is exceeded. Likewise, as long as the sperm cells are properly diluted with extender there does not appear to be an increased risk of inducing endometritis in susceptible mares when insemination with larger volumes is performed correctly. It does not make sense to overload a mare's tract with more fluid than necessary. In this case, more is not necessarily better.

The required dilution rate of extender to semen is typically greater for chilled, transported semen (4-5:1), than for fresh AI (1-2:1). As previously mentioned, prolonged contact with seminal plasma and dead sperm cells is detrimental to the viability of the live sperm cells in the ejaculate. To improve transported semen's survival rate and fertility, extender must be added so that the final diluted concentration of cells is 25 to 50 million/ml. The final volume of the extended dose is determined largely by the concentration of progressively motile sperm in a given stallion's collected ejaculate. Stallions producing concentrated semen will end up with an overall relative smaller volume in a dose that provides one billion-plus progressively motile sperm cells extended 4-5:1 extender to semen. Stallions producing less concentrated semen will have larger relative breeding dose volumes (all other parameters being the same) as the initial volume of raw semen required to produce the dose will be greater, requiring a larger volume of extender to achieve the proper final dilution.

It is the responsibility of the stallion management to evaluate, extend, and package the semen properly to provide the minimum number of sperm in the proper dilution for each stallion's ejaculate. It is the mare management's responsibility to identify the optimal point in her breeding cycle and to handle and inseminate the received semen properly.

As the saying goes, "It takes two to tango."

Chilled semen should remain undisturbed in the unopened transport container until insemination time. Once the mare has been prepped, the dose of semen is removed from the container, gently agitated within the packaging to redistribute the sperm cells in suspension, and drawn up into a non-spermicidal, pre-warmed syringe. A drop of semen is quickly placed onto a pre-warmed slide and examined under the microscope to determine whether the sperm cells, though sluggish in the chilled state, are at least motile. A small quantity (approximately 1 ml) is then reserved to be warmed slowly to 37 degrees Celsius (in an incubator, on a warming plate, properly sealed in a water bath, or in a syringe next to someone's skin), and the majority of the semen dose is then inseminated into the mare. The chilled semen placed in the mare is not pre-warmed. The mare's tract is exactly the right temperature and will do a much better job of gently warming the inseminated semen to body temperature.

There is always the chance of overheating the sperm and effectively "cooking" it or of inadvertently contaminating it with water if a water bath is used. Counterproductive to say the least. The approximately 1 ml of reserved extended semen is allowed to warm slowly to body temperature over five to 10 minutes. It then is examined under the microscope for post-chill motility and quality (i.e., is it just twitching or is it zinging about the slide?).

The syringe should be kept safely tucked in an inner pocket to protect it as much as possible from extremes in ambient temperature and from light.

Insemination Timing

From the standpoint of semen longevity, the goal of breeding with transported, fresh, chilled equine semen is to inseminate the mare 24 to 48 hours before ovulation. Obviously the closer the mare is inseminated prior to ovulation the better. Ideally the mare managers are able to orchestrate the breeding so only a single, well-timed insemination is required. The cost of repeated semen shipments can add up quickly (there are usually separate charges for each collection as well as the cost of shipping the semen container). From the mare's health perspective, her chances of developing post-breeding endometritis increase with multiple breedings during a single estrus period.

Accomplishing the task of exactly timing the mare's insemination requires diligent management. Daily teasing and rectal examinations are frequently required as the mare progresses through her heat so the progression of tract changes and follicular development can be carefully monitored and pending ovulation predicted.

In most instances, orders for semen delivery must be made in advance, usually by 48 hours before the semen actually needs to arrive on the farm and the mare bred. This requires the veterinarian to predict with good accuracy that a mare will be within 24 to 48 hours of ovulation two days in advance of the event.

Many stallion managers are cooperative and happy to allow mare managers to make adjustments to semen orders within reason in the form of confirmation calls prior to the stallion's actually being collected. Stallion owners appreciate any increases in the accuracy of timing the shipments, as proper timing lessens the need for repeated collections of a busy stallion. It is common courtesy and behooves the mare managers to keep the stallion owners informed as the mare comes into and progresses through her heat. Mare managers also need to respect preset collection schedules (frequently, collected stallions are on a Monday, Wednesday, Friday, and sometimes Saturday schedule) and ordering deadlines set up by an individual stallion station.

Agreeing to breed two horses establishes a working relationship between the parties. Stallion managers frequently do everything they can to accommodate the needs of the mares they are breeding (after all, they want the mares to become pregnant just as much as the people on the mare's end).

However, it is rude to expect the stallion's owners to compensate repeatedly for poor planning or poor communications. No matter how well managed a mare is, sometimes she will not ovulate as expected, and a second (or even a third) insemination will be required before she finally goes on to ovulate.

As previously discussed, an average fertile stallion's semen will remain fertile within a mare's tract for at least 48 hours after breeding with fresh semen (live cover or AI). This is also true using good-quality, transported semen (even though the shipped semen is not inseminated into the mare until it is already 12 to 24 hours old). Therefore, except in those cases where an individual stallion's semen longevity is poor, it is not necessary to breed a mare more often than every 48 hours while waiting for ovulation. Sperm cells incite an inflammatory reaction in the mare's uterus that will routinely clear within 36 hours (older and susceptible mares with uterine clearance problems will take even longer). Each additional dose of sperm cells given before 48 hours has passed will be entering a hostile environment and will leave the mare at an increased risk of developing a persistent endometritis.

The simple rule to follow is to time the initial breeding as close as possible to ovulation, but if a repeat breeding/insemination is required do not breed a mare more often than every 48 hours.

It has become standard practice for two doses of a stallion's semen to be sent within a single shipping container meant for one mare so a second dose is on hand if necessary. A nice idea, but if a mare requires a second insemination, it is far better to order an entirely new second shipment and breed her with a more recently ejaculated dose of semen.

For starters, the mare's reproductive tract is far more capable of storing and preserving the fertility of the sperm deposited in the first breeding than any extender/container system designed by man. If the sperm in the second remaining dose of stored, transported semen are still mobile 48 hours after the first dose was inseminated, then the sperm from the first dose probably are still well maintained in the mare's oviduct.

As already discussed, the overall fertility of chilled extended sperm begins to decline markedly after the first 24 hours of storage. (It is always best to place the transported dose of semen into the mare's tract as soon as possible after its arrival as her tract will take the best care of the sperm.) The sperm in that second, now 72-hour-old dose will not be as good in quality as what is already in the mare.

A completely new, freshly ejaculated and transported second dose of semen obviously is going to add to the cost of the breeding. But not providing a second ejaculate when the mare truly needs it increases the likelihood that all of the cost associated with the mare management and first insemination will be a loss if the mare does not become pregnant.

An order for a second collection and shipment in this situation can be delayed until after the mare has been examined the morning of the second day following breeding and only ordered once it has been determined that the mare truly needs to be bred again. If she still has not ovulated, then the semen can be ordered to arrive that same day and she can be inseminated again.

Breeding with Frozen Semen

Breeding a mare with frozen semen presents an even greater management challenge than breeding her with chilled, transported semen. A wide variation in post-thaw semen fertility exists among stallions. Some stallions' semen freezes well, and others, not at all. Sperm cells that survive the freezing and thawing processes with reasonable fertilization capabilities intact also do not appear to have the longevity within the mare's tract of viable sperm cells in fresh or chilled semen. Mares bred with frozen semen need to be inseminated within a window of less than 12 hours before but not more than two to six hours after ovulation. This requires very intensive management. Even when management is excellent and frozen semen with at least reasonable fertility is being used, average conception rates per cycle only range from 30 percent to 60 percent. In general, it is reasonable to anticipate that it could take two to three cycles to get a mare to settle using frozen semen. Better success rates have also been reported using an increased breeding dose of 800 million progressively motile sperm (PMS) post-thaw as opposed to the standard 500 million PMS used for transported semen.

Frozen semen theoretically can be stored indefinitely in liquid nitrogen. The advantage to the stallion owner in this instance is obvious. The stallion's frozen semen is ready and waiting and can be shipped to the mare at the beginning of the breeding season or at the beginning of each estrus period in a liquid nitrogen tank until the moment it is needed. Frozen semen eliminates the need for collecting the stallion and shipping fresh, extended, chilled semen on daily demand. This is especially convenient for managers of stallions that compete, as the stallion's training and showing schedule does not need to be interrupted by breeding. Collections can be scheduled when the stallion is not otherwise occupied and the collected semen processed and stored until it is needed. Due to seasonal changes in a stallion's libido and semen quality, it is obviously better if the semen collection and subsequent freezing are performed during the physiological breeding season (late spring and early summer).

Another advantage of freezing a stallion's semen is that his stored genetic material remains viable and available should the stallion become injured or die. The disadvantage of frozen semen on the stallion's end is the storage and shipment of the semen. Commercial services are available for storage and shipment, but these come at a price. If a stallion's managers elect to store the semen themselves, then it becomes their responsibility to provide the necessary storage and shipment tanks and to ensure that the liquid nitrogen tanks containing the semen are properly maintained. Stored semen that is accidentally warmed or thawed while in the tanks is irreparably lost.

Semen is most commonly packaged in 0.5 or 5 ml straws, but it also can be packaged in glass ampules or in pelleted form. The volume of the final breeding dose depends on the number of sperm cells packaged per straw and the post-thaw motility. For example, a total of eight, 0.5 ml straws containing 200 million sperm cells with a post-thaw motility of 50 percent will be required to provide the 800 million PMS breeding dose (an end total of 4 ml of semen).

The frozen semen straws are not removed from the tank until the exact moment they are to be thawed for use. Once thawed, the semen needs to be inseminated into the mare without delay. Thawing protocols vary depending on the method used to freeze and package the semen. Some methods call for a quick thaw of the semen in a 79 degree Celsius water bath for seven seconds; others may call for a slow thaw at 38 degrees Celsius for about 30 seconds. Thawing instructions for different batches of semen should be followed to the letter. Failure to follow the proper thawing protocol can damage the sperm and affect fertility.

Thawed semen is loaded into a pre-warmed syringe (or specialized breeding gun) and placed in the mare. A small air bolus usually follows the semen as it is pushed through the syringe, through the pipette, and into the mare to make sure as much semen as possible makes it inside and does not remain clinging to the walls of the inseminating pipette. In general, the frozen semen dose is deposited through the mare's cervix to the uterine body in the same manner as fresh or transported semen inseminations. In extreme cases the semen may be surgically inseminated or, more commonly, placed directly onto the oviductal

A container for frozen semen

opening via endoscopic insemination or deep-horn pipette insemination. These techniques are usually reserved for semen that has limited fertility/sperm numbers.

To identify the optimum time for successful insemination with frozen semen, the veterinarian must examine the estrus mare at least every 12 hours once her dominant follicle reaches a diameter of 35 mm. Using that examination schedule, mares are then bred when the veterinarian determines that the mare is likely to ovulate within the next 12 hours. In an effort to ensure that this will be the case, frozen semen mares are frequently treated with hormonal therapies (HCG or Deslorelin) to help induce timely ovulation. The mare is then re-examined and inseminated as needed every 12 hours until ovulation is detected. Breeding in less than 12 hours before or at the same time as ovulation is ideal but is not always possible. A veterinarian does not always have the luxury of inseminating a mare multiple times. Frequently there are only a limited number of frozen breeding doses available. In other instances, the mare is the limiting factor.

As already discussed, some mares have an extreme reaction to frozen semen (they will go so far as to pool large quantities of luminal uterine fluid and develop a sterile but purulent vulvar discharge post-breeding). These extremely reactive mares demonstrate this response largely because of the sperm's concentrated nature as well as the removal of the stallion's seminal plasma from the semen during the freezing process. The mare's immune system will recognize the sperm cells as foreign and will respond with an influx of white cells into the uterine lumen. The lack of seminal plasma and the extremely concentrated number of sperm cells within the breeding dose (and not, evidence also suggests, the freezing extender) produces these extreme post-breeding reactions in some mares. Mares that have extreme reactions to the frozen semen may benefit from the frozen semen's being diluted with pre-warmed Kenney's Extender post-thaw, prior to insemination. For some mares, frozen semen breeding is just simply not an option.

Frozen semen mares are sometimes palpated and examined with ultrasound every six hours around the clock once they reach a 35 to 40 mm follicle, and the mares are inseminated as soon as ovulation has been identified. Intensive monitoring of the mare every six hours pinpoints when ovulation has occurred and, therefore, eliminates the need for more than one insemination per estrus period.

One final comment about breeding mares with frozen semen. Many infectious viruses readily survive the freezing process and so are readily communicable through the semen. In particular the virus that causes EVA can be so transmitted (infected shedder stallions are thought to be the primary reservoir for this disease). Semen coming from any stallion that is sero positive for EVA is suspect for carrying this virus unless he has been vaccinated and has the documentation to prove he was negative before his first vaccination.

A negative semen analysis for the presence of the virus pre-freezing does not eliminate the possibility that the semen, in fact, contains the virus. Infected semen sometimes tests falsely negative as a result of improper handling of the semen at collection, during transport to the laboratory, or within the laboratory itself. A number of EVA outbreaks have occurred as a result of supposedly negative semen.

Stallion owners are typically candid about the status of their positive stallions. But many stallions have not been tested, or frozen semen is marketed by people other than the stallion's owners and the EVA status of the stallion might not be clear. Mare owners should carefully investigate the status of the stallion they wish to breed to, and if his overall status is questionable or unknown, the mare should be vaccinated for EVA by a veterinarian prior to breeding season.

Post-Breeding Management of the Mare

Even after a mare has been covered or inseminated successfully, the task of monitoring her uterus and ovaries is not complete for that estrus period. It is important to continue to tease the mare and perform rectal examinations daily to confirm that the mare has ovulated and gone out of heat. Examination of the mare's tract within the first 12 to 24 hours post-breeding also allows any abnormal accumulations of uterine fluid to be identified quickly and her uterus treated as needed. Rapid identification and treatment of mares that do not appear to be effectively clearing post-breeding contamination and inflammation can help prevent persistent endometritis or infection and save a pregnancy. (Such an environment is not conducive to embryo survival when the young embryo reaches the uterus at about six days post-ovulation.)

Repeated examination and teasing of the mare post-breeding also aids in the detection of double ovulations when they occur. The preference is to continue following normal mares through the first 48 hours post-ovulation to ensure that there are no lingering problems (problem mares are monitored longer). Mares that will receive early progesterone supplementation beginning four to eight days post-ovulation are closely monitored. Any sign of post-breeding infection must be detected because infections in a mare's uterus will worsen with progesterone supplementation.

Routine teasing should continue into and throughout the mare's diestrus period. Mares that fail to establish a pregnancy as a result of breeding activity during the previous estrus period are expected to begin teasing back between 16 to 18 days post-ovulation. Open mares (especially those with endometritis) will sometimes return to heat earlier than expected, i.e., they have short-cycled. That makes it important to keep teasing mares a minimum of two to three times a week for the first two weeks following ovulation.

In this way infections can be handled, and estrus in normal mares that have short-cycled for an unexplained reason are not missed along with the opportunity to breed them back.

Manipulation of the Breeding Season

L
eft to her own devices, a mare cycles more or less between April and October. Each estrous cycle (or the length of time between ovulations) lasts approximately 21 days, and the mare ovulates 24 to 48 hours before the end of her behavioral estrous period after a variable number of preceding days in heat. Unfortunately, these patterns are not always the most convenient for humans imposing their own schedules on the breeding process. Equine reproductive physiology lends itself to manipulation in a number of ways, and the mare's seasonality, ovulations, and interestrous interval all can be manipulated to suit manmade demands.

Because the mare's gestation length is approximately 11 months, the equine breeding season begins during late spring and ends in early to mid-autumn. Over time, natural selection pressures favored individuals born during the warmer seasons, and, consequently, the genetics of those mares that cycled during May, June, and July in the Northern Hemisphere. However, at some period during man's Western development, January was chosen as the start of our calendar year. Many stud books once recorded a horse's actual day of birth as its official birthday. But for racehorses in particular, this manner of measuring a horse's age started to cause considerable confusion as horses might compete as three-year-olds one week, then turn around and run as four-year-olds the next. As a matter of convenience, it was decided that all Standardbreds and Thoroughbreds should have the same designated birthday, and January 1st became the chosen date. It is unfortunate that the decision-makers did not stop to think the matter through a little better.

In order for a mare to foal on or a little bit after January 1, she needs to conceive during February. Left alone, mares are still in late anestrus or spring transition at this time (not the optimal time to be trying to breed a mare!). There are strong incentives for trying to breed mares so that they foal as close to January 1 as possible. A foal born in January will be older and thus more mature than a foal born in June. The older foal will have developmental advantages when the two race against one another as two- and three-year-olds in particular. Older foals generally will be larger when it comes time to sell them as weanlings and yearlings and might command a higher price at the sales. Other breed registries also adopted a January 1 birthday, so racehorses are not the only horses placed under this kind of winter birthing pressure. Breeds, such as Morgans and Quarter Horses, which have richly rewarded futurity competitions for weanlings and yearlings, also are under the "bigger is better" dilemma. Any time money is involved, there is obviously a strong incentive to meet the requirements, and so it is with breeding mares in what, in effect, is the non-physiological breeding season.

The Use of Lights

Increasing day length, or photoperiod, is the signal that initiates the mare's hypothalamic-pituitary axis to resume production of gonadotropins following winter anestrus. In natural conditions this stimulus begins shortly after the winter solstice (on or about December 21) and culminates in the mare's first ovulation of the breeding season, typically in mid-to-late March or early April. It is possible to trick the mare's system into believing spring has arrived earlier by placing her under lights to increase the day length artificially. Mares exposed daily to an artificial photoperiod of 16 hours will experience their first ovulation 60 to 90 days after the light program starts. The light can be fluorescent or incandescent and must be bright enough so that a book can be read easily anywhere within the mare's stall or enclosure (a 150- to 200-watt bulb is usually sufficient although mares in paddocks might be under flood lights). The light must bathe the mare in such a way that no dark stall corners or low stall doors or fences allow the mare to place her head in the shadows.

AT A GLANCE

◆ Equine reproductive physiology can be manipulated in a number of ways, including hormonally, to suit manmade demands.

◆ Many breed registries have adopted January 1 as the universal birthday for horses.

◆ Placing a mare under lights could trick her system into having ovulatory cycles earlier than under natural conditions.

To have a mare up, cycling, and ready to begin breeding between February 15 to March 1, she must be placed under the daily extended photoperiod sometime between November 15 and December 1. It is wise to wait until at least February 15 to begin breeding horses with January 1 birthdays to avoid the possibility of producing a foal in late December. This foal would technically celebrate its first birthday when it was only a few days old!

It is a good idea to maintain mares under lights until their natural photoperiod has caught up (i.e., until May). Many farms stable their mares under lights with timers set to turn the lights on at 6 a.m. and off at 10 p.m. Mares can spend the day outside, provided they do not go out until the day is well advanced and they are back inside under the lights well before sunset.

Other lighting regimens that successfully stimulate mares to begin cycling are "end of the day" and "night interruption" techniques. Studies have shown that extending lighting at the end of the day for two to three hours can stimulate mares to cycle as long as the 60- to 90-day protocol is followed. There is something special about these first few hours after darkness as this method does not work if the light is provided at the beginning of the day. The night interruption technique involves daily exposing the mares to an hour-long period of light, 9 1/2 hours after sunset. It also is not clear why this method works, but apparently this time period is a light sensitive time for the mare and is sufficient to trigger her system. Different farms will choose methods that suit their particular management system best, but traditionally farms have used the 16-hour daylight/day approach.

Increasing day length is the primary stimulus that brings the mare out of estrus and through spring transition, but diet and ambient temperature also can act, to some degree, as additional modifiers to a mare's response. In colder climates, mares protected from temperature extremes might be more responsive to a lights program. The gradual warming of the seasonal environment in the spring probably does play some small role in stimulating the mare's continued progression towards her first ovulation. (A single late March snowstorm, while depressing to the spirit, probably is not enough to delay mares a great deal.) This is not to say that broodmares are best shut up in a barn in the winter. Fresh air and freedom help keep horses healthy, and horses with chronic respiratory allergies might not tolerate being stabled, even in a well-ventilated barn. What it does mean is that if the goal is to try and trick the mare into believing it is spring, then it is probably best that she not spend every day in blizzard conditions. In those areas of the country where the snow doesn't leave until May, the use of a well-lighted and ventilated covered arena for

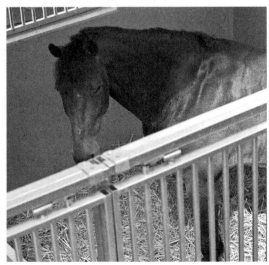

A mare under lights

turnout might have an advantage over placing the mare out in the snow.

It is also worth mentioning that some managers consider it counterproductive to blanket a mare while she is under lights. However, the light signal travels to the mare's pineal gland via the eye, so blanketing should not have a disruptive effect provided the mare's head is not covered. It is always best to keep an open mind. Therefore, if blanketed mares appear to be slow to respond, and are not moving through transition within six to eight weeks as would be expected, perhaps it might be a good idea to leave off the blankets as long as the mares have an adequate winter coat.

Another somewhat controversial (depending on whom one asks) management practice is manipulating an open mare's plane of nutrition in conjunction with a lights program to mimic what she would experience naturally with the change of seasons. During the winter, food is scarce and a horse in the wild gradually would lose condition until the grass returns. In spring the mare would start to regain weight at the same time she would be breeding. "Flushing mares," as it is sometimes referred to, involves reducing a mare's plane of nutrition in the early fall so that she is mildly underweight (ribs showing somewhat) in November and December. When she is placed under lights, the energy level in her diet is gradually increased so that she is on a slowly rising plane of nutrition. In this manner she gradually begins gaining weight daily as she progresses through her transitional period and continues to gain throughout the time she is being bred. The goal is to have her back up to her optimal weight after she has established her pregnancy, then decrease her diet just enough so that once pregnant she maintains her optimal condition without becoming fat.

Unlike "flushing" in ewes, this method does not necessarily increase the incidence of multiple ovulations per cycle in a mare, but it is thought by some to optimize her fertility and increase her overall chances of conception. This management practice should only be undertaken by experienced horse managers because it is possible to overdo the dieting and make mares too thin. Rapid shifts in a horse's diet can lead to GI upset and colic. When in doubt, it is always best for a mare to get a consistent diet that maintains her optimum body condition (i.e., not too fat and not too thin, but glossy and happy with ribs that can still be felt, but not seen). An additional caveat is that flushing probably should not be practiced on older broodmares as it has been shown that aged mares in general seem to perform better reproductively if they are not thin entering the breeding season.

Placing mares under lights is the tried and true method (when performed correctly) of stimulating most mares to enter transition earlier than they normally would under natural lighting conditions. But lights programs do not speed up a mare's normal, six- to eight-week spring transitional period. That is the reason it takes 60 to 90 days from the start of a lights program for a mare to begin cycling normally. Rather, lights reset the mare's seasonal clock so that she enters transition sooner during the calendar year, and, therefore, ultimately begins cycling normally earlier in the season than she otherwise would. The use of lights is quite common across the industry in those breeds that profit from late winter foaling. However, it does have some associated drawbacks, such as the cost of lighting over such a long period, the additional workload associated with caring for confined horses, and the effort required to time the lighting exposure properly. While to some these inconveniences are small and well worth the effort, it is man's nature to try to find better, faster means of accomplishing a goal.

Hormone Therapy

To this end, a great deal of research has gone into trying to identify ways to manipulate mares hormonally in order to speed them toward earlier ovulations. Work with various GnRH protocols has produced variable results, and in many instances is too labor intensive (hourly injections over 24-hour periods) to have much practical use. Recent studies using dopamine antagonists such as sulpiride and domperidone have shown some promise of rapidly inducing a percentage of mares to enter transition and go on to ovulate, but preliminary results have not been consistent with all mares. These responses have improved and become more consistent with the addition of stabling, consistent grain intake, and lighting to the treatment protocols. (Again, photoperiod appears to be the most consistent and important stimulus required to return the mare to cyclic activity, and the addition of this stimulus seems to improve drug treatment responses in those mares that are going to respond.) These drug protocols are not without some side effects, such as mammary development and the early shedding of winter coats along with localized muscle soreness in those protocols requiring multiple daily injections. And they are still somewhat labor intensive without producing 100 percent effectiveness. However, these treatments do show promise of eventually becoming an additional management tool that mare managers and veterinarians could have at their disposal.

Breeding on the Second Cycle

Breeding a mare to conceive on her very first ovulation of the year might not be as successful at establishing a viable pregnancy as waiting and instead breeding on the next cycle. It has been mentioned by some researchers that the oocyte released by the first ovulatory follicle of the year is not the same as oocytes released on subsequent ovulations during the season. For instance, there are differences in shape. This possibly supports the notion that perhaps an embryo resulting from the first ovulation could be more susceptible to early embryonic loss in some way than an embryo resulting from later ovulations. In addition, the endometrial biopsy samples of anestrous and transitional mares differ in appearance from samples taken from cycling mares. Anestrous mares have little glandular activity, and the endometrial tissues reflect the inactive state of their ovaries, whereas the glands and other endometrial tissues in cycling mares, which are under the influence of the ovarian steroid hormones, reflect that activity and are productive. The uterine environment of a mare that is ovulating for the first time that season possibly might not be as ready to support a developing conceptus as an established cycling mare. More study is required on both counts to make more definitive judgments.

From a practical standpoint, it is easier to predict the timing of the second ovulation of the season than it frequently is to predict the first. Mares in transition express wide variations in the intensity and duration of their estrous behavior as transitional follicles come and go. Transitional follicles also can become quite large without going on to ovulate, and so it is possible to be fooled and begin breeding a mare to no avail. Once the mare has passed that first ovulation of the year, she will settle into her normal 21-day pattern and thus can be bred with more certainty.

Given these reasons, it is the preference of some practitioners to allow the mare's first ovulation to pass and either wait for her to return to estrus on her own or short cycle her back with prostaglandin to breed preferentially on the second or an even later heat during the season. The occurrence of the first ovulation can be identified either by the presence of a CL on an ovary during rectal ultrasound examination or by an elevated blood progesterone level. It is a good idea to monitor transitional mares once a week using either method so that their progress can be monitored and their ovulations identified. In this way, management stays on top of these mares and little time is lost getting them bred.

Manipulation of the Estrous Cycle

Ovulation Induction

The ability to induce a mare's ovulation so she will require only a single breeding is extremely useful to managers. It is especially helpful when a mare is being bred either by live cover to a busy stallion or with transported semen. It also helps to limit a mare's exposure to possible uterine contamination. In the world of frozen semen breeding, manipulating a mare so that an ovulation most likely will occur within a 36- to 48-hour time frame also means the mare requires less monitoring to pinpoint her ovulation. Veterinarians have two hormonal therapy protocols available to them, using either human chorionic gonadotropin or Deslorelin, to help induce ovulation.

Human chorionic gonadotropin (HCG) has a luteinizing hormone (LH)-like effect and will cause most estrous mares with a viable follicle that is at least 35 mm in diameter to ovulate within 48 hours of treatment. However, an estrous mare's ovaries still must be examined by rectal palpation and/or ultrasound to determine the presence of a follicle that is at least 35 mm in diameter. Using a shotgun approach to treat mares with HCG will not yield reliable results, as mares with follicles less than 35 mm in diameter frequently will not respond (i.e., they are unlikely to ovulate within 48 hours). In addition, many mares tease hot with only a 30 mm follicle. When used correctly, however, HCG is fairly but not absolutely reliable in inducing mares to ovulate, and as such is a particularly useful tool in a veterinarian's arsenal when combined with good overall estrous management.

Mares that have been monitored accurately so that they are being bred at the optimal point in their cycle can be injected with HCG at the time of breeding with the relative assurance that they then will ovulate within 48 hours and not require rebreeding. (The mare still needs to be monitored post-breeding to make sure this is indeed the case.) Some veterinary managers even prefer to give the mare an HCG injection the day before a scheduled trip to the breeding shed or the day before the shipped semen arrives. This management technique assumes that the mare who is bred 12 to 24 hours post-HCG injection is within 24 hours of ovulating. This works well unless: the mare ovulates sooner than anticipated, the transported semen is delayed, or the breeding shed appointment has to be shuffled at the last moment.

In most cases, once a mare with at least a 35 mm follicle has received the HCG, there is no turning back the clock. The mare is going to ovulate, and all the managers can do is hope the semen is found or she can make it to the stallion in time. On more than one occasion, a commercial carrier has misplaced a semen shipment. It may be preferable to wait until the semen has arrived and the mare is actually being inseminated to give her HCG.

The drawback to using HCG is that not every mare treated will ovulate within 48 hours as expected. In addition, HCG is a controlled substance and subject to tight handling regulations. All things considered, though, HCG is a time tested and useful tool and the most economical method available for inducing ovulation.

Deslorelin is a GnRH analogue. Treatment with Deslorelin stimulates the mare's pituitary to produce her own endogenous LH, which in turn stimulates the estrous mare to ovulate within 36 hours provided she has a follicle that is at least 35 mm in diameter at the time of treatment. Practitioners report Deslorelin to be more reliable than HCG in inducing ovulation in some instances, especially if follicular parameters vary somewhat from the ideal (i.e., the mare's follicle is less than 35 mm in diameter at the time of treatment). Deslorelin can be more reliable in inducing timely ovulation in mares that must be bred earlier in their heat period than is ideal. At the time of this writing, Deslorelin is only available in the United States from compounding pharmacies and only in

AT A GLANCE

◆ Different hormonal therapies can induce or inhibit ovulation.

◆ Hormonal therapy can be useful when the objective is to breed a mare only once during her cycle.

◆ Use of prostaglandin may produce side effects such as sweating, cramps, and colic.

◆ Use of hormonal therapies must be done in conjunction with good management.

an injectable form. The implant formulation is no longer available.

Estrous Synchronization

Estrous synchronization means manipulating a mare's cycle so that she enters estrus on or around a particular date. This is accomplished by either shortening the diestrous phase with the use of prostaglandin or prolonging it with progesterone. Short cycling mares with prostaglandin is most often done to bring a mare into heat as quickly as possible so that she remains open a minimum number of days. Delaying a mare's estrous period by prolonging the diestrous phase with supplementation of exogenous progesterone can be done to synchronize her estrous period with that of another mare or to coordinate her estrus so that it occurs when a stallion is available. It is also possible, using a protocol that gives both exogenous progesterone and estrogen simultaneously, to program a mare's estrus so that she comes into heat at a predetermined time and also ovulates predictably from the start of treatment. This programming method is particularly useful when more exact timing is required to schedule a breeding in advance. An example would include arranging a breeding with a stallion that has an active competition schedule.

Prostaglandin, as we discussed earlier, is normally released by the non-pregnant mare's uterine endometrium 14 days post-ovulation in order to end the functional life of the ovarian corpus luteum (CL). Progesterone production ends, and the mare returns to estrus. The mare's CL is susceptible to the lysing effects of prostaglandin at any point during diestrus once it has reached functional maturity (i.e., it is susceptible from about five days post-ovulation onward). Therefore, it is possible to short cycle a mare with exogenous prostaglandin beginning five to six days post-ovulation. There has to be a functional, mature CL present on the ovary for this to work. If the mare is not yet cycling (anestrus or transitional) or is less than five days post ovulation, prostaglandin will not trigger estrus.

How long it takes for a mare with a mature CL to return to estrus after she receives a prostaglandin shot depends on the size of the largest actively developing follicle at the time of the injection. Remember, mares continue to develop a new wave of follicles once or twice during diestrus, so the size of a developing follicle varies on any given day during diestrus. If the largest follicle is 25 to 30 mm, then the mare may well be back into behavioral estrus within 48 hours. If the largest growing follicle is only 5 mm, then the mare could take six or more days to return to estrus. Mares that have 40-plus mm follicles when the prostaglandin is given can ovulate within 24 to 48 hours without ever having the chance to show behavioral estrus. The bottom line about using prostaglandin is that a veterinarian needs to examine a mare's ovaries rectally before giving the injection to verify a CL and ascertain the status of her follicular activity. The

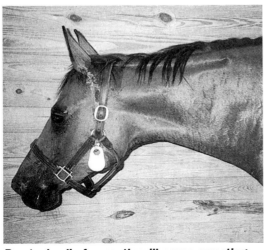

Prostaglandin frequently will cause sweating

mare then needs to be monitored with daily teasing and examination after prostaglandin treatment to pick up the ensuing estrus and ovulation. In a small percentage of mares, prostaglandin will fail without any discernible reason. These mares could require a second dose 12 to 48 hours after the first. Apparent failure to respond to treatment typically is due to the presence of an immature CL or a rapid ovulation without the mare having time to return to estrus.

Prostaglandin is administered by a veterinarian intramuscularly and is available in a couple of different preparations. PGF2a (Lutalyse) is a naturally occurring form of prostaglandin. Fluprostenol (Equimate) is a synthetic analogue (other synthetic analogues exist but are less commonly used to short cycle mares). Either PGF2a or Fluprostenol can be used to short cycle mares. However, some mares appear more sensitive to the use of PGF2a and experience fewer or less severe side effects from the synthetic analogue. Potential side effects of prostaglandin are usually transient (15 to 60 minutes) and include sweating, crampiness, diarrhea, and mild decreases in rectal temperature. Most mares will sweat within minutes of treatment but otherwise appear comfortable and will continue to eat. A few mares will become quite colicky. It helps to use the lowest possible dosages necessary to induce luteolysis or synthetic preparations and to hand walk them through the worst of the crampiness.

For a small percentage of mares, it is probably best not to use prostaglandin as it makes them too uncomfortable. It is important to point out that the use of prostaglandins (PGF2a or synthetic analogues) can cause life-threatening bronchoconstriction in mares with respiratory disease. Prostaglandin, therefore, should be used with caution in any mare that suffers from chronic respiratory allergies (chronic obstructive pulmonary disease or heaves). Another important point to emphasize is that prostaglandin will readily terminate pregnancy in early gestation mares. So unless the intent is to terminate an unwanted pregnancy, the examiner must be absolutely positive that the mare is open before short cycling her.

One final comment on the use of prostaglandin to short cycle mares. In some instances, mares will begin to show signs of behavioral estrus earlier than normal with a smaller follicle, and these heats will last longer than perhaps the mare would normally demonstrate. Premature removal of progesterone will make a mare more responsive to smaller levels of estrogen being produced by the young, developing ovulatory follicle. The rate of follicular growth is not affected, but because the mare begins teasing in on a smaller follicle, she continues to tease in throughout that follicle's development until it finally ovulates, making the overall behavioral estrus longer.

Another subjective observation is that the intensity of the heats demonstrated by some short-cycled mares appears to increase (these mares will actually posture, wink, and urinate so continually in their stalls that the urine scalds their vulvas and lower perineums). The exceptions to this are the mares that are given prostaglandin when they already have a large follicle present. They might actually ovulate without developing strong behavioral signs of estrus because there just isn't enough time for them to do so. In general, however, most mares demonstrate fairly typical heats following short cycling with prostaglandin, and conception rates on short-cycled heats are typically the same as for naturally occurring estrous cycles.

Exogenous progesterone — either oral altrenogest (Regu-Mate®) or injectable progesterone in oil — can be given daily to extend a mare's diestrous period artificially and keep her out of estrus. In general high progesterone levels will suppress final follicular development and prevent ovulation from occurring. In this manner, a number of mares can be synchronized somewhat by keeping them all out of heat, then allowing them to come into estrus together at roughly the same time by simultaneously removing the exogenous progesterone. Conversely, the estrus of a single mare can be delayed to synchronize her heat to fit a stallion's busy schedule. (Many mare owners are also familiar with the common use of oral altrenogest to keep performance mares out of estrus for long periods.)

Typical protocols call for a minimum of 10 days daily treatment with exogenous progesterone. After the last progesterone dose on the 10th day, the progesterone is discontinued, and many mares are given prostaglandin to lyse any remaining luteal tissue. For instance, if therapy were arbitrarily begun the day after she ovulated, the mare would still have an active CL present on her ovary 10 days later that would prevent a return to estrus. Just as with prostaglandin therapy, the mare must be examined rectally to ascertain her follicular development when the progesterone is discontinued. Exogenous progesterone will suppress ovulation but not the overall development of subsequent follicular waves. Therefore, the mare could have a variably sized, viable follicle at the end of treatment; thus, her return to estrus also could vary.

A combination of injectable progesterone and estradiol given to a mare for 10 days under a veterinarian's supervision not only will suppress ovulation but also will suppress follicular development during that time. Mares so treated usually will have fairly inactive ovaries follicle-wise after 10 days. Follicular activity will resume and progress at a more predictable rate following discontinuation of the progesterone:estradiol (P:E) treatments on day 10. A mare should have a rectal exam at the start of the therapy and again on day 10 before getting prostaglandin. Mares generally will return to estrus within four to five days after the P:E treatments are discontinued and will ovulate nine to 11 days later. A total of 19 to 21 days will elapse from the start of the therapy protocol. The ovulation date can be tightened up further with the additional use of HCG or Deslorelin. The more predictable response of mares to this protocol makes its use highly advantageous in those instances when timing is crucial, such as when trying to synchronize donor and recipient mares for embryo transfer. A number of practitioners also use this method as a means of synchronizing the mare's first ovulation of the season. Therapy is initiated on mid- to late-transitional mares that demonstrate the development of at least multiple, 20-plus mm follicles. The major drawback is that many of the mares become muscle sore during treatment due to the multiple daily injections required.

The most important point to remember about any of the manipulation protocols just discussed is that none of them will take the place of good breeding management. All of these methods require careful observation of the mare and diligent teasing and rectal examinations. If the necessary criteria are not followed, none of these protocols will work and frustrated mare managers will still have an open mare staring back at them. Mares are not toasters or VCRs. Giving a mare a dose of this or that and expecting her to behave in a certain fashion just will not work. I often find that during the course of breeding a mare it is always best to be diligent in your management and work with the mare's natural rhythms as much as possible. Use manipulation techniques only if the mare will be better served by their application.

Causes of Infertility in Mares

Non-Medical Causes of Infertility in the Mare

Mares on the whole are very fertile creatures. Under natural conditions, when food and water are readily available and other environmental stresses are not extreme, healthy, mature mares conceive readily (often on their foal heats) and produce foals with great regularity from year to year. Horses reproduce much better without man's interference, and the unrealistic expectations we sometimes place on mares can make it difficult for them to conceive. The number one reason fertility rates in domestic mares are perceived as being low is poor overall breeding management. This is followed closely by the fact that we are often asking mares to breed outside of their normal physiological breeding season and, in some instances, are making futile attempts to breed mares that are still in spring transition. It is also unfair to expect an old mare past her reproductive prime to become pregnant and carry a foal to term as easily as a young mare will. For all of these reasons, the somewhat low average per cycle pregnancy rates (40 percent to 60 percent) seen nationwide really cannot be blamed entirely on the mare.

As stated previously, "It takes two to tango." One constant in breeding mares is that they cannot become pregnant, no matter how well they are managed, if fertile semen is not placed into them.

The stallion is a critical player in the mare's becoming pregnant. If he fails to produce semen of good quality or if he fails to deposit it into the mare's uterus during coitus, the mare cannot be held responsible for not becoming pregnant. Likewise, in AI breeding, if humans mishandle the semen at any point in the process, or if a stallion's semen just doesn't ship or freeze well, those factors aren't the mare's fault either. Careful assessment of the stallion and his semen's performance are important elements to consider when trying to sort out why a mare has failed to become pregnant following a breeding.

One stallion factor sometimes overlooked is the fact that normally fertile stallions can experience periods of infertility, either because an insult to their testicles (heat or injury) has hurt their sperm production, or because of overuse. Overuse problems are more commonly encountered in busy stallions that are live covering all of their mares. Remember, stallions whose semen is collected for AI usually produce more than enough breeding doses in a single ejaculate to breed numerous mares. Consequently, the number of ejaculates they produce a week often does not need to go up as mare demand increases. Sometimes an overuse problem takes the form of ejaculatory failure due to decreased libido that develops as the stallion is asked to breed more frequently. In other instances the stallion might have plenty of will, but no horse is a machine and sperm count begins to decline with too frequent ejaculations. The daily sperm output of each stallion will dictate how many fertile ejaculates he can produce over a week's time. This number will differ somewhat from stallion to stallion, but on average a normally fertile stallion should be able to cover up to 10 mares a week. Covers typically are spread out so that a busy stallion might breed one to three times per day, four to six days a week.

Once individual ejaculate/week thresholds are exceeded, stallions will begin to miss on their mares. In the Thoroughbred industry, late April through early May is typically the busiest time of the season for a stallion. Mares that miss during this time should not always be condemned out of hand. Good stallion managers know their stallion's limits and are careful not to overbook as this is a disservice to the mare owner. Tactful questioning of the stallion's managers when poor-quality transported semen arrives or when an apparently normal, well-managed mare misses is usually well received by responsible horsemen. The stallion's managers are just as anxious to identify any potential problems on

their end as are the mare's managers. Good communication helps put foals on the ground.

Conception Failure

With good management and good timing, fertilization rates in young, fertile mares have been shown to be about 90 percent. In subfertile or old mares, the rates are between 80 percent and 90 percent. Properly managed mares almost always conceive. What happens to the embryo's survival after conception is another story. For conception to occur, viable sperm must be present in the mare's oviducts at the same time that a viable oocyte is present. Many stallions produce sperm with good longevity, and those fertile sperm are stored safely in the mare's oviducts for at least 48 hours. Every sperm has its limits, however, and if a mare is bred too early relative to her ovulation, no viable sperm will be left to fertilize the ovulated oocyte by the time it reaches the oviduct. On the other hand, if the mare is bred too late after her ovulation, the oocyte no longer will be fertilizable even though swarms of vibrant sperm have just arrived to do the job. Even if fertilization still occurs, embryos resulting from aged oocytes frequently do not survive long.

In general, mares mated (even with fresh semen) 12 or more hours after ovulation fail to establish a viable pregnancy. Remember, the mare still might be teasing in for 24 to 48 hours post-ovulation. Even with careful palpation and ultrasound, it is sometimes difficult to determine how many hours have passed since a follicle ovulated if 12 hours have elapsed since the mare's last examination. Conception rates and embryo survival are far better in mares bred pre-ovulation rather than post-ovulation. For this reason, post-ovulation breeding should be avoided unless ovulation is known to have occurred within the last 12 (and preferably fewer) hours. If frozen semen is being used, the mare needs to be bred no later than about four to six hours post-ovulation.

Early Embryonic Loss

The death of developing embryos prior to 50 days of gestation is common in all equine pregnancies and makes a significant contribution to the reproductive failure in infertile and aged mares. On average, up to 20 percent of all equine pregnancies in young, reproductively normal mares are lost by 50 days of gestation. In subfertile mares, the percentage of failed pregnancies by day 50 is even higher, 70 percent or more. Most failures in subfertile mares occur before the time when pregnancy can first be diagnosed reliably with ultrasound at days 12 to 14 post-ovulation. The reasons for the loss of early embryos in otherwise healthy mares are not well understood. One way this normal attrition is viewed is that nature eliminates genetic errors that might have occurred at some point before or at conception or during the early cellular divisions of the very young embryo. In subfertile mares, the high rates of embryonic loss are attributed to both embryonic factors and mare factors. Mare factors are generally considered to be those age-related changes or pathologic conditions that lead to poor overall uterine and/or oviductal environments. A poor or even hostile environment is not conducive to normal embryonic survival and development.

Poor Uterine Environment — Endometritis

Simply defined, endometritis is an inflammation of the uterine lining, the endometrium. Pre-existing uterine inflammation can interfere with conception as accumulated inflammatory products and pathogens within the uterine lumen are injurious to normal sperm motility and survival. Abnormally persistent post-breeding uterine inflammation (unresolved at approximately four days post-ovulation) can harm the embryo that is newly arrived in the uterus five to six days post-ovulation. There are many different causes of uterine inflammation, including, as the reader no doubt remembers, the presence of semen within the uterine lumen. It becomes necessary at this point to conceptualize the existence of "resistant" and "susceptible" mares. Resistant mares have uterine defense mechanisms that function normally and can deny uterine access to irritants or rapidly eliminate them. Normal, healthy mares experience transitory contamination and inflammation post-foaling and post-breeding, which they can clear in a timely fashion so that there are no adverse effects on their subsequent fertility. Susceptible mares have one or multiple breakdowns in their uterine defense mechanisms such that the uterine environment is easily contaminated. Once contaminated, these mares cannot readily clear inflammatory debris and invading organisms. Contamination and insults that normally would result only in transitory inflammation in a healthy mare result in persistent inflammation in a susceptible mare. Susceptible mares easily develop established inflammation and infections within their uterine environments, and even when cleaned up, these mares often succumb to recurrent infections with each new insult (i.e., breeding).

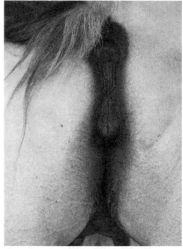

The uterine defense mechanisms include good conformation, anatomic barriers to contamination, uterine clearance, and the actions of white blood cells. All of these can be adversely affected by phase of cycle, aging, parity (number of births),

Good vulvar conformation is important

injury, and poor condition.

A majority of infertile, susceptible mares have one or more anatomic predispositions toward developing endometritis. As we discussed earlier, the mare has three anatomic barriers between the lumen of her uterus and the outside word: the vulva, the vestibular-vaginal sphincter, and the cervix. A compromise to the integrity of any of these three barriers increases the likelihood of vaginal and uterine contamination with feces, urine, or air. Mares with poor perineal conformation — their vulva is sloped and raised above the pelvic floor, and/or whose vulvar lips fail to join together in a tight seal — are predisposed to developing pneumovagina. Poor conformation can exist from the beginning or develop as the mare experiences trauma to these structures, ages, or grows thin. This problem is further compounded in mares that, because of multiple births or injury, no longer have a tight vestibular-vaginal sphincter that could compensate for a somewhat defective vulvar conformation to block incoming air. During estrus the mare's cervix is open, and the air that slips by the poorly conformed vulva and vestibular-vaginal sphincter has ready access to the uterine lumen. In addition, the tissue-softening effects of estrogen produced by the ovulatory follicle during estrus can cause a mare with seemingly normal perineal conformation and adequate seals during diestrus to windsuck intermittently. Air that gains access to the vagina and uterus often carries fecal debris and is, therefore, a source of contamination and chronic irritation.

Visual examination of a mare's perineal and vulvar conformations along with careful listening for an intake of air when the vulvar lips are parted are ways of assessing the likelihood of developing pneumovagina. The relative ease of passing a vaginal speculum through a mare's vestibular-vaginal sphincter provides a means of grossly assessing the integrity of this second anatomical barrier. Pneumovagina is confirmed by the finding of pre-existing air distension of the vaginal cavity along with a reddened vaginal mucosa and also sometimes a frothy exudate with or without contaminating debris. The presence of air within the uterus detected during the course of an ultrasound examination of a mare that has not had any recent vaginal manipulation also confirms the occurrence of wind-sucking.

The mare's muscular cervix normally forms a tight, impenetrable seal under the influence of progesterone during diestrus. The seal's integrity is vital in protecting a developing pregnancy from bacteria and irritants that might breach the cervix and gain access to the uterine lumen and endanger the pregnancy. Cervical trauma incurred during foaling can affect the muscular, cervical ring, compromising the cervix's ability to form a tight enough seal. Such deficits often lead to an increased incidence of poor early embryonic survival or to the development of placentitis and subsequent abortion of a fetus farther down the road. The integrity of a mare's cervical seal is best assessed with direct digital palpation of the cervix while she is in diestrus.

Foaling injuries to and changes in vaginal conformation also anatomically predispose the mare's uterus to contamination. Recto-vagina fistulas are formed as a result of a foal's malpositioned or snagged hoof pushing through the vaginal wall and into the mare's rectum during birth. The resulting hole typically will not reseal completely as it heals without surgical intervention and is the source of chronic fecal contamination in the vaginal lumen. The deficit and the presence of contaminating fecal debris in the vagina can be identified during a vaginal speculum examination, but some recto-vagina fistula may be quite small and far back, requiring direct vaginal or rectal palpation for diagnosis. Normally, the mare's vagina slopes upwards at a 10-degree angle from the vestibular-vaginal junction to the cervix. If the vagina instead slopes downhill to the cervix, the mare may begin to pool urine in her cranial vagina. During urination, urine normally exits from the urethral opening behind the vestibular vaginal junction and on out the vestibule and vulvar lips. A mare's vagina that slopes down to the cervix has the urethral orifice at the top of that slope and some of the voided urine ends up running forward into the mare's vagina to pool at the cervical os. This pool of urine then chronically bathes the cervix, causing inflammation. The inflamed cervix is less capable of forming a tight seal, and urine and bacteria are more likely to reach the uterine lumen during diestrus as well as during estrus when the cervix is normally relaxed and open. (It should also be remembered that urine is damaging to spermatozoa.) As with pneumovagina, some mares might pool urine only intermittently during estrus when the vaginal tissues are more relaxed and the weight of the edema-filled uterus pulls the vagina forward and downward. Likewise, some mares experience transient urine pooling post-foaling that resolves as the uterus involutes and the vaginal and perineal tissues tighten up. Gravity is no woman's friend, however, and as mares age and have multiple foals the supportive tissues generally become lax and the weight of the uterus tends to pull everything forward. This problem predisposes mares to chronic pneumovagina and urine pooling. This sagging and dropping forward of the mare's reproductive tract not only increase the likelihood of uterine contamination and inflammation but compromise the uterus' ability to clear itself of contaminating materials and accumulated fluid. Urine pooling can be diagnosed during a vaginal speculum examination, or histologic evidence of its occurrence may be detected upon examination of uterine cytologic and endometrial biopsy samples.

It is pretty well accepted at this time that delayed uterine clearance plays a major role in a mare's susceptibility to chronic and repeated bouts of endometritis and subsequently decreased overall fertility. Transient post-breeding uterine inflammation is a normal reaction to the presence of semen, and normal mares can clear the fluid, dead sperm, inflammatory debris, and bacterial contamination from their uterus within 24 to 36 hours of natural cover or AI. Contractions of the myometrium (the muscular layer of the uterus) clear the uterus by expelling accumulated fluid out of the uterine lumen through the open estrous cervix. This expulsion promotes uptake and removal of additional particulate matter via the uterine lymphatic duct network.

Susceptible mares in general have a delay in their ability to clear post-breeding endometritis in a timely fashion. A number of factors can lead to delayed uterine clearance. Poor pelvic or overall conformation in which the mare has a flat croup or is built downhill from her hindquarters to her front, respectively, impairs fluid expulsion from a mare's uterus, primarily because the flow of fluid runs counter to gravity. Likewise, a mare that has a non gravid (not pregnant) uterus pulled forward over the brim of the pelvis so that it sags into the abdomen or that has uterine horns that sag from their broad ligament attachments to form a "V" is more prone to accumulating uterine fluid. Sacculated areas in the base of the uterine horns also are frequently associated with abnormal retention of uterine fluid. Decreased myoelectrical activity leads to poor overall uterine contractility and is a large component of delayed uterine clearance. Another problem contributing to delayed uterine clearance is the failure of the cervix to relax and open during estrus. Failure of the cervix to relax blocks the flow of fluid expulsion. A number of mares simply do not experience good cervical relaxation during estrus; others have cervices that have become scarred and fibrotic and cannot relax appropriately. Taken to the extreme, a severely fibrotic cervix will predispose a mare to the development of a pyometra (an abscessed, pus-filled uterus).

Susceptible mares fail to clear normal post-breeding contamination and inflammation within a normal time frame. In instances in which a mare is bred multiple times during a single estrous period, spermatozoa entering the uterus subsequent to the first breeding are adversely affected by the persistent inflammatory environment, thereby compromising a mare's chance of conceiving. The chances of embryo survival are compromised in instances in which the mare conceives but her uterus remains inflamed in the early diestrous period and through the time the six-day-old embryo reaches the uterine lumen. The embryo can perish as a direct result of exposure to inflammatory products and bacteria, or it can be lost if the inflammation provokes the mare's endometrium to release prostoglandin, which lyses the CL. Another point to realize is that the longer contaminating bacterial or fungal organisms remain in the uterine lumen without being expelled, the more likely the organisms are to flourish and overwhelm the mare's cellular defenses and establish an infection. A primary failure of the immune defenses of susceptible mares has yet to be demonstrated. White blood cell function, opsonization (the process by which bacteria or other cells are targeted for destruction by immune cells known as phagocytes), and antibody production in susceptible mares appear to be normal. It appears that a decreased uterine clearance capability is the major contributing factor leading to chronic, repeated uterine infections in susceptible mares. Abnormal accumulations of retained uterine fluid are readily seen on rectal ultrasound examination.

The uterus normally is free of bacteria, and unlike the vestibule and vagina, no known normal resident microflora reside on the mucosa. Transient contamination of the uterine endometrium occurs during breeding and foaling, but normal resistant mares rapidly eliminate the presence of these organisms before an infection can develop and become established. Susceptible mares, as we have said, fail to clear this normally occurring bacterial contamination on their own, and in many cases become infected even in the absence of breeding or foaling as a result of chronic pneumovagina or other predisposing condition. Bacterial endometritis in mares is diagnosed based on a combination of uterine culture and cytology findings. Mares with bacterial uterine infections sometimes will outwardly display a vaginal discharge. On rectal palpation, the infected uterus frequently will feel somewhat thickened and heavy and on ultrasound there might be edema and echogenic fluid. On vaginal speculum examination, uterine exudate might be visible exiting the cervix and/or pooling in the cranial vagina, and the cervix and vaginal mucosa might appear red instead of a normal, healthy pink. The organisms isolated most commonly from mares with bacterial endometritis are those normally found on the mare's skin surface, in her feces, or in the soil. These include *Streptococcus zooepidemicus* and *Escherichia coli* in particular. *Pseudomonas auerogenosa* and *Klebsiella* are also recovered with some frequency. Some practitioners think that certain strains of these latter two organisms are more than just opportunists; they are primary pathogens in their own right. This could be true although susceptible mares in general are more likely to turn up with a *Pseudomonas* or *Klebsiella* infection than are normally resistant mares. Therefore, the host susceptibility of a given mare often appears to be a major factor in the establishment of these two organisms.

Yeast (especially *Candida* species) and fungal organisms also can be responsible for causing established, persistent endometritis. Chronic, indiscriminate intrauterine antibiotic use in many cases seems to be a predisposing element in the establishment of uterine yeast or fungal infections in mares. Yeast organisms also can establish themselves in the vestibule and clitoris of mares, so the mare's own tract serves as a ready source of contamination by these organisms during breeding, insemination, or uterine sampling by a veterinarian. Lastly, endometritis can result from the exposure of the mare's uterus to irritating chemical substances. Urine is one. Sterile saline in and of itself is enough to incite a mild inflammatory response in the uterus of some mares. The variety of substances put into a mare's uterus in the quest for a cure for infertility never ceases to surprise me, and the use of strong disinfecting agents and other harsh substances actually can cause additional irreversible damage to the endometrium and should be avoided.

Degenerative Endometrial Changes

Cystic formations within the endometrium develop from two separate structures. Glandular cysts arise from the dilation of endometrial glands secondary to endometrial periglandular fibrosis. These cysts are small (less than 10 mm in diameter) and are primarily a histologic diagnosis based on microscopic examination of an endometrial biopsy. Lymphatic endometrial cysts arise from enlarged lymphatic ducts and can become quite large (several cen-timeters in diameter). These lymphatic cysts may be contained within the uterine wall or bulge into the uterine lumen. The fluid-filled lymphatic cysts are readily identifiable on rectal ultrasound examination of the uterus. If they are extremely large, they might even be identifiable on rectal palpation.

Lymphatic cysts are the "uterine cysts" a veterinarian may diag-nose following a gross examination of the mare's tract. The etiology behind the formation of lymphatic cysts is not well understood, but they are quite common in many mares. These cysts tend to appear as the mare increases in parity (number of births) and age, and they could be a "red flag" that the mare is experiencing some deteriora-tion of her uterine clearance capabilities. The direct role the pres-ence of cysts might play in contributing to early embryonic death and infertility is somewhat unclear. Very large luminal cysts may impede the migration of the early embryo throughout the mare's uterine lumen, thereby interfering with maternal recognition of pregnancy. Large and/or numerous cysts also might interfere with nutrient exchange to the fixed embryo and in embryonic implanta-tion. However, many embryos continue to develop quite happily nestled amongst large cysts in the base of a uterine horn. In gener-al, unless the cysts are very large (more than 20 to 30 mm in diam-eter) or extremely numerous, it is the author's opinion that the cysts themselves do not cause a problem. Instead, they are a sign that a mare's tract is undergoing degeneration. Deterioration of the defense mechanisms (in particular uterine clearance) results in an overall decrease in fertility, not the presence of the cysts themselves. The vast majority of mares with one or few, small endometrial lym-phatic cysts conceive and carry a foal to term without too much dif-ficulty. A few, small lymphatic cysts within the endometrium is expected with time and wear and tear and not immediate cause for panic.

Many studies have shown a relationship between an increased severity of endometrial fibrotic changes and decreased foaling rates in affected mares. Pregnancy losses after 28 days of gestation seem to be most highly correlated with the presence of increasing degrees of uterine fibrosis, and a history of repeatedly lost pregnancies between 35 to 80 days of gestation is highly suggestive of this condition. Formation of the diffuse microvillous attachment of the equine placenta has its rudimentary beginnings around day 40 of gestation, and the equine placenta is not firmly established until after 100 days of gestation. Therefore, the developing foal would appear to be very dependent on the nutrition supplied by the endometrial glands in the form of histotroph (uterine milk) during much of its early development. It is believed that periglandular fibrosis somehow compromises the ability of the endometrial glands to support a developing pregnancy. Diagnosis is based on the finding of fibrotic changes on endometrial biopsy, and a biopsy grade is assigned to the mare's sample, based largely on the degree of fibrosis and inflammation present on histological examination. The poorer the biopsy score the less likely the mare is to conceive and carry a foal successfully to term.

The reason behind the development of fibrosis in the endometrium is not entirely clear. Endometrial damage incurred in the course of repeated episodes or in single, extreme episodes of uterine inflammation likely results in the formation of some of this "scar tissue." Mares with severe endometrial fibrosis appear to be more susceptible to developing bacterial endometritis, so it became a sort of "chicken or the egg" kind of puzzle. The development of uterine fibrosis also might be a wear-and-tear type change that occurs along with parity in the mare. However, the degree of uterine fibrosis also is observed to increase in mares as they age but which have no history of previous breedings or endometritis. Therefore, it might occur normally, in part, as a result of aging.

Fibrotic changes within a mare's endometrium are permanent, and there are presently no known effective means of treatment though many, such as chemical and physical curettage, have been tried. It is feared that many of the methods described as possible treatments to decrease the severity of endometrial fibrosis in a mare's uterus actually end up causing more damage. Producing live foals from moderate to severely affected mares is largely a result of excellent management and luck.

The Role of Progesterone

The production of histotroph by the uterine glands and other endometrial proteins that support the growth and development of the young embryo, such as uteroferrin, are stimulated by progesterone. Some studies suggest that some aged and/or infertile mares might require higher levels of progesterone (above those that are considered to be normal for early pregnancy) early on in gestation (i.e., within the first days following ovulation) in order to establish a successful pregnancy. Remember, much of the embryonic loss that occurs in subfertile mares happens prior to the time a positive pregnancy diagnosis can be made. Some infertile mares only become diagnosibly pregnant and successfully deliver foals when they are supplemented with an exogenous source of progesterone beginning approximately four days after ovulation. Some research findings support the idea that early progesterone supplementation might increase early embryonic growth and survival. Increasing amounts of progesterone before 14 days post-ovulation (in normal mares) results in a higher production of uteroferrin by the endometrium. Embryos that develop within this kind of "enhanced" uterine environment are often larger at 14 days than would normally be expected. So perhaps the promotion of increased production of endometrial proteins in a subfertile but otherwise noninfected uterine environment may rescue an otherwise doomed embryo. Progesterone suppresses the response of white blood cells to invading bacteria and decreases the uterine clearance of materials from the uterine lumen by decreasing lymphatic uptake as well as by causing the cervix to tighten and close. This is one of the reasons that uterine infections can "take off" during the diestrous phase of the mare's cycle. Therefore, the risk of giving a mare additional progesterone to enhance her uterine environment as described above is inadvertently causing a pre-existing uterine contamination or infection to "explode." A mare must be free of any signs of possible uterine infection or delayed uterine clearance (uterine fluid or edema) before therapy with exogenous progesterone begins. At present, the only means of supplementing mares is with daily oral altrenogest or with daily injections of progesterone in oil.

Old Mares

As mares reach 12 years of age, their fertility begins to decline with each subsequent birthday. The incidence of early embryonic death increases as mares age, and a percentage of mares require more breeding attempts on multiple estrous cycles to establish viable pregnancies. Compounding this is the fact that some old mares experience a delay in their return to cycling in the spring, resulting in fewer fertile cycles during the breeding season.

Older mares experience a one-two punch to their fertility in the form of increased incidence of degeneration to their reproductive tract and uterine defense mechanisms along with an increased incidence of primary embryonic abnormalities. As previously discussed, the amount of endometrial fibrosis within a mare's tract tends to increase with age, and the incidence of lesions within the oviducts also increases with age. The presence of oviductal lesions has particular ramifications for the survival of the developing embryo during the first five to six days as it is the oviductal environment that provides nourishment and support during initial embryonic development. As mares age, the overall tone and resiliency of their reproductive tissues tend to decrease (especially if the mare has had multiple foals). Perineal conformation suffers, and the uterus tends to drop somewhat forward into the abdomen. Associated with these changes is an increased tendency for aging mares to windsuck and accumulate increased amounts of luminal uterine fluid during estrus.

As mares age, so do their oocytes. Mares, like women, are born with their full lifetime complement of oocytes within their ovaries. Oocytes obtained from older women demonstrate an increased incidence of aneuploidy (abnormal number of chromosomes). It is likely to be the same situation in the aged broodmare. Embryos that result from the fertilization of such abnormal oocytes will be defective. Experiments over the years have shown that embryos recovered from older mares have poorer survival rates when transferred to healthy recipients than do those recovered from young mares. Primary embryonic defects appear to be a major cause of early embryonic loss in older mares. The tendency for poor embryonic quality, combined with an aged uterine environment that is also less than optimal, results in overall decreased foaling rates for this class of mares.

Managing Infertility

Breeding Soundness Examination

The first step in managing a subfertile or infertile mare is to identify the cause(s) for her apparent decreased ability to reproduce successfully. The standard complete breeding soundness examination (BSE) includes a complete review of the mare's health and reproductive history, a general physical examination, assessment of the mare's perineal conformation, rectal palpation and ultrasound of her reproductive organs, vaginal speculum examination, manual vaginal and cervical examination, samples taken for uterine cytology and culture, and an endometrial biopsy. Ancillary procedures such as blood profiles or hormonal levels, karyotyping, and/or direct endoscopic examination of the uterine lumen also may be performed if results from the basic BSE indicate a need for additional information.

A thorough reproductive history is perhaps the most important aspect of the entire examination and should never be overlooked. Factors such as the intensity and appropriateness of previous mare breeding management; the fertility of stallions bred to; whether breedings were with fresh, transported, or frozen semen; and how many cycle attempts have been made to get the mare pregnant are all important clues as to whether a mare's apparent infertility is likely to be entirely her fault. Many mares are dubbed infertile simply because they have failed to become pregnant on a single attempt, and that is not really fair. Remember that the average per cycle conception rate is somewhere in the neighborhood of 60 percent, and a single failure could just mean she was merely part of the unlucky 40 percent. Unsuccessful mares that have been bred only in February or early March could merely be victims of the season. Remember, a mare exposed to a stallion in the 11 months before the examination could be pregnant. A fair percentage of mares presented to veterinarians for BSE are, in fact, pregnant! This condition, then, must be ruled out fairly early during the course of the examination before invasive uterine sampling (which would likely terminate a pre-existing pregnancy) is performed.

Once the gross anatomy and condition of the perineum vulva, vestibule, vestibular-vaginal sphincter, vagina, cervix, uterus, and ovaries have been thoroughly checked, then conditions such as pneumovagina, urine pooling, abnormal uterine fluid accumulations, and abnormally enlarged ovaries can be assessed. A determination of whether the mare is cycling and, if so, the status of her cycle (i.e., estrus or diestrus) also is made and compared with the season. The overall consistency between ovarian structures and uterine and cervical findings (tone, fluid accumulations, presence of edema) also is evaluated. Just as important, her present pregnancy status is identified.

Once the mare is determined to be open, the veterinarian then begins directly sampling the uterus (cytology, culture, and biopsy) so that the mare is next examined on a cellular level. In this way, a determination is made of the state of her endometrium relative to the existence of infection, inflammation, and degeneration. The sampling of a mare's uterus in the form of a uterine culture is very common practice in the breeding world and not only just a part of a full BSE. Many stallion owners routinely require the mare owner to verify that the mare's uterus is free of infection before she is bred. This is particularly true of live covers. It is very important to realize, however, that to reach the lumen of the mare's uterus, the culture swab first must be passed through the non-sterile environments of the vestibule, vagina, and cranial cervix. Thorough cleansing of the mare's perineum prior to sampling, the use of guarded culture swabs, and careful sampling technique are all employed in an effort to avoid incidental contamination of the sample with organisms not originating from the mare's uterus. Even with the most conscientious sampling techniques, however, contaminants sometimes make it onto the swab and are cultured

AT A GLANCE

◆ All subfertile or infertile mares should have a breeding soundness exam before the start of the breeding season.

◆ It is important to make sure the mare isn't pregnant before performing invasive procedures.

◆ The first step in treating endometritis is to correct any anatomic predispositions.

◆ Many susceptible mares benefit from post-breeding uterine lavage and ocytocin therapy.

in the laboratory just the same. These contaminants are most likely to be the very same sorts of organisms commonly found in mares with uterine infections (i.e., organisms that are commonly present on or in the mare's skin or feces). One way to determine whether the organism in the petri dish truly came from the uterus is the purity of the growth and the number of colonies present. One or a few colonies of a mixed assortment of organisms are unlikely to represent anything more than contamination (although there is concern any time *Pseudomonas*, *Klebsiella*, yeast, or a Beta hemolytic *Streptococcus* is present). A heavy, pure growth of a single organism is likely to represent the source of the uterine infection in the mare that was sampled. The best way to determine whether a mare is truly infected and the culture results are believable, however, is to retrieve a uterine sample for cytology at the same time the uterus is sampled for a culture. These samples can be obtained using the same swab technique employed to obtain the culture (the swab for the cytology is pre-moistened with some sterile saline) or by flushing a small volume of sterile saline into the uterus using a sterile pipette, then aspirating it back out with a syringe. There are even some commercially available uterine swabs that also are designed to gather a sample for cytological examination simultaneously.

With the rare exception of the occasional mare with a very recently established yeast infection, the presence of an infecting organism will incite inflammation in the endometrium. The presence of the white blood cells rushing in to defend the integrity of the uterine environment is readily observable on slides with the cytological samples. The presence of more than one neutrophil (a type of white blood cell) per five high-power (40x) microscopic fields on a slide is proof positive that there is inflammation within the uterine lumen. The corresponding growth of an organism obtained on culture should be considered a truly positive culture. Except during the first 24 to 36 hours post-breeding, neutrophils are relatively absent from the normal mare's uterus. Without the cytological evidence, it is difficult to confirm that a mare truly has endometritis, and a cytology should be performed routinely any time a mare's uterus is cultured; otherwise, the culture results are meaningless. An additional advantage of examining uterine cytologies is that it is possible to find evidence of other reproductive tract problems (pneumovagina and urine pooling) based on cells or debris found in the sample. The presence of bacteria, yeast, and fungal organisms also can be readily apparent upon viewing the cytology, and it is possible to get at least some idea of the likely causative organism and some indication of how to initiate treatment while waiting for positive culture results and antibiotic sensitivity testing.

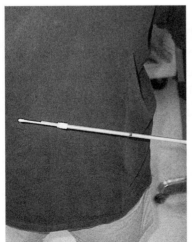

A uterine culture swab

One final comment about culturing a mare's uterus. Opinions differ as to whether it is better to culture a mare's uterus when she is in diestrus or in estrus. It is certainly easier to obtain a sample through the open cervix of an estrus mare than it is through the closed cervix of a diestrus mare, but sampling a diestrus mare actually is not that difficult. During estrus, the mare's uterine defenses are at their optimum and so it is thought by many that any organism present within the uterus at that time truly represents an infecting organism. The exception, of course, is during the foal heat when mares are normally contaminated but not necessarily infected with a number of organisms immediately post-foaling. The other thought behind sampling a mare when she is in estrus is that she is better able to clear any uterine contamination that might occur during sampling and so runs a lower risk of inadvertent infection at that time. Careful sampling is successful at identifying true uterine infection irrespective of the mare's phase of cycle, provided a cytology is performed at the same time. Sampling a mare during early estrus also has the added advantage of the veterinarian being able to treat any identified infection more effectively while the mare is actually in estrus. If a BSE is performed on a mare that is in diestrus, the mare often will be given a dose of prostaglandin at the completion of the examination to short cycle her back into estrus immediately following the examination. That way, she is better able to deal with any bacterial contamination of her uterus that might have occurred during the examination.

The routine BSE is completed by performing an endometrial biopsy using a long, sterile jawed biopsy forceps. The biopsy instrument is introduced through the mare's cervix manually just the same as the uterine culture and cytology swabs. Once the forceps are placed within the uterine body, the veterinarian then withdraws his or her arm from the mare's vagina and places it in the rectum. The forceps in the uterus then are palpated rectally and positioned at the base of one uterine horn or at any other point in the

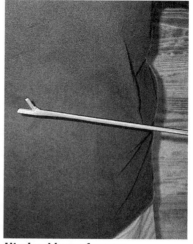

Uterine biopsy forceps

uterus that has been deemed suspect, and a small piece of the endometrium is retrieved. As long as the forceps are manipulated gently so they do not bang around in the mare's cervix, the endometrial biopsy procedure is painless and well tolerated by most mares. The retrieved piece of endometrium (usually a piece approximately 0.5 to 1 cm long) is typically placed into a fixative solution (Bouin's or formalin) and sent to the lab for histological examination. A sample of the endometrium occasionally is submitted for deep culture of a mare's uterus. Examining the endometrium histologically is done primarily to obtain an overall picture of the degree of acute and (in particular) chronic inflammation and degeneration (fibrosis, dilated lymphatics, endometrial gland atrophy). When considered in context with the mare's history and examination findings, the endometrial biopsy represents the most objective means available at this time to assess a mare's potential reproductive capabilities. Even though the size of the tissue sample is small compared to the overall surface area of the uterine lumen, studies have demonstrated that lesions in the uterus tend to be uniform and evenly distributed throughout. Therefore, the findings in a single biopsy sample are usually representative of the uterine lining as a whole. (Sometimes a practitioner may take multiple samples from different points within the mare's uterus if there is any question that one area might be more problematic than another, perhaps as a result of a past localized uterine injury.)

A prognostic scoring system is used by the veterinary pathologist examining the endometrial samples to describe the cumulative changes present. Named the Kenney-Doig system after the men who developed it, this system rates and correlates the mare's endometrial findings with her ability to conceive and carry a foal to term, provided she is well managed. (Please refer to the table.) Endometrial biopsies from cycling mares are more revealing and more accurately assessed than those from anestrous mares. Endometrial biopsies from anestrus mares are normally inactive and somewhat atrophied in appearance. For this reason, it is best to biopsy a mare during the physiological breeding season as that is the time when many changes and pathologies reveal themselves.

Kenney-Doig Equine Endometrial Biopsy Grading System

Biopsy Category	Endometrial Changes	% Chance of Mare Carrying a Foal to Term
I	normal or only slight changes	80%-90%
II a	mild changes (fibrosis, inflammation, Lymphatic lacunai, endometrial atrophy)	50%-80%
II b	Moderate changes	10%-50%
III	Severe changes	<10%

(No mare is ever labeled as having a zero percent chance of foaling [unless she has had an ovario-hysterectomy]. Occasionally even a grade III mare manages to beat the odds and produce a foal, although the chances of her making it all the way to term are very small.)

Taken together, the role of a complete BSE is to identify any problems in a mare's reproductive system and to make a judgment call about her future reproductive capabilities, provided any identified problems can be fixed and she is properly managed during future breeding attempts. As previously stated, many mares undergo a BSE because they have demonstrated an inability to get in foal. Other instances when a BSE might be indicated are as part of a broodmare pre-purchase examination, post-abortion or multiple embryonic resorptions, or before corrective reproductive surgery. In the latter case, a pre-surgical endometrial biopsy is recommended because if a mare already has a grade III uterus, it could be somewhat pointless (unless the mare is an extremely valuable producer) to spend a lot of money and put the mare through the stress of a surgical procedure that might have negligible results because her uterine environment is pretty much shot. In instances when a BSE is performed primarily as an infertility work up, it is best to perform the examination as far in advance of the next breeding season as possible. This way there is plenty of time to remedy any correctable problems and less time will be lost during the next season. Barren mares should have a BSE performed during the late summer or early fall. This is well in advance of the next season, and the mare in question likely will still be cycling during this time. Whether a full BSE is performed at the initial work up of a mare depends on the circumstances. A potential buyer of a young maiden mare that presents for a pre-purchase examination with no identifiable physical abnormalities on visual or palpable examination may opt to forgo a uterine cytology, culture, and biopsy. During the breedings season, a well-managed mare that already has a Caslick's and clean specs initially might require only a culture/cytology following an unsuccessful breeding attempt. The bottom line, however, is that if a mare has had recurrent problems for no apparent reason, and her management pre- and post-breeding has been excellent, it is probably time to take a second full look at her and get a uterine biopsy.

Treatment of Endometritis

Successful handling of a mare with endometritis includes the following three objectives. The first objective is to correct surgically any anatomic pathology a mare might have that predisposes her to developing uterine infections. The second objective is to clean up any existing uterine infections before rebreeding her. The third objective is to prevent the mare's uterus from becoming reinflamed and reinfected following any future breeding attempts.

Any defects in the three anatomic barriers (vulva, vestibular-vaginal junction, and cervix) between the outside world and the inside of the uterus need to have their integrity restored to eliminate the affected mare's predisposition toward uterine contamination. Many foaling injuries to the cervix often heal well and do not compromise the ability of the cervix to form the tight seal so critical during diestrus. The best way to assess the integrity of the cervical seal is by direct manual palpation of the diameter of the internal cervical canal during diestrus. Many times even a complete tear in the vaginal cervical os does not compromise the ability of the cervical body and internal os to close completely. However, in those instances where the cervical lumen

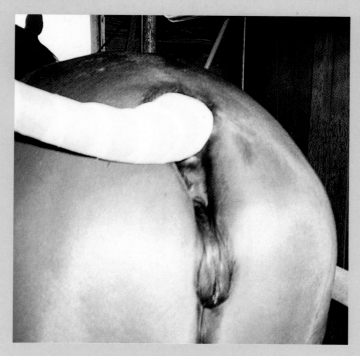

Signs of impending foaling include elongation of the vulva (above) and teats that begin to drip milk (below).

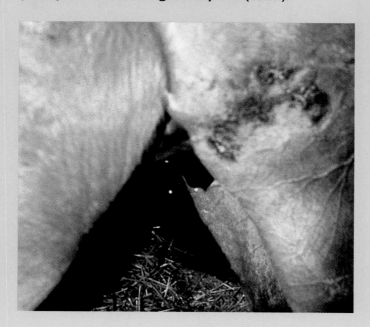

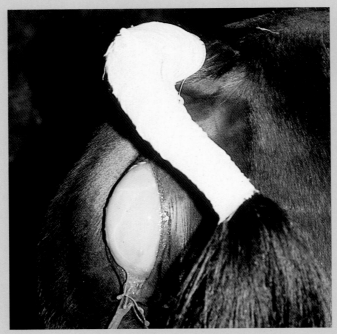

The appearance of the white amnion and discharging allantoic fluid (above); the foal's forelegs (below) present first in a normal birth.

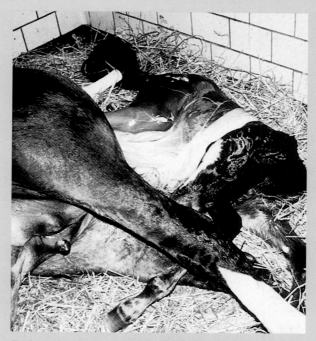

Delivery is nearly complete (above); the mare and
foal greet each other for the first time (below).

Allantoic surface (above) and chorionic surface (below) of an equine placenta; a so-called red bag delivery is characterized by the presentation of the red chorionic membrane rather than the white amnion.

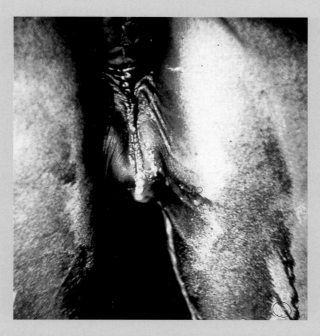

Post-foaling discharge that is pus-tinged (above) is abnormal; ultrasound (below) can detect free fluid in the abdomen in post-foaling mares with hemorrhage or peritonitis.

A plank separates a mare that has rejected her foal but allows the foal to nurse (above); a nurse mare (below) is often used for a rejected and orphaned foal.

Colic in a two-day-old foal due to a meconium impaction. This foal (above and below) is demonstrating some typical colic behavior — rolling from side to side and getting up and down frequently.

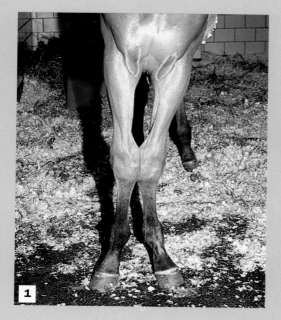

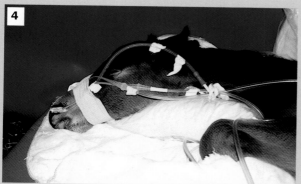

1) A two-month-old foal with angular limb deformities on both front legs; 2) a severe clubfoot; 3) a foal with a scrotal hernia; 4) a newborn with pneumonia from complete failure of passive transfer.

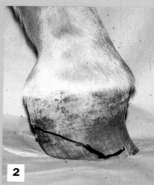

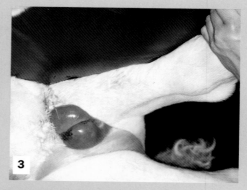

remains somewhat dilated due to the presence of a previous tear, it needs to be surgically repaired by an experienced surgeon. It should be remembered that once a mare tears her cervix she is likely to do it again at subsequent foalings even after it has been surgically repaired once (scar tissue has a tendency to tear again instead of stretching). Mares that have had cervical tears need to have their cervical integrity re-evaluated following each subsequent foaling. Laxity in the vestibular-vaginal sphincter is difficult to address, but reconstructive surgery on the roof of the vestibule to reconstruct the perineal body somewhat could help those mares that continue to windsuck despite having a Caslick's. Far and away the most common problem found in a majority of sub-

fertile mares is the presence of poor perineal/vulvar conformation. For these mares, a simple Caslick's procedure can turn around fertility literally overnight provided there has not already been too much damage done to the endometrium as a result of the chronic pneumovagina.

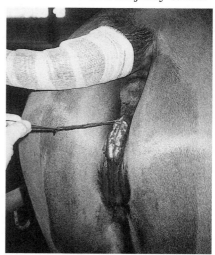

A Caslick's is a surgical procedure in which the edges of the vulvar lips are surgically cut and then sewn together starting from the top of the vulva and ending

Performing a Caslick's

at or just below the level of the pelvic floor. The sewn portion of the vulvar lips heal together to form a protective barrier that prevents the mare from windsucking. The vulvar lips are not sewn completely together so the mare is still able to urinate freely and discharge can still drain through the vulvar lips. Depending on the diameter of the remaining vulvar opening, the mare might have to have her Caslick's opened and reclosed to permit natural breeding or AI, but in all instances these mares require opening approximately two weeks before foaling so that they do not tear themselves trying to push the foal through.

If intermittent, vaginal urine pooling does not always warrant surgical repair. Many mares will urine pool in the immediate period post-foaling but spontaneously resolve once the pelvic tissues tighten up and uterine involution returns the uterus to a more normal non-pregnant size. Some mares that only urine pool for a brief time during estrus and are not inflamed can be managed by literally sopping up the urine with sterile gauze before breeding or inseminating to dry up the mess in the vagina. Other practitioners use specific acupuncture points that sometimes will cause a mare's perineal and pelvic tissues to tighten up enough to resolve the problem. Mares that chronically pool urine in their vaginas require reconstructive surgery to extend the length of the urethra artificially and effectively place the urethral opening on the downside of the vestibular slope so that the stream of urine can no longer partially backflow into the vagina. This procedure is technically a little tricky, and sometimes the tissues forming the artificial urethral extension fail to heal together without the formation of little gaps in the tissue seal. When this occurs, the mare will frequently leak a little urine through these gaps each time she urinates, and this escaping urine again will pool in the cranial vagina. For this reason, it is not uncommon to perform a urethral extension procedure more than once.

Recto-vaginal (R-V) fistulas, likewise, must be surgically repaired to prevent chronic fecal contamination of the vagina. Like urethral extensions, R-V repairs might require more than one attempt before the reconstructed tissues (in this case the reconstructed tissue shelf between the rectum and vagina) heal to form the desired complete barrier seal.

A quick mention of surgical removal or obliteration of endometrial lymphatic cysts is warranted at this point. Remember, the vast majority of so-called endometrial cysts do not have an impact on fertility. But a mare occasionally might have one or two extremely large cysts that perhaps interfere in a direct physical way with embryonic development and survival. These large cysts sometimes can be removed using laser surgery through an endoscope placed in the uterine lumen or by direct manual removal using a surgical snare if the cyst is on a stalk of tissue. Whether removal of such cysts helps is up for debate, depending on whom you consult. Some mares successfully get pregnant following this kind of endometrial cyst removal and others do not. Don't forget that the formation of lymphatic cysts is expected as a mare ages and in many instances is a sign that the mare's uterine clearance mechanism is beginning to work less effectively. Removing the cyst will not cure the uterine clearance problem.

The successful treatment of a mare with an established uterine infection depends on helping the mare help herself by eliminating any accumulated uterine fluid and debris, accurately identifying the offending organism, and subsequently treating that mare with an effective antibiotic or antifungal. The uterine defenses of the mare are heightened during estrus. Uterine drainage is facilitated by an open cervix, and the seek and destroy activities of the white blood cells are heightened in the absence of progesterone. It makes sense, then, to short cycle an infected diestrous mare back into estrus when her own immune system is best able to fight a uterine infection. A number of mares that when Caslicksed and short cycled, rapidly cleared uterine infections on their own without need for any additional therapies. When additional means of treatment are required, however, the open cervix of the estrous mare makes the veterinarian's application of intrauterine therapies that much easier.

Mares with significant accumulations of fluid (inflammatory products, white blood cells, and organisms) will benefit from their removal. Just returning a mare to estrus frequently is enough to help her clear this kind of a mess, but many mares benefit from initial uterine lavage therapy using sterile saline or lactated ringers to flush the debris from their uterine lumen. It also helps to follow lavage therapy with oxytocin treatment, which makes the uterus contract and push out fluid accumulations. Harsh disinfectant solutions such as concentrated iodines and especially chlorhexidine solution (Nolvasan) should be avoided, as they are much too irritating to the mare's endometrium and actually can cause more damage than the infection itself. The exception to this is in the case of some resistant yeast or fungal infections where lavage with a very diluted iodine solution (1 percent iodine diluted 1:10 with water or sterile saline to form a weak tea-colored solution) can sometimes help.

Bacterial endometritis frequently is treated successfully with antibiotics, but the occurrence of bacterial antibiotic resistance needs to be addressed. It is a waste of time to use an antibiotic that doesn't work. Shotgun, indiscriminate antibiotic use in mares not only can lead to the use of an ineffective antibiotic but also might cause a contaminating yeast or fungal organism to jump into the mix and take hold. Antibiotic treatment of bacterial endometritis of mares is most effective when it is based on antibiotic sensitivity testing. In addition, not every antibiotic to which a given bacteria is sensitive may be appropriate to place in the uterus of a mare. Many antibiotics or their carrier solutions are irritating to the endometrium. So where a choice exists, only uterus-friendly drugs should be used for direct intrauterine infusion treatments.

It is also possible to treat a mare's uterine infections using systemic (oral, intramuscular, or intravenous administration) antibiotics at the proper dose and frequency. The advantage of intrauterine therapy with antibiotics is the high endometrial tissue levels of the antibiotic obtained by placing the antibiotics directly into the uterine lumine at the site of infection. Typically a mare will be treated daily throughout her estrous period with uterine antibiotic infusions. Follow-up cultures and cytologies are performed at the beginning of the mare's next heat period (short cycled or naturally occurring) to see whether treatment has been effective, and the mare is now clean. If the mare's uterus is still infected, antibiotic sensitivities should be repeated on the cultured organism as its antibiotic sensitivity pattern might have shifted during the previous round of therapy and a different antibiotic might be required.

Yeast and Fungal Infections

Nothing will ruin a veterinarian's day quite like the discovery that a mare's uterus is infected with a fungal or yeast organism. These types of uterine infections can be extremely difficult to clean up, and it is not unusual to lose an entire breeding season once a mare develops a yeast or fungal infection. There are many different available treatment protocols for dealing with these mycotic infections, which immediately serve as a red-flag warning that none of them is 100 percent effective in every mare. It helps to run sensitivity pattern testing on these organisms as well, as some cultured yeast organisms are resistant to some of the available antimycotic preparations. Daily uterine lavage while the mare is in heat using dilute iodine solutions is sometimes successful. So is lavaging the estrous mare's uterus daily with dilute vinegar and sterile water or saline solutions. Daily, long-term (21 days in some protocols) intrauterine therapy with Nystatin or Clotrimazole is occasionally successful as well, as is a combination approach using lavage and an antimycotic. However, some mares with yeast infections fail to clear these organisms no matter what you try until their own immune system finally gets around to joining the fight. There is little to be done but hang in there and be patient.

Breeding the Susceptible Mare

Once a mare finally comes clean after a yeast infection, it is extremely important to handle her with the proverbial kid gloves so that she does not become reinfected down the rode. Her own lower tract could serve as a source of reinfection, so vaginal and uterine manipulations should be kept to an absolute minimum, and of course intrauterine antibiotic therapy should be avoided completely in these kinds of mares unless it is desperately needed. Long-standing yeast infections can do extensive damage to a mare's endometrium, so on the whole it is really best to prevent mycotic infections from occurring rather than to have to treat them.

Once the susceptible mare has been cleaned up and steps taken to prevent casual reinfection via pneumovagina and or urine pooling, the question now becomes how to get her bred without causing re-infection upon the introduction of semen. The hallmark of suscepti-ble mares is that they reinfect easily. Such mares will tolerate very lit-tle in the way of repeated intrauterine manipulation, and so not only does the act of breeding pose a threat but so does the possible con-tamination that could occur during uterine manipulation for sam-pling and treatment. The best approach to these mares is to work very hard at managing their breeding correctly!

Breeding management of a susceptible mare needs to be highly accurate. The best approach for a mare like this is a minimum breed-ing contamination technique. The idea is to follow the mare very closely so that ideally she only needs to be bred one time, and that one time happens within 24 hours or less before ovulation. It is best that the mare is already cycling with at least one ovulation under her belt when it is time to begin. In that way, her estrus will be more pre-dictable, and hopefully it will be easier to determine the optimal time to breed her. In general, too, her fertility will be better as May and June approach. It would be ideal not to breed this kind of mare until the normal peak of the physiological breeding season, although this approach needs to be balanced with the fact that starting late leaves fewer cycles with which to work. It is many practitioners' opinion that the best chance of successfully establishing a pregnancy in a susceptible mare will be on the very first attempt of the season. The rationale behind this thought is that susceptible mares frequently will have chronic inflammation in their uterus as a result of previous repeated or long-term infections. Once she is cleaned up and caslicksed the preceding fall, the still somewhat inflamed, infection-free uterus finally has a chance to quiet down and rest over the fall and winter anestrus. If everyone has done his or her job well and luck is smiling on the mare, she will not become reinfected over the course of the winter and early spring before her first breeding of the new season. By the time her first breeding arrives, the chronic inflammation in the endometrium most likely will be as subdued as possible. Once she is bred for the first time, however, and experiences that first post-breeding inflammatory response, everything begins to flare up. Over time, this inflammation becomes cumulative with each successive cycle in which she is breed. Also, her chances of becoming reinfected increase with every cycle bred. For these reasons, the first shot of the season is frequently the best shot for a susceptible mare.

The semen going into a susceptible mare needs to be of the highest quality possible. A stallion that has marginal fertility breeding young fertile mares is not a good selection for a mare like this. Likewise, the use of frozen semen with its overall reduced conception rates (compared to fresh or transported semen) and its increased tendency to incite uterine inflammation should not be considered an option for breeding a susceptible mare. The only exception to these considerations is if a particular stallion is the only possible pairing for the mare, and if she cannot produce a foal with that particular stallion then there is no need to breed her at all. In that kind of situation, there is nothing to lose, and it is worth a try as long as everyone is aware that the chances for success are guarded and the risk of reinfecting the mare with nothing to show for it is good.

In those breed registries that permit the registration of foals resulting from artificial insemination, breeding a mare with fresh, antibiotic extended semen (or in some cases where the stallion ships well, transported semen) is the preferred method for breeding a susceptible mare. AI results overall in less contamination of the mare's tract than does natural cover. A sterile pipette and carefully inserted, sterilized gloved hand result in less contamination of the mare's uterus with air and bacteria than does even the cleanest, thrusting stallion penis. Secondly, the actual number of inflammation-causing sperm cells is far fewer in an inseminating dose (100 million to 500 million) of extended semen than it is in the average stallion's ejaculate (5 billion to 10-plus billion). If at all possible then, AI breeding has a better chance of successfully impregnating a susceptible mare while still managing to keep her clean.

The next critical step in managing a susceptible mare so that she becomes pregnant without becoming reinfected or persistently inflamed comes during the post-breeding period, especially the first 24 to 48 hours. If all has gone well, the mare has ovulated as you predicted within 24 hours of the breeding. In addition to monitoring the mare for ovulation, it is important to monitor the mare's uterus closely with ultrasound and treat her as needed to ensure that post-breeding inflammation is kept to a minimum and uterine clearance is accomplished in a timely fashion. Susceptible mares tend to accumulate fluid in their uterus (it's the main reason why these mares are susceptible). Ultrasound monitoring of normal mares through estrus and post-breeding show them to have normal trace accumulations of clear fluid that are less than 1 cm in diameter and that clear rapidly from the uterus without intervention. Susceptible mares tend to have much larger accumulations of clear to cloudy fluid that persists without treatment. The longer seminal by-products (seminal plasma, dead sperm, etc.) remain in the uterus the greater the generated inflammatory response. This inflammatory response peaks within 12 hours of insemination, and begins to rise exponentially after that in response to the presence of accumulated inflammatory by products in and of themselves. Those sperm that form the group that make it to the oviducts to wait for their chance to fertilize the mare's oocyte reach the safety of the oviduct within four hours post-breeding. Once within the oviducts, these sperm are safe from being flushed during the act of uterine lavage with sterile saline.

Post-breeding uterine lavage performed within eight to 12 hours of breeding, combined with intramuscular treatments of oxytocin every eight to 24 hours post-breeding, has proven extremely beneficial at cleaning up mares post-breeding. It is important to remember that the very act of lavaging the mare's uterus runs the risk of contaminating it with bacteria, and so if at all possible it is best only to have to lavage the mare once during the post-breeding period. This first lavage hopefully rinses all the initial contaminants and inflammatory debris out of the uterine lumen and breaks the abnormal inflammatory accumulation cycle in these mares.

The use of oxytocin daily as needed one to three times a day for one to three days following breeding and ovulation is particularly useful to help the uterus clear itself of any remaining fluid. Oxytocin works by increasing the contractility of the uterus. These contractions help push fluid and debris out the open cervix and also through the uterine lymphatic system once the cervix begins to close down following ovulation. The goal is to have a quiet, fluid-free uterus at five to six days post-ovulation to welcome the embryo. Some practitioners routinely monitor all mares with daily ultrasound for at least the first 48 hours post-ovulation and susceptible mares daily up through at least the first four days post-ovulation. The question of whether it is appropriate to put post-breeding antibiotic infusions into the uterus is a controversial one. In mares that are bred AI with antibiotic extended semen there is probably no additional benefit to infusing these mares further. In mares that are live covered it is unclear whether the use of post-breeding antibiotic infusions help prevent a contaminated mare from becoming an infected mare. Many thousands of mares in the Thoroughbred industry in particular are routinely infused in this manner within 24 hours of breeding. The antibiotics used vary with the experience and preference of the veterinarian administering them. The majority of normal mares handle these treatments without any apparent harm. In mares that tend to accumulate fluid post-breeding, however, it makes better sense to lavage the mare before administering the antibiotic so that the infused antibiotic is not being merely dumped into a "cesspool" and overwhelmed by all the accumulated fluid and debris. In mares with histories of previous mycotic uterine infections, the routine administration of post-breeding uterine infusions with antibiotics is probably best avoided.

Early Post-Ovulatory Progesterone Supplementation

As discussed earlier, some infertile mares seem to establish successful pregnancies only when they are supplemented with exogenous progesterone beginning prior to 14 days post-ovulation, typically starting as early as four days post-ovulation. It is extremely important to stress that individuals chosen as candidates for this form of therapy have to be monitored carefully during the post-breeding period and throughout the supplementation period for signs of inflammation and infection. The use of exogenous progesterone in mares with endometritis is absolutely contraindicated as the additional progesterone will drive the infection and make an already bad situation a lot worse.

Advanced Assisted Reproductive Technologies

It is beyond the scope of this text to go into a detailed description of the techniques and management involved in successfully performing some of the advanced assisted reproductive technologies that are available commercially. A few appropriate points relative to breeding options for infertile mares are worth mentioning. In discussing these technologies, the two presently available techniques are embryo transfer and oocyte transfer. Embryo transfer involves the harvesting and transfer of a (usually) seven-day-old embryo from the uterus of one mare (the donor) and placing it into the uterus of a synchronized recipient mare that then will hopefully carry the foal to term. Oocyte transfer, simply described, is the process of harvesting an oocyte directly from the ovary of a donor mare, then transferring it to the oviducts of a recipient mare. The recipient mare is then bred with the desired stallion's semen to fertilize the donor's oocyte while it is within the recipient's oviduct. If all works out well, the donor's oocyte is fertilized and the recipient mare carries the resultant foal to term.

The best candidates to be embryo transfer donors are young, healthy mares (better embryo quality and better reproductive tract to support the embryo to the seven-day stage). The older or more infertile the mare, the lower the chances for success with embryo transfer. On average, the success rate on embryo flushes from young mares and then the success rates of establishing a viable pregnancy in a recipient mare are somewhere around 60 percent and 60 percent, respectively. The procedures are not technically difficult and can be performed on the farm, but usually mares are brought into clinic settings for management and embryo harvest. Mare owners can nominate their potential donor mares to one of several different recipient programs around the country. These programs make it possible to flush an embryo from the donor mare at home. Then the embryo can be packaged and sent same day (preferably) to a recipient center for transfer. This eliminates the need to provide and synchronize recipient mares at home. In general, a mare owner should anticipate as many as three cycle attempts before an embryo is transferred successfully and a foal results. This can become fairly expensive with the possibility of having several thousand dollars in costs with no pregnancy to show for it. Even so, embryo transfer remains a nice way of obtaining offspring from mares that are in active competition or increasing the total number of foals produced by a valuable mare over the course of her lifetime. Unfortunately, it is frequently not the answer for obtaining one more foals from an old mare or from a mare that has a uterus that is beyond redemption. Also, registration of embryo transfer foals is not permitted by a number of registries.

The main advantage of oocyte transfer is that it makes it possible for a mare with a terrible uterine environment to produce a foal. For old mares, however, it is still a challenge to be successful as you are forced to work with an aged oocyte; the resulting poor embryo viability from these old mares makes success more elusive. Disadvantages include difficulty of harvesting and maturing the oocyte prior to transfer, cost, and the presently limited availability of this technique. At the time of this writing, there are only a limited number of large referral institutions set up to offer this service to mare owners.

Switching Stallions

Although there is no concrete evidence at this time to support this theory, it sometimes helps to change stallions if a mare has failed to establish a pregnancy after several attempts with the same stud. Some things are not meant to be, and some pairings appear just to be incompatible. For example, the stallion has good fertility and settles other mares without any difficulty, or the mare management has been first rate, the mare does not appear to have anything wrong with her, and she is not getting infected. It has been the experience of many mare managers and veterinarians that switching stallions at the end of the season after multiple failed attempts to settle a mare with one stallion often results in the mare's becoming pregnant to the new stallion on the first jump. Is there some as yet unknown immune incompatibility between certain individuals? Or is it just breeding luck? Hard to say.

The Pregnant Mare

The role of the broodmare on any farm is to produce a live, healthy foal and thereby pass her genes on to a new generation of horses. All of an owner's hopes and management efforts culminate in that hour when the mare begins to labor to deliver her foal, and success is measured in the foal's first breaths and unsteady steps. In the wild, the mare must rely on strength, experience, instinct, and luck to deliver her foal and the placenta. She needs those same qualities to see that the foal nurses that first vital colostrum and bonds with her so that it recognizes and follows her. Failure to accomplish any of these tasks could result in the death of the foal and even the mare.

The foal's initial strength and vitality also determine the outcome, as the foal plays an active role in its own birth and survival right from the beginning. When considering the potential for disaster at almost every point in this scenario, along with the fact that mares have been delivering foals on their own for eons, it becomes apparent that nature knows what she is doing. Intervention by humans, on the other hand, actually can be counterproductive.

Having said that, it is also important to recognize that our domestic environment imposes conditions (such as concentration of disease pathogens) that can interfere with or create problems for the broodmare and her foal. Those who undertake the responsibility of managing the foaling mare must learn to recognize what is normal and what is not, to identify potential problems, and to troubleshoot. Planning and preparedness can help prevent illness or loss of the mare and foal.

The wild mare has no choice but to rely on luck. It is best for the domestic mare that her caretakers leave as little to luck as possible. Otherwise, all of the time, effort, and money that went into bringing the mare to this moment of delivery may have been for nothing.

Pregnancy Physiology

Fertilization of the mare's ovulated egg (oocyte) by the stallion's sperm occurs in the mare's oviducts (uterine tubes). For the first five to six days after ovulation, the developing equine embryo is nourished and supported by the oviduct. During this period, the embryo is dividing so that by the time it reaches the uterus on the fifth or sixth day after ovulation it has grown from a single-cell embryo to a multi-cell embryo (late morula or early blastocyst stage) still surrounded by a protective coat (the zona pellucida).

The mare's oviducts can distinguish between viable embryos and unfertilized oocytes. How they are able to make this distinction is unclear. With few exceptions, only developing embryos enter the uterus. Unfertilized eggs are retained within the oviduct where they degenerate over time.

The embryo undergoes rapid growth and expansion upon entering the uterus. The expanding blastocyst emerges from its zona pellucida about eight days after ovulation. After hatching, the embryo is still surrounded by a protective glycoprotein coating that formed underneath the zona pellucida. This capsulated coating is thought to provide mechanical protection and support to the embryo; it also might protect the embryo against any organisms that still might be infecting the uterus.

The embryo is mobile within the uterus for the first 15 to 17 days after ovulation. The capsule likely helps the embryo maintain its spherical shape and prevents the embryo — the cells of which by this time have reconfigured from a tight mass (morula) to a hollow ball (blastocyst) — from becoming damaged as it traverses the lumen of the uterine horns and body. The embryo's diameter greatly increases during this time. By 10 days after ovulation, the embryo has grown from the microscopic so much so that on ultrasound it will be about 3 mm in diameter, and by 15 days it will be 15 to 20 mm in diameter.

The mobility of the equine embryo within the uterus for such a long time after ovulation is one of its unique features. The embryo journeys back and forth throughout the uterine lumen from the time of its arrival in the uterus until it fixes in the base of one of the uterine horns usually by days 15 to 17 after ovulation. It is thought that this mobility is necessary for maternal recognition of pregnancy. In the cycling, non-pregnant mare, the uterus normally will produce prostaglandin on the 14th day after ovulation to terminate the progesterone-producing corpus luteum on the ovary. In this way the diestrus period is brought to an end, and the mare cycles back into estrus to begin a new cycle and another chance to become pregnant.

If the mare is pregnant, however, it is vital that the corpus luteum be maintained so that progesterone production by the ovary (which is vital to the maintenance of the early equine pregnancy) is not interrupted or terminated. Maternal recognition of pregnancy is the event by which the equine embryo signals the uterus that it is present and prevents the endometrium from producing prostaglandin. The mechanism by which the embryo signals the endometrium is not clearly understood, although it likely involves the production of an embryonic product. What is understood, however, is that the embryo must take this message to the entire surface area of the uterine lumen; otherwise, the endometrium will produce prostaglandin, and the pregnancy will be lost. Therefore, anything that obstructs embryonic movement or in any other way interferes with the signaling process will likely result in termination of the pregnancy.

The embryo migrates frequently from one end of the uterus to the other during a 24-hour period. This movement picks up in intensity between days 11 and 14 so that the embryo is likely covering the entire surface area of the endometrium every few hours. The embryo's movement through the uterine horns and body is facilitated by uterine contraction, which is likely further modulated by direct signaling from the embryo.

By days 15 to 17, the embryo comes to rest in the base of one of the uterine horns, becoming fixed in this location. The embryo has continued to grow (usually it is about 2.5 cm by day 17) and the increase in uterine tone effectively decreases the size of the uterine lumen so that the growing embryo becomes stuck. Embryos that are the result of foal-heat matings almost always become fixed in the smaller, previously non-pregnant horn. Those few pregnancies that fixate in the uterine body as opposed to the horns seem to be lost at a higher frequency than horn pregnancies.

Once the embryo fixates, it continues to develop, and the embryonic vesicle loses its spherical appearance about 19 to 20 days after ovulation. At this point it takes on an irregular outline that conforms to the uterine folds. This change corresponds to the loss of the glycoprotein capsule. By days 21 to 22, the embryo proper starts to become visible in the bottom of the fluid-filled vesicle, and by days 23 to 25 an embryonic heartbeat first becomes discernible on ultrasound as a tiny flicker.

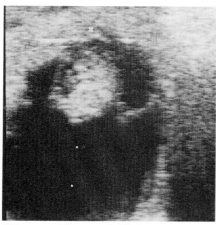
Ultrasound image of 37-day pregnancy

On ultrasound, the fluid-filled chamber above the embryo proper is the embryonic yolk sack that has helped nourish the embryo. Beginning around day 23, the developing allantois becomes visible as a line suspending the embryo from one side of the vesicle to the other. This membrane line starts out along the bottom of the vesicle and gradually migrates upward through the vesicle as the allantois expands and the yolk sack regresses. The expanding fluid cavity below the embryo is the developing allantoic cavity. By 28 days the embryo is suspended in an equatorial position by the allantoic membrane, and by 36 days the allantoic cavity and membrane have expanded so the embryo is now hanging from the "roof" of the fluid-filled embryonic vesicle. The yolk sack disappears as the umbilical cord forms, and the embryo gradually descends toward the bottom of the vesicle.

Diameter-wise the vesicle has expanded very little between days 20 and 30 compared with its expansion between days 10 and 20, but the size of the pregnancy continues to increase so that it is palpably 3 to 5 cm in diameter by about 30 days and about 8 cm by about 45 days. The changes in size and sequential orientation of the pregnancy as the embryo first ascends and then descends through the vesicle, as well as the presence of a heartbeat at the expected time, are helpful in both assessing how old the pregnancy is and whether it is developing at an expected rate. Many embryonic losses after day 18 seemingly occur sometime between days 20 and 25 and are first recognizable as such by the fact that the embryo proper and/or its heartbeat fail to appear at the expected times. Also, embryos that fail to take on the normal alignment (i.e., arise from the side or "roof" of the vesicle initially as opposed to the "floor") also seem to be at a higher risk for loss than normally aligned embryos.

Implantation of the equine embryo does not occur until nearly day 40 of gestation. Implantation is when the uterus and fetal membranes begin to attach to one another and direct exchange of nutrients and waste products between the mare's and the developing foal's circulatory systems begins to occur. The fact that the embryo relies on the histotroph (uterine milk) for its nourishment and support for so long is unique. It is easy to understand, therefore, why mares that have damaged uterine endometriums with large amounts of fibrosis choking off the uterine glands have a more difficult time maintaining an embryo. The mature equine placenta has a diffuse attachment of microcotyledons (tufts of finger-like microvilli) that interlock with the uterine endometrium over its entire surface area so that there is a one-to-one exchange of nutrients.

The expansion and attachment of the fetal membranes is a slow and tenuous, beginning at around day 40 with the first villi forming an attachment with the uterus at the base of the pregnant horn. The membranes gradually expand to cover the entire uterine lumen by about day 75, but the microvilli's attachment to the endometrium is not fully developed until 100 or more days. As the attachment becomes stronger and nutrient exchange increases, the role of the glandular histotroph becomes less important.

At about the same time as implantation, structures that are unique to the equine placenta — the endometrial cups — begin to form. These cups are important because they produce the hormone equine chorionic gonadotropin that causes the formation of secondary corpora lutea on the ovaries. These corpora lutea serve as backup to the corpus luteum that formed at ovulation to ensure that the mare's ovaries continue to produce enough progesterone to maintain the pregnancy until the placenta assumes pregnancy maintenance at approximately 120 to 150 days of gestation. The endometrial cups are formed from embryonic trophoblast cells that migrate from the chorionic girdle of the embryo into the endometrium of the mare at about 35 days of gestation. The trophoblast cells become embedded as aggregates of cells in the wall of the endometrium and begin producing equine chorionic gonadotropin.

Once formed, the endometrial cups will persist and function, regardless of whether the pregnancy is still viable, until they are rejected by the mare's immune system. The mare normally will not return to estrus while the cups are functioning. The mare's immune system begins to reject the cups around 60 to 80 days of the gestation, and they are usually gone by 120 days. Equine chorionic gonadotropin levels are detectable beginning about day 40, peak around days 60 to 70, and are low usually by day 100 but still detectable sometimes until about days 120 to 150.

Pregnancy Diagnosis

In general, pregnant mares will fail to return to behavioral estrus as expected 17 to 19 days following ovulation and will reject the advances of a teaser. However, failure to return to estrus does not ensure that a mare has a viable pregnancy.

Horses experience a relatively high percentage of early embryonic loss, and many mares might have had an embryo or embryonic remnants that were able to signal their presence successfully to the uterus at the time of maternal recognition of pregnancy but were no longer viable a few days later. Therefore, these mares still would have an active corpus luteum (CL) and fail to return to estrus. There are also some mares that will ovulate again during mid to late diestrus (greater than or equal to day 10 after the first ovulation) and still have a second, active CL at 21 days even though the first CL is no longer present. (The mare's endometrium still produces prostaglandin 14 days after the first ovulation, which eliminates the first CL, but the second CL is too young to respond to the prostaglandin and so persists.)

Likewise, teasing behavior cannot be relied upon to indicate pregnancy in mares that regularly do not show heat well. On the flip side, some pregnant mares will display signs of estrus if they develop a large follicle. Typically this will occur 18 to 20 days into gestation (right when you would expect an open mare to return to her next heat cycle), but these mares usually will tease half-heartedly. They might stand quietly and raise their tails and even wink, but they usually don't break down well for the teaser and object to being mounted. Attempting a live mating with a mare like this is dangerous for her, the stallion, and their handlers. The estrogen being produced by the large follicle causes this mild positive response, but in the end the progesterone being excreted by the primary pregnancy CL makes her less than receptive. Some pregnant mares will demonstrate this lukewarm teasing at later points in gestation, usually around 35 to 50 days, when the mares have multiple follicles destined to become secondary CLs. On palpation, however, these pregnant mares (especially those around 18 to 20 days) will have tremendous uterine tone and a very tight cervix, indicating an active CL.

In some cases a pregnancy bulge might be palpable as well, and if examined by ultrasound the pregnancy is readily discernible. If artificial insemination is being used, it is important that the mare be examined thoroughly for pregnancy before being rebred so that an established pregnancy is not lost when the cervix is violated and semen is dumped on top of the developing embryo. If the cervix is tight in an estrus mare that has been previously bred, double-check to be sure she is not pregnant before attempting to breed her!

Lastly, there is that group of mares that short-cycle themselves before the 18th day after ovulation. Usually this occurs because the mare has developed a uterine infection and is trying to clear it by coming into heat early. This early estrus could have been missed if the mare was not teased after ovulation or examined prior to 18 days by a veterinarian trying to detect an early pregnancy (10 to 18 days after ovulation) with an ultrasound examination. These mares already might have a new CL established or forming at what would have been 18 to 20 days from the observed previous estrus and therefore will also not show heat at the previously expected time.

Direct rectal palpation of the mare's reproductive tract by an experienced veterinarian can verify a mare's pregnancy status. Changes in the mare's uterine tone (which is quite tubular during early pregnancy, especially around 18 to 20 days) and increased firm cervical tone indicate early on that the mare might be pregnant. The embryo itself becomes palpable as a ventral bulge in the base of the pregnant horn as early as 18 to 20 days in some mares (maiden mares usually) and reliably in most mares by 25 to 30 days gestation.

AT A GLANCE

◆ Direct rectal palpation by a veterinarian can verify a mare's pregnancy status.

◆ Ultrasound can identify a pregnancy as early as 10 days after ovulation.

◆ Twins that survive are usually small and weak.

◆ Mares that double ovulate usually do so repeatedly.

The age of the pregnancy can be roughly estimated in days up until about 90 days by palpation. After that time the uterus is over the brim of the mare's pelvis and its true size not readily discernible. However, finding that the cervix is closed and pulled forward and the uterus has a normal resilient tone and is enlarged and fluid-filled all indicate to the person palpating that the mare is pregnant. The fetus becomes readily palpable after four months of gestation provided it is not lying too deeply in the abdomen. As pregnancy advances, the fetus cannot hide and will be readily palpable to the veterinarian.

The palpable size of the pregnancy relative to the breeding or ovulation dates indicates to the experienced veterinarian whether the pregnancy appears to be progressing normally. Pregnancies that are small for gestational age can indicate pregnancy loss and warrant further investigation either by serial palpations or by ultrasound to definitively diagnose the viability of an embryo or fetus. Pregnancies that seem larger than they should be or pregnancies where bulges are discovered in the base of both horns are immediately suspect for twin pregnancies and warrant an ultrasound. Once the fetus is palpable, the presence of spontaneous movement indicates to the veterinarian that the fetus is literally alive and kicking.

Lack of fetal movement in an otherwise palpable fetus does not necessarily mean there is a problem (sometimes the foal is asleep), but failure to find or elicit movement (or the finding that the foal is hyperactive) after several minutes of assessment could indicate a problem

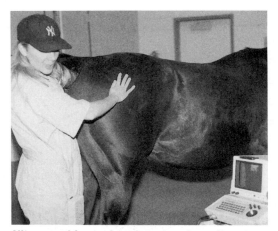

Ultrasound is used to detect and monitor pregnancy

and should be investigated. Changes in uterine tone quality at any point also can signal a problem. The tone of the uterine horns early on should be pronounced and tubular. Later, as the uterus becomes distended with the fetal membranes, fetus, and fluids, the pregnant uterus is resilient and somewhat thin-walled. Except at the very end of pregnancy, the cervix should be pronounced and tight with no edema or softening. Once the foal itself is palpable, the uterus should be soft and pliant and not thickened or tightly distended with fluids. Any findings that differ from the norm indicate there might be a problem.

Veterinary ultrasound examination has been a boon to broodmare practice. When used to detect and monitor pregnancy, it offers management advantages that cannot be implemented when using teasing and/or palpation alone to determine a mare's status.

First, ultrasound examination can identify a pregnancy as early as 10 days and reliably by 14 days after ovulation. The obvious advantage to early detection is confirming that the mare carried an early embryo to this point. Ultrasound also lets the veterinarian interpret the status of the pregnancy. The embryo should appear perfectly round and be a characteristic diameter for a given day after ovulation. From time to time it might be difficult for a veterinarian to determine if the fluid-filled structure he or she is examining within the uterine lumen is an embryo or an endometrial cyst. In general, cysts will not be perfectly round, and they will appear to be off center, but sometimes it can be hard to tell. A cyst, however, is stationary and will not grow appreciably over a one- to three-day period, and so when in doubt, serial examinations might be necessary. If the embryo is undersized for gestational age or has an abnormal contour or if there is edema or free fluid in the uterus, the risk for early pregnancy loss is greater.

Simultaneous assessment of palpable tone of the reproductive structures also can indicate how well the pregnancy is developing. A small embryo or decreased uterine tone does not necessarily mean the pregnancy is in trouble, but it does warrant closer monitoring. Examining the mare before the 18th day after ovulation also identifies those mares that are not pregnant and assesses the status of the ovarian structures and tubular tract changes so the next cycle is not missed and the mare can be promptly bred again. It also offers the chance to identify those mares that might retain a CL and require prostaglandin therapy to bring them back into estrus in a timely fashion. A note of caution here: It is always best to delay giving prostaglandin if there is any chance the mare might have a viable but undetected pregnancy. Some mares do not have a demonstrable embryo at 14 days after ovulation, but when a follow-up examination is performed within the next four days (or if the mare fails to return to heat) a small but viable embryo is found and the mare often goes on to have a normal pregnancy. Treating too hastily with prostaglandin can terminate the pregnancy.

Probably the greatest advantage of using rectal ultrasound for determining pregnancy is detecting twins early. Twin pregnancies that persist past 40 days rarely end successfully. The majority end in abortion during the late second or third trimester or produce dead or small, weak foals at term. Detecting twins before the embryos are fixed in the base of one or both horns allows for more options for reducing the twin pregnancy to a singleton before the endometrial cups form. Lastly, ultrasound offers a chance to monitor the viability of a pregnancy during the early stages right on up to foaling (after 70 to 90 days the foal's heartbeat is imaged across the mare's abdomen). It is advantageous to be able to monitor a pregnancy for the first 35 to 40 days to detect the loss of an embryo in a timely fashion so a previously pregnant mare with a persistent CL is not permitted to go open unnoticed as the breeding season ticks away.

Measurement of progesterone, equine chorionic gonadotropin (ECG), and estrone sulfate in the blood of pregnant mares at specific periods during gestation also can be useful to equine pregnancy diagnosis. Blood hormone testing could be particularly useful in those situations when rectal examination cannot be performed safely (i.e, with an extremely uncooperative mare or a mare that is physically too small to be examined such as some miniature mares). Progesterone levels are *not* specific for pregnancy. All an elevated blood progesterone level means is that there is an active CL(s) somewhere on the ovary. It gives no information whether there is a viable pregnancy. If, however, progesterone levels are low (less than 1 nanogram per ml) at 18 to 20 days after the last ovulation, it is likely the mare is not pregnant. If progesterone levels are elevated, the mare indeed might be pregnant, but further examination will be necessary to confirm it.

The endometrial cups produce equine chorionic gonadotropin. This hormone can be detected at 35 to 40 days of gestation, with levels peaking around 60 to 70 days, then declining (as the mare's immune system rejects the cups) to undetectable levels by days 100 to 150. ECG in the mare's blood between days 40 and 100 and beyond indicates the mare had a viable pregnancy at least at the 35- to 40-day mark. Remember, the endometrial cups will function for their set period regardless of whether the pregnancy is lost.

The live fetal-placental unit produces estrogen during pregnancy. Increasing levels of estrone sulfate detectable in the mare's blood and urine reflect fetal estrogen production after 60 to 90 days of gestation (peak levels occur at about 210 days). If the fetus dies, estrogen production ceases and the estrone sulfate levels drop precipitously. Therefore, measurement of elevated blood or urine estrone sulfate levels after 60 to 90 days positively identifies the presence of a viable pregnancy. The main disadvantage of this diagnosis method is that the levels do not become significant until later in gestation.

The following recommended schedule for detecting and monitoring pregnancy in mares summarizes and addresses the points discussed.

Number of Days Post-Ovulation	Procedure	Questions Looking to Answer
Day 14	Rectal palpation/ ultrasound; tease	Normal embryonic vesicle present? Twins? Quality of uterine and cervical tone? Normal diestrus appearance to uterus? What structures are present on the ovaries?
Days 18-20 (single check)	Rectal palpation/ ultrasound; tease	Normal embryonic vesicle? Twins? Quality of tone and appearance of uterus and cervix? If not pregnant, is she in heat or does the CL appear to be retained?
Days 25-30 (single check)	Rectal palpation/ ultrasound; tease	Normal embryo with a heartbeat? Twins? Quality of tone and appearance of uterus and cervix? If pregnancy is no longer present, has it been resorbed or are there still remnants visible? If not pregnant, is she in heat or does the CL appear to be retained?

Number of Days Post-Ovulation	Procedure	Questions Looking to Answer
Days 35-45 (single check)	Rectal palpation/ ultrasound	Normal fetus with a heartbeat? Twins? Quality of tone and appearance of uterus and cervix? If pregnancy is no longer present, has it been resorbed or are there still remnants visible? Has she returned to heat or have secondary CLs already begun to form?
Days 60-80 (optional check unless the mare is being) supplemented with progesterone)	Rectal palpation	Normal uterine and cervical tone? A palpable pregnancy that is the appropriate size and distension for the state of gestation?

Days 100-120	Rectal palpation; ultrasound (optional)	Normal cervical tone? Uterine tone and distension normal for stage of gestation? Live foal? If being supplemented with progesterone, decision on whether to begin weaning the mare off needs to be made (usually starting at 120 days)

Depending on the finding at each evaluation, more frequent checks or further diagnostics might be needed. For example, if a second, previously undetected CL is discovered at the 14-day check but only one embryo is detected at that time, it might be prudent to check daily or every other day between 14 and 20 days to look for a possible twin. Mares on progesterone need to be checked more regularly between 35 and 120 days in the event the fetus dies but abortion is prevented. In general, mares that are pregnant at 35 to 45 days are unlikely to cycle back if the pregnancy is lost until what would have been 90-plus days of gestation. Therefore, mares that are otherwise normal may not be looked at again until 100 days, but, again, prompt detection of pregnancy loss will allow the mare to be managed so that she can be bred back as soon as she does begin cycling back.

The combination of teasing, rectal palpation, rectal ultrasound, and blood hormone levels (when indicated) helps the veterinarian get an appreciation for the progress of the pregnancy. A mare is never 100 percent safe in foal, but the longer the gestation progresses the more established the foal becomes and the more likely it is to stay put. Obviously economics is a factor, and the cost of frequent veterinary examinations must be weighed against the potential value (monetary and emotional) of the foal the mare is carrying and the cost of the mare coming up open at the end of the season.

Management of Twin Pregnancies

While it seems that every person you meet has a tale about a mare that successfully delivered and raised twin foals, the truth is that the majority of equine twin pregnancies that survive beyond 40 days end in abortion during the second or third trimesters. The small percentage of twin foals that make it to birth are usually small and weak, and often one or both are born dead or die within the early neonatal period in spite of good nursing care and medical support.

Mares that deliver twin foals frequently have complications (foals get tangled during delivery and/or weak or dead foals are malpositioned) and frequently retain their placenta(s). Due to trauma and resultant inflammation (and sometimes infection) caused to the mare's reproductive tract by the late-term abortions, it is typically difficult to breed back the mare the subsequent breeding season. This means two years of the mare's reproductive life are lost. It is potentially three years from conception of the twins until she carries a viable, singleton pregnancy to term and a foal hits the ground.

The reason horses are not usually successful carrying twins to term has to do with the equine's placentation. As we have discussed, attachment and nutrient exchange between the foal's placenta and the mare's uterus is accomplished in a one-to-one ratio. If two foals occupy the space originally designed for one, the best-case scenario is that they share the uterus 50-50, but this still means each foal is receiving only half the support and nutrient exchange it would receive if it were the only foal. If, as in most twin pregnancies, there is an uneven sharing of the uterus so that one foal gets more than half, the foal receiving less will be at an extreme disadvantage. Nutrient demand by the developing foal is greatest during the end of the second and throughout the third trimesters of pregnancy (i.e., the last three to four months). At this time, the twin that has the least amount of surface area for placental exchange starves.

The death of one of the foals frequently causes the death of the other, and the pregnancy is aborted. Occasionally there is an extreme discrepancy in the uterine surface area each foal has so that one foal is limited to perhaps the tip of a uterine horn. In this scenario, the limited foal might die much sooner without compromising its twin, and the pregnancy is maintained as a singleton with the dead twin being completely or partially resorbed. With the latter, the dead fetus will be delivered as a mummified remnant at the time of foaling.

There seems to be a breed predilection for the occurrence of twins (Thoroughbreds, Standardbreds, and draft mares in particular), and twins seem rarely to occur in ponies. However, twin pregnancies occur in a wide variety of breeds. Equine twins are fraternal twins (there has been only one reported case of identical equine twins, and that was not verified by DNA testing). Therefore, multiple equine embryos result from a double (sometimes triple) ovulation during a single estrus period. Both follicles usually ovulate roughly simultaneously or within 24 to 48 hours of each other.

The incidence of double ovulations seems to be a little higher late in the breeding season and also seems more common in older mares and barren mares (as compared to younger mares and foaling mares, respectively). Individual mares that double ovulate once tend to repeat this pattern. It is recommended to breed all cycles regardless of whether there is the potential for a double ovulation, then manage the twin pregnancy to ensure reduction to a singleton. It is not uncommon for double ovulations to go undetected initially. The average longevity of a fertile stallion's semen in the mare's tract also makes it highly likely that if both ovulations occur within 72 hours of a given single breeding that the mare will conceive twins. Therefore, it is important that a mare be checked via ultrasound before 30 days gestation at least once to detect the possible presence of twins and manage them so as to ensure one has been eliminated before the endometrial cups have formed.

It is possible for an experienced veterinarian to maneuver the embryos manually via rectal palpation (with the aid of ultrasound) so that one embryo can be guided to the tip of a uterine horn and manually crushed (pinched) while leaving the second embryo undisturbed. This is most easily accomplished when the two embryos are occupying different horns. Ideally, the smaller of the two embryos is chosen as the reduction candidate. However, it is important that the embryo be pinched off with minimal handling of the uterus, so whichever embryo is positioned to most easily accomplish this should be pinched.

Sometimes, however, the embryos are adjacent to one another and it is not possible to separate them without risking damaging them both. In this situation, some experienced practitioners can manipulate the embryos as a unit and crush only one of them, but this is risky. Where practical, if the mare is left alone and then re-examined within a few hours, the two embryos will have moved apart and one can then be easily maneuvered and crushed. Follow-up examinations are recommended within 48 hours of pinching off a twin to confirm that the remaining embryo is continuing to grow and thrive and that the pregnancy is indeed only a singleton.

It is also important to note at this point that if a mare has endometrial cysts, it is vital that a cyst not be mistaken for a twin embryo and the real single embryo be crushed by mistake. It is useful to have mapped out a mare's cysts (numbers, sizes, and locations) with ultrasound before breeding so the veterinarian can refer to this information. Once the embryos have become fixed in the horns, it is no longer possible to reposition them. If the embryos have settled in separate horns, one can still be manually crushed, but the older the embryos become the more difficult it is to crush them.

When twins fix together side by side in the base of the same horn (unilateral twins), the veterinarian can't eliminate one manually without damaging the other. The good news about unilateral twins is that 80 percent of them self reduce to a singleton pregnancy by day 30 or so once fixation has occurred, especially if one embryonic vesicle is larger. If this does not happen, a decision needs to be made before the 33rd day of gestation on how best to proceed.

Once the endometrial cups have formed, the mare likely will not begin to cycle again until sometime after what would have been 90 days of gestation, even if the whole pregnancy is lost before that time. (This was dramatically demonstrated by the mares that lost their pregnancies after more than 35 days gestation due to mare reproductive loss syndrome in central Kentucky.) Therefore, if the owner wants to breed the mare again that year, it is better to abort a persist-ent twin pregnancy with prostaglandin by the 33rd day and try again on another cycle. If the mare will not be bred again that season, the decision can be made to watch and wait a little longer to see if the pregnancy still won't self reduce. In general, however, the longer the twin embryos remain, the less likely self reduction is to occur, and after 40 days a twin pregnancy will most likely go on to abort.

There are two remaining veterinary options for reduction of the twin pregnancy. The first is a transvaginal approach using transvagi-nal ultrasound and rectal palpation simultaneously to place a sterile needle into one of the developing fetuses and aspirate the fluid from around it and thereby kill it. This procedure can be performed between 40 and 50 days by an experienced veterinarian using spe-cialized equipment. Success rates are about 50 percent. The second option is to use a transabdominal ultrasound and aseptic technique to image one fetal heart across the mare's abdominal wall and then guide a sterile needle into the fetal heart and inject it with potassium chloride to kill the fetus, leaving the remaining twin alive. This pro-cedure usually is most successful when performed around 120 days gestation, and the success rate is about 50 percent. This latter pro-cedure is best performed by an experienced veterinary ultrasonogra-pher in a hospital setting.

CHAPTER **14**

Gestation Length

The equine gestation length averages 340 days based on a given ovulation date. However, normal length can range from 325 days to 355-plus days. Mares that foal early in the year (i.e., January, February, and March in the Northern Hemisphere) tend to have longer gestations than mares that foal later (i.e., April, May, or June). Consequently, many mares do not foal right on their due dates. Annual foaling records will help identify a more accurate date for a given mare as mares tend to repeat their previous gestation lengths, especially if they have been bred to the

 same stallion and are foaling around the same time each year.

A recent study also suggests that gestation length might be correlated with individual sires as well, and it appears that colts tend to have longer gestations (one to two days) than fillies. Bottom line: Watch the mare for signs of approaching foaling as she often chooses to ignore the calendar.

Gestational length can vary

Foalings that occur outside the accepted normal range result in foals that are premature, postmature/dysmature, or result in abortions, depending on when the delivery occurred. Foals born between 300 to 325 days of gestation are considered premature and require intensive nursing and medical care to survive. The earlier the foal is born relative to its expected due date, the less well equipped it is to handle life outside the womb. Fetuses delivered before 300 days of gestation are considered abortions, and if not dead at delivery, they die soon afterward despite human assistance.

On the other end of the spectrum are those foals considered overdue, born after 355 days or more. Many mares have carried for a year or longer and still delivered apparently normal foals. In general, however, overdue foals tend to be smaller rather than larger than normal-term foals, and they tend to be thin. Often, too, they will resemble premature foals in that they are down in their fetlocks and pasterns, have silky hair coats, and other signs of prematurity. Such foals are labeled postmature or dysmature. In these pregnancies, it is thought that the rate of nutrient exchange to the foal across the placenta might be decreased, which slows the foal's development and results in a prolonged gestation. This condition is more commonly observed in older mares that have foaled before and could be caused by age changes and wear and tear in the endometrium. In these cases, it is always best to allow the mare to continue her gestation until she is ready to foal.

Inducing labor poses a danger when an overdue mare shows no other signs that she is close to foaling — udder development, relaxation of the ligaments around the tailhead, etc. Induction can result in a foal that is not ready to be born and is in fact premature despite what the calendar says. The exception to this overdue scenario is the mare that is experiencing a prolonged gestation due to fescue toxicity.

Tall fescue (*festuca arundinaceae*) is a common pasture grass of the southeastern and northwestern United States. Its hardy nature and ease of growth make it a popular forage and an acceptable source of nutrition for horses. Trouble arises when the grass is infected with a fungal endophyte, *Acremonium coenophialum.*

This endophyte lives in a symbiotic relationship with the grass and is the source of toxins associated with causing prolonged gestation (13 to 14 months), dystocia, neonatal morbidity and mortality, agalactia (absence of milk), and retained placenta in mares consuming infected fescue during late

AT A GLANCE

◆ The average gestation is 340 days.

◆ Foals born after 355 days or more are considered overdue.

◆ Inducing parturition before a mare is outwardly ready can have dire consequences for the foal.

◆ Infected fescue grass can cause a number of problems for pregnant mares.

gestation. Diagnosis usually is based primarily on the signs of poor udder development and prolonged gestation in pregnant mares known to have ingested infected fescue.

Pastures should be tested each fall before the breeding season to determine whether they are endophyte-infected and to what extent. The best way to manage this problem is to avoid it by removing mares from infected pastures and not feeding hay made from infected fields after day 300 of the gestation. In addition, pastures should be managed to minimize the amount of endophyte. Reseeding with endophyte-free seed, mowing frequently to prevent formation of seed heads, and over-seeding infected pastures with a legume are beneficial. Late-term mares that have been exposed to the fescue endophyte toxins should

Test pastures for the presence of fescue

be monitored for failure of normal mammary development.

To treat or prevent agalactia, the attending veterinary might recommend administering a prolactin-stimulating agent (reserpine, domperidone, or acepromazine). Foalings should be attended closely because dystocias are common. Foals are often oversized and weak, and frequently they are malpositioned for delivery. The mare's pelvic ligaments frequently are not relaxed, which often makes delivery more difficult. These foals require good nursing care and medical treatment to survive, and the foaling must be managed to safeguard the mare's future fertility. Fescue mares often retain their placentas, which tend to be thick with edema.

CHAPTER **15**

General Broodmare Management

Thehe pregnant mare, like all horses, thrives on routine. Changes in the mare's housing, diet, companions, exercise, and handling should be avoided or made gradually when possible. Chronic medical conditions should be addressed, as should routine upkeep of feet, deworming, etc. Ideally, any procedures that might be extra stressful to the mare (such as teeth floating) should be performed before the mare is bred so it does not become an issue during the pregnancy, and all vaccinations should be up to date at least two weeks before the first breeding, if possible. Pregnant mares that are stressed by vanning should stay home, and all pregnant mares should not be hauled for long periods or over great distances if at all possible. If a long trip home from a breeding facility is necessary, it should be done when the pregnancy is well established, and stress should be kept to a minimum.

Pregnant mares ideally are housed at pasture in small, compatible groups and have separate stabling from transitory horse populations. They should be kept in seclusion. All new horses brought to a farm should be isolated for a minimum of four weeks and closely monitored for any signs of illness before coming into contact with the resident population. This is particularly important on farms that house pregnant mares.

Pastures should be well maintained and safely fenced, and barns should be well ventilated and comfortably bedded with clean shavings, paper, or straw. Large box stalls (14 x 14-foot minimum) are ideal so that the mares can move around and lie down and get up easily.

A pregnant mare needs adequate daily exercise. Ideally, this means turnout into a good-sized paddock or pasture. Mares that are able to stay in work and conceive at the time of breeding can continue at their previous level of conditioning provided they do not become overly sweaty or tired. Now is not the time to begin training her for an event course or prolonged park class. Opt instead for a leisurely trail ride. Strenuous exercise and jumping should be curtailed from the start of the pregnancy, and riding probably should be discontinued by the time the mare is beginning to show (i.e., halfway into the second trimester).

Open and maiden mares should receive all their annual vaccinations before breeding. These include Eastern-Western encephalomyelitis, tetanus toxoid, herpesvirus types I and IV (rhino), influenza (flu), and Potomac horse fever, West Nile virus, and rabies in endemic areas. Strangles vaccine also may be given prior to breeding if the mare is at risk of exposure. In general, no vaccinations should be given during the first 90 days of gestation (the period during which the mare's immune system is adjusting to the pregnancy and the foal's vital organs are forming). Pregnant mares should be vaccinated against rhino/herpes viral abortion at three, five, seven, and nine months of gestation. In endemic areas, botulism toxoid also should be administered to previously unvaccinated

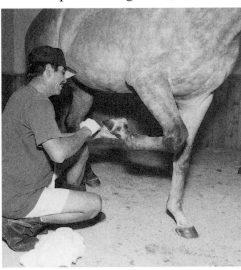

Maintain routine care of the mare

mares at eight, nine, and 10 months of gestation, and at one month prior to foaling in previously vaccinated mares. The protocol for botulism toxoid is designed to boost the level of antibodies against botulism in the mare's first milk (colostrum) to provide her foal with immunity against botulism (shaker foal disease).

In general, with the exception of rhino and botulism, all other vaccinations in pregnant mares should be avoided until one month prior to foaling. Late-term mares receive their annual boosters of

Eastern-Western encephalomyelitis, tetanus, flu, and rabies (where endemic) one month before foaling, again to boost the foal's colostral immunity.

Control of parasitic infections in pregnant mares is extremely important. She should not have to compete with intestinal worms for the nutrients she eats, and the damage caused to the mare's intestinal lining and blood vessels by migrating larvae is debilitating to her and potentially life-threatening. Parasite control will differ from farm to farm as factors such as pasture stocking rates, climate, and degree of parasite infestation will differ. However, most parasite control plans will combine the use of anthelmintics (dewormers), pasture management, stocking rates, and routine fecal monitoring.

Under a veterinarian's direction, rotational treatment of pregnant mares with the three classes of anthelmintics (Avermectins [Ivermectin], Benzimidazoles [Fenbendazole, Febantel, etc.], and Pyrimidines [Pyrantel Pamoate and Tartarate]) can be performed using varying schedules tailored to best meet the requirements of the season and given farm situation. Mares should be dewormed before being bred, and administration of anthelmintics to pregnant mares probably should be avoided for the first 60 days of gestation. All hors-

Parasite control is important

es on a given farm should be dewormed along with the broodmares.

Organophosphate dewormers and combination products containing organophosphates should be avoided in pregnant mares. Ideally, pasture stocking rates are kept low (i.e., a minimum of one to five acres of pasture per horse if possible) as "dilution is the solution" to pasture parasitic infestation rates. Parasitic larva and eggs are passed in an infected horse's feces. The pasture becomes increasingly infested with infectious stage larva as manure buildup increases. The fewer horses there are on a given piece of land, the less manure produced. Likewise, the less manure that is left on a pasture, the fewer parasitic larva with which the grazing or feeding horse can reinfest itself. Rotating, chain harrowing, and mowing pastures and picking up manure help decrease exposure.

Individual fecal samples on all horses are important as some individuals seem to be more susceptible to increased parasitic loads than others. Lactating mares, for instance, often appear to be infected more easily with intestinal parasites than non-lactating mares. These "weak sisters" serve as a chronic source of reinfection for the other horses and could require different anthelmintic schedules and frequency. As always, pregnant mares should be medicated as little as possible. Effective parasite management for the entire farm and individually tailored anthelmintic treatment schedules help maintain the pregnant mare in premium condition while minimizing her drug exposure.

Feeding

Following appropriate guidelines to ensure that a mare is achieving a properly balanced diet is the obvious goal of any nutrition program, but make adjustments as needed to maintain pregnant mares at an optimal body condition. Mares that are too thin at foaling will not milk well. Mares that are too fat are susceptible to developing laminitis and metabolic disorders, especially during late pregnancy or after foaling.

The optimally conditioned mare should have a shiny coat and bright eye, and you should be able to just feel her ribs and not have to dig for them or be able to see them from five steps back. Her back, loin, and croup areas should appear rounded and smooth with muscling. The back, pelvic, and tail head bones should not feel or look prominent, and her neck should not be thin and "ewe" shaped from lack of condition. At the same time she should not have rolls of fat over her back and withers, her crest should not be rock solid and ready to fall over, and there should not be pads of fat around the root of her tail.

Once you have established that your mare looks optimal, weigh her (or tape her), and record her weight. Eyeballing any animal can be misleading, because changes might be subtle from day to day. Pregnant mares should be weighed every one to two months to accurately assess their progress. For a 1,000- to 1,200-pound mare to maintain her optimal pre-pregnancy condition, she should gain somewhere between 150 to 200 pounds during the last trimester to allow for the weight of the foal, the fetal membranes, and fluids. (The average birth weight of a healthy foal is approximately 9 percent to 10 percent of

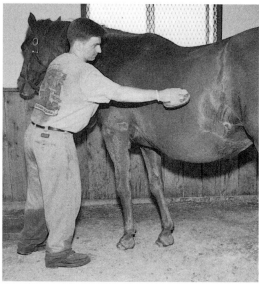

Good condition is important during pregnancy

the mare's body weight.) Remember the foal's greatest nutrient needs and weight gains occur during the last three to four months of gestation. Correspondingly, that is also when the mare's nutrient requirements increase above maintenance levels and she needs to be fed a more nutrient-rich ration.

Feeding any animal is a matter of supplying energy, protein, vitamins, minerals, and (in the case of herbivores) roughage in the correct amounts to meet the metabolic needs of the animal and keep the digestive tract functioning smoothly.

A pregnant mare's energy and protein requirements are at maintenance levels during the first eight months of gestation provided she was in the proper body condition at the start of her pregnancy. During the ninth, 10th, and 11th months of gestation the digestible energy requirements of the mare increase to 1.11, 1.13, and 1.20 times the maintenance requirement, respectively. Non-pregnant mares require a total ration that is 7 percent to 8 percent protein on a 90 percent dry matter basis. Pregnant mares require 9 percent to 10 percent protein of the total ration, and early and late lactating mares require 12 percent and 10 percent total dietary protein respectively. Grains are more protein and energy dense than grass hay. As nutrient demands increase, the amount of grain in the total ration also should increase. Likewise, as pregnancy advances, the mare's gastrointestinal tract competes with the growing foal for available space in the mare's abdomen, and she is inclined to consume less hay. This "available space" issue also makes it difficult for some mares to consume enough food during the third trimester to keep up with the increased energy demands of late pregnancy. Because of this, it may be advisable to increase feed levels earlier, during the second trimester, so that these mares are actually a little "overconditioned" coming into the last trimester.

Horses require a diet that is largely made up of forages to keep their digestive system functioning properly. Concentrates (grain mixtures with added vitamins and minerals) complement the nutrient content of the forage portion of the ration. At maintenance requirements, mares in general will eat about two pounds of grass hay per 100 pounds of body weight per day, and late gestation mares will eat one to two pounds of hay per 100 pounds of body weight and about one pound of grain per 100 pounds of body weight per day. Grain meals should be divided over the day so no more than five pounds are provided at any single meal. Assuming a grass hay protein content around 8 percent, a pregnant mare needs a grain ration that is about 14 percent protein to round out the overall protein content of her diet to meet her 10 percent need.

The nutrient content of grass pasture changes from season to season, and the quality of hay changes depending on the phase of plant growth when the forage was cut, the weather conditions when it lay drying on the fields, and the quality of the field from which it was cut. The nutrient content and quality of all forages need to be analyzed routinely throughout the year. Without knowing the quality of the forages being fed, it is impossible to know what mixture of grain, vitamins, and minerals is required to properly complement the forage. Most commercially available feeds are formulated to be balanced and complete, but again this is based on suppositions on the quality of the forages that will be fed. Every horse manager should have forages routinely analyzed two to four times annually and adjust the concentrate rations accordingly to complement the forages properly. Properly balancing a ration is best done with the advice of an equine nutritionist. Many veterinary or agricultural colleges have nutritionists who will consult with individual mare owners. County extension agents also can refer you to to qualified equine nutritionists.

Lastly, mares should be able to take full advantage of the feed that is offered to them. They should have regular dental care and should have their teeth floated before breeding so they are not stressed by the procedure while pregnant. Mares should not have to compete with stronger, greedier pasture mates for their meals. Proper bunk space and spacing of feed should be provided so all mares housed in a group can eat their full ration in peace.

Where the management system permits, bring mares in at meal-times and feed their concentrate rations individually in stalls along with their hay. Hay and/or grass, clean water, and mineral salt blocks should be available to mares at all times. Mares turned out onto lush green pastures for the first time should be introduced to these pastures slowly so as not to disrupt their normal gut function. Mares should be fed a hay ration before turnout so they are not ravenous when they reach the grass, and it is nice to have hay available in racks in the pasture as well so the mares can have a choice.

High-Risk Pregnancies

Supplementing the pregnant mare with progesterone is sometimes controversial. Therapy can be overused and is not always necessary in every mare that receives oral altrenogest (Regu-Mate®) or injectable progesterone in oil. However, in specific situations, supplementing a pregnant mare with progesterone is necessary to maintain the pregnancy. There also are some infertile mares that maintain accepted, normal progesterone levels but seem to be better able to establish and maintain a pregnancy if they receive additional progesterone supplementation.

Circulating progesterone is necessary for the mare to maintain and support a pregnancy. The minimal level of progesterone required appears to be 2 nanograms per milliliter (ng/ml). Reference values will differ from laboratory to laboratory, but at the New York State Diagnostic Laboratory at Cornell University Veterinary College, the accepted normal range for an early pregnant or mid- to late-diestrous mare is 5 ng/ml or above. After ovulation, it takes the corpus luteum (CL) on the ovary four to six days to mature and produce progesterone at this level. In the pregnant mare, this primary CL will continue to produce this hormone for the first 120 days of gestation. Once the endometrial cups are formed and begin producing equine chorionic gonadotropin, secondary CLs form on the ovaries as a backup to ensure that the ovaries will produce adequate levels of progesterone until the placenta is producing adequate levels of progestogens.

The placenta begins producing progestogens between days 50 and 70 of gestation. During the second half of the pregnancy, placental progestogens are responsible for pregnancy maintenance. The assays available for measuring progesterone in the mare usually do not measure the placental progestogens but only the ovarian progesterone. Therefore, it is normal to measure progesterone levels in a mare after 150 or so days of gestation and find them numerically low even though the placental progesterone is maintaining the pregnancy just fine.

Any cause of decreased production of ovarian progesterone during the first 100-plus days of the pregnancy endangers the pregnancy. Primary failure of the corpus luteum to produce adequate progesterone levels is rare. Progesterone production is not constant over a 24-hour period, so measured levels at any given moment might be low even though overall production is fine. It might be necessary to sample a mare twice during a 24-hour period to get an accurate picture.

If the ovary is exposed to prostaglandin during the first 100-plus days of gestation and progesterone production is decreased or terminated, the pregnancy is in danger of being lost. Inflammation of the endometrium (endometritis, usually due to infection) or failure of maternal recognition of pregnancy will result in prostaglandin being produced and destruction of the CL(s). The most common reason for luteal (and embryonic) failure before day 20 is a chronically infected uterus. Progesterone has been shown to inhibit the action of white blood cells within the uterus to clean up infection. Progesterone also stimulates the uterus to produce glandular secretions and histotroph to help support a possible pregnancy. These fluids provide a wonderful medium for bacteria or fungal organisms to set up residence. For these two reasons, it is not advisable to give a mare exogenous progesterone if a uterine infection is suspected, as progesterone has the potential to make the infection worse and damage the endometrium.

In a worst case scenario, mares with undetected infections that are placed on supplemental progesterone then not closely monitored can develop a pyometra (uterus that is filled with fluid and pus) as the additional progesterone keeps the cervix closed and might not permit the infection to drain. Pyometra causes severe damage to the mare's uterine lining.

Mares that have free fluid in their uterus on ultrasound examination during the diestrous period or vulvar discharge are suspect for having an infection. Infected mares also could have uterine edema on ultrasound, and their tract could be palpably heavy and/or thickened. A uterine infection is not always readily apparent, however, and any mare placed on progesterone therapy needs to be watched closely just in case her uterus "blows" with an obvious infection.

Mares that lose pregnancies due to a failure of maternal recognition require supplementation before or by the 14th day after ovulation. Mares that are suspect for this condition likely will benefit from supplementation if it is initiated very early (i.e., about four days after ovulation). It is important to examine these mares closely during the post-breeding period to ensure they have no signs of lingering inflammation before treatment starts. In the experience of some clinicians, early supplementation also seems to help some mares that have no discernible reason for not being pregnant after two to three cycles of breeding. Many of these mares fail to show a discernible embryo the 12th day after ovulation and breeding, and often they retain their CLs. The mares have clean uterine cytologies when examined during the beginning of the next estrus. The semen being used appears to be of good quality or the stallion is impregnating other mares, but this particular mare is still not pregnant. Some of these mares seem to benefit from early progesterone supplementation and successfully go on to carry a pregnancy after it is instituted, although the reason why is not clear.

A normal pregnant mare that becomes injured or ill is also at risk of losing her pregnancy. Progesterone supplementation could help her maintain the pregnancy until she is recovered and able once again to support the developing foal herself. Any condition that releases endotoxins into the mare's circulation (a strangulating intestinal colic or diarrhea, for example) will induce prostaglandin release. While the pregnancy depends on the ovarian CLs, subsequent pregnancy loss is due to the loss of ovarian progesterone. Later on during gestation, it is thought that perhaps prolonged exposure of the uterus to high levels of endotoxin-induced prostaglandin results in contractions and subsequent abortion of the fetus. Supplementing endotoxic mares with exogenous progesterone has proved effective in preventing pregnancy loss in many affected individuals. Initiate progesterone therapy as soon as possible once the insult to the mare's system has begun. Fetal viability needs to be monitored (usually by checking for a fetal heartbeat with ultrasound). Affected mares at less than 120 to 150 days of gestation will need supple-

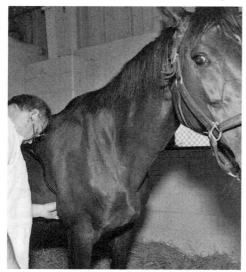

mentation at least until placental maintenance of the pregnancy begins (i.e., days 120 to 150) because once the CLs have been destroyed they do not come back. Progesterone therapy in later gestation mares with well-established placentas can be discontinued at the discretion of an attending veterinarian once the mare has fully recovered from her illness.

Stress can make a mare a candidate for progesterone therapy

The role stress plays in

causing sick or injured mares to abort is unclear. Levels of adrenal corticosteroids rise during times of stress, but in practice very high levels given repeatedly over several days are required to cause a mare to abort or go into labor. It also has been proposed that periods of stress could suppress progesterone production, although experiments have not shown this. Without a doubt, however, some stressed mares do seem prone to pregnancy loss. Therefore, any injury or illness is cause for concern, and veterinary advice should be sought.

Options for supplementary progesterone therapy are limited. Injectable progesterone in oil is given daily in the mare's muscle and is the only proven available alternative that is safe and adequately maintains blood progesterone levels when the mare is unable or fiercely unwilling to accept oral supplementation. Altrenogest is a synthetic progesterone (Regu-Mate®) that is given orally on a daily basis. It can be administered by dose syringe or put in the feed if the mare is being fed individually and will lick up all of her grain ration. Altrenogest should be handled with care because it can be absorbed across a person's skin. The person handling and administering the drug should wear gloves and wash thoroughly afterward. Both forms of progesterone should be administered at the direction of a supervising veterinarian.

Once supplementation begins, the next question for the veterinarian is when is it safe to discontinue treatment? The whole purpose of initiating therapy is to provide added or replacement support of ovarian, luteal progesterone. Therefore, supplementation should not be discontinued prior to 120 to 150 days of gestation. In general, once the placenta is producing adequate levels of progestogens and its uterine attachments have matured, an ovarian source of progesterone is no longer needed. This occurs sometime between 100 and 150 days of gestation. If the pregnancy is progressing normally, it is possible to wean mares off supplementation beginning around day 120 so it is discontinued by day 150. This is done by decreasing the oral dose by half and giving it daily for seven days, then decreasing the frequency of the half dose to every other day for seven to 10 days.

While it has been shown that treatment can be stopped cold turkey, it is less of a shock to the mare's system and the pregnancy to do so gradually. The mare should be rectally palpated and an ultrasound examination (both rectally and transabdominally) performed to assess cervical and uterine tone and to check on fetal viability and placentation before weaning off supplementation. Sometimes blood progesterone levels can be checked as well. If the levels are still above 2 ng/ml (and preferably more than 5 ng/ml), the decision to discontinue therapy can be made with the feeling of a little extra security. (Progesterone assays will only reflect endogenous production of progesterone if altrenogest is being given, but do not discern between ovarian and injected progesterone so measured levels will be misleading in the latter instance.) Likewise, estrone sulfate levels can be checked to assess that the fetal-placental unit appears to be functioning normally.

Many mares are maintained on progesterone supplementation until just before term (usually discontinued by 325 days) with no adverse effects. If a doubt exists, the pregnancy is particularly valuable, or the owner is nervous, continue therapy.

Once therapy is initiated, the uterus needs to be monitored for infection and also fetal death. While the mare is on progesterone, she will not return to estrus. Failure to detect the loss of an embryo needlessly maintains the mare in a diestrous state and is a waste of time and money because of the increased amount of time the mare spends open and the cost of the supplementation itself.

Lastly, progesterone keeps the uterus quiet and the cervix closed. Once the pregnancy reaches the fetal stage, the fetal tissues might not be resorbed fully by the uterus if the developing foal dies. Supplemental progesterone could prevent these retained tissues from being aborted. If this occurs, it is possible that the fetal remnants will become mummified as the fluid is slowly removed from them by the mare's tract. Once a mummy has formed, it might not be possible to remove it from the uterus. Should this occur, the mare's reproductive career is over. In addition, an infection could enter the occupied uterus and become established in the mummified tissues. The result would be a severe and dangerous infection.

Abortion

Equine abortion generally refers to the premature expulsion of the fetus between the 50th and 300th day of gestation. Mares abort for any number of reasons. Abnormalities in the placenta or the endometrium also place the developing foal at risk. Late-developing or long-standing reproductive tract infections can cause inflammation and damage to the placenta, resulting in pregnancy loss. A number of infectious diseases that affect the horse also can cause abortion. Nutrition, genetic mistakes, exposure to environmental toxins, and injury can all cause abortion.

Abortion rates are in the neighborhood of 10 percent of all equine pregnancies, and unfortunately only about 50 percent of equine abortions receive a definitive diagnosis as to why they occur. The placenta and the uterine lining are the developing foal's lifeline to the outside world. The connection between the two supplies oxygen and nutrition to the foal and helps remove waste products throughout the foal's uterine life. Scar tissue or fibrosis of the mare's uterine lining is formed at the expense of the uterine glands and other supportive tissues of the endometrium. Endometrial glands that are choked off by fibrosis are unable to produce histotroph to support the pregnancy early on, and placentas from mares that have an endometrium that is atrophied and fibrotic often show corresponding abnormalities in the development of the microvilli on the chorionic surface. Developing foals from these mares likely experience poor nutrient exchange across the uterine and placental interface. There is a higher incidence of abortion and pregnancy loss in mares with uterine pathology.

The equine umbilical cord is quite long compared to those in other domestic species. As a result, the equine fetus, wrapped in its amnion, is quite mobile on its umbilical tether within the allantoic cavity for a long period during early to mid gestation. Excessively long umbilical cords can be prone to torsion if the fetus somersaults excessively, and abortion due to strangulation of the blood supply within the umbilical cord is sometimes recognized in aborted equine fetuses. However, the umbilical cord of horses often contains many twists without compromising the fetus, and this condition should only be suspected if bruising, clotting, or rupture of the aborted fetus' cord is seen in addition to twisting.

Placentitis is an inflammation of the placenta. Usually it is caused by an infection on the surface of the placenta. It is thought that infecting organisms come from long-standing uterine infections or gain access to the placental surface via a bacteremia in the mare's bloodstream. The most common scenario is a placentitis caused by an ascending infection through the mare's cervix. Any condition that compromises the integrity of the cervical barrier predisposes a mare to developing placentitis and subsequently aborting. Severe cervical trauma (lacerations) at foaling can result in scar formation or deficits in the cervix that prevent the mare from forming a tight closure of the cervix during diestrus and pregnancy. Chronic irritation and bacterial contamination caused by pneumovagina, urine pooling, or small recto-vaginal fistulas can cause the cervix to become

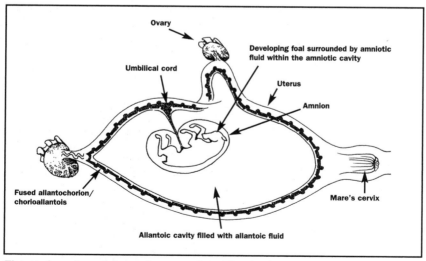

The equine placental membrane and cavities in the pregnant mare

inflamed and open, allowing the bacterial or fungal organisms access to the uterine environment. A variety of organisms have been isolated from placentitis cases with the majority of them (such as *Streptococcus* species, *Escherichia coli*, and *Staphylococcus* species) being opportunists that were in the right place at the right time to cause a problem.

Most placentitis abortions occur during the last 60 days of gestation. Outwardly the mares typically demonstrate signs of premature mammary development and a vaginal discharge that can range from serous to hemorrhagic to frank pus. Diagnosis may be made by simple speculum examination, which might show an inflamed cervix discharging an exudate through the external cervical os. If the vaginal discharge is bloody, a speculum examination will help distinguish a placentitis case from a case of vaginal varicose veins.

(Bleeding from vaginal varicose veins is sometimes seen in mares during pregnancy and occasionally during estrus and is most likely due to the increase in blood circulation and pressure seen in the vaginal region. Unless the bleeding is excessive and the mare is becoming anemic, usually no attempt is made to ligate or cauterize the offending vessel, and the mare is simply kept quiet and under close observation. Frequently she will also have a Caslick's procedure to decrease the likelihood of any further vaginal irritation to the engorged veins. The condition usually resolves spontaneously after the mare foals, but foaling should be closely attended in case the mare ruptures a particularly large vessel.)

Placentitis also can be confirmed via rectal ultrasound, which might show placental thickening in the caudal uterine body and adjacent to the internal cervical os of the cervix. There could also be evidence of premature placental separation in this region. Detection of these changes early (i.e., before the mare shows a discharge or begins to develop her udder prematurely) can save some endangered pregnancies by allowing therapy to be initiated as early as possible. For this reason mares are now routinely scanned with ultrasound every one to two months during the second and third trimesters as an early detection screening exam.

Treatment for placentitis includes broad spectrum, systemic antimicrobials, anti-inflammatory drugs, and stall rest. Using progesterone for uterine infections is somewhat controversial. Exogenous progesterone can help quiet the uterus in placentitis cases in an attempt to maintain the pregnancy. If progesterone is used, fetal viability should be monitored closely and supplementation discontinued the moment fetal death is recognized. A veterinarian also might choose to use other uterine quieting agents such as isoxsuprine or clenbuterol (where available).

Frequently, placentitis is too advanced when first noticed to save the pregnancy, but treatment occasionally succeeds and the fetus makes it to term. Foals born with affected placentas are frequently septic and weak and require intensive nursing and medical care to survive. The mare likewise should be treated aggressively for endometritis after aborting or foaling with sterile saline, uterine lavage, and antibiotics or antifungals as indicated by culture and sensitivity results. Damage caused to the mare's uterus by a placentitis could hurt her future reproductive capabilities, and any predisposing anatomical conditions should be repaired before the next breeding to prevent the condition from recurring.

In spring 2001 a new condition resulting in the loss of established pregnancies, neonatal deaths, pancarditis, and ocular pathology was recognized. Named Mare Reproductive Loss Syndrome (MRLS), this outbreak was largely confined to Central Kentucky. It had a devastating effect on the number of live births that year and on the number of pregnancies that resulted in 2002 foals. The pathogenesis of this condition is still unclear but a direct link to exposure and likely consumption by pregnant mares of the eastern tent caterpillar has been made. An abnormally large hatch of these caterpillars occurred in 2001, providing an explanation for the outbreak. In subsequent years this new entity has remained rare. At this time, limiting pregnant mares' exposure to these insects is highly recommended as is taking steps to eliminate the caterpillars on the farm.

There are several infectious equine diseases that can cause abortion in mares. Among these diseases the most common are equine herpesvirus (type I and type IV), equine viral arteritis, Potomac horse fever, and leptospirosis. The key to managing any pregnant mare is to isolate her from any possible sources of infection, keep stress levels to a minimum, and vaccinate her appropriately. Equine herpesvirus type I typically causes respiratory disease (rhinopneumonitis) in young horses but also can cause abortion in pregnant mares, neurologic disease occasionally in any horse, and neonatal pneumonia and mortality. Herpesvirus type IV typically only causes respiratory disease, but has been associated with abortions in mares. Clinically, the abortions caused by type I and type IV are indistinguishable.

As with other herpesviruses, equineherpes virus will lie dormant within a previously infected horse and become active during periods of stress. These silent carriers can infect other horses, and they could shed the virus without showing any outward clinical signs. The virus gains access to its host when horses inhale it as an aerosol transmission or sniff aborted fetal materials. Infected pregnant mares could show varying degrees of respiratory signs and fever, or show no sign of illness until they abort. Abortions typically occur after seven months of gestation and could occur anywhere from 14 to 120 days after exposure to the virus.

In the past, it was common for an abortion storm to go through a farm. Today, the incidence of mass abortions has decreased because horsemen have become better at managing their mares to decrease their exposure, and vaccination of pregnant mares has become widespread. However, no vaccine is 100 percent effective in preventing disease, and some mares will not mount a good response to vaccination and remain susceptible if exposed. Typically these days rhino abortions occur sporadically but are still responsible for a large percentage of the equine abortions diagnosed. Pregnant mares should be kept apart from all young horse and transient horse populations (i.e., weanlings, yearlings, show horses, racehorses, and sales horses). Any and all aborted membranes, fetal fluids, and tissues should be removed promptly, and contaminated bedding should be removed and stalls disinfected in such a way that there is no chance of other horses being exposed to the virus (i.e., do not spread contaminated bedding on pastures, and do not leave aborted materials in a bucket or wheelbarrow).

Mares should be vaccinated at a minimum at five, seven, and nine months of gestation. Immune response to herpes viral antigens are short-lived, so vaccinations must be repeated regularly for an animal to maintain a good level of immunity. All other horses on the premises should be vaccinated regularly for rhino as well to decrease the likelihood of an outbreak.

Equine viral arteritis abortions have been observed sporadically, and positive titers confirming exposure to the virus are more common in Standardbreds than in any other breed. EVA causes widespread vascular necrosis in affected individuals, resulting in fever, depression, swelling of the limbs and sometimes the face and abdomen, conjunctivitis, temporary infertility in bred mares, and abortion in pregnant mares anywhere from three to eight weeks after exposure to the virus. Airborne transmission can result in outbreaks, and the virus also is transmitted venereally to mares from infected shedder stallions. (The virus resides in the accessory sex glands of the stallion and can be shed in the semen in some individuals.) A note of caution to breeders: This virus will freeze readily and contaminate frozen and shipped semen as well as fresh.

Vaccination efforts are aimed primarily at the stallions. Stallions should be checked for negative titers and vaccinated around four weeks before the start of the breeding season. Stallions that have positive titers and were not previously vaccinated should be tested to see if they are shedding the virus in their semen (shedding can occur for years after initial clinical disease affected the stallion). Stallions that are confirmed to be shedding virus should only be bred to mares that have a positive titer against the disease (either through previous natural exposure or by vaccination at least three weeks before breeding). Mares bred to shedder stallions should be isolated from other in-foal mares and sero-negative mares for a minimum of three weeks just in case these recently bred mares do manifest clinical disease and shed the virus despite precautions. Vaccination of pregnant mares with the modified live vaccine is not recommended. Depending on the horse's export status, preventive vaccination may not be pursued because of export regulations barring sero-positive horses and/or their semen from entering certain countries. With the increased popularity of using frozen semen in certain breeds, it might become prudent to vaccinate mares without positive titers before breeding with frozen semen if the stallion's status is unknown.

Potomac horse fever is caused by the ehrlichial organism, *Ehrlichia risticii*, and is thought to be transmitted by some form of biting insect, although the exact vector is unknown. An increased incidence of this disease is usually seen in endemic locations during the late spring through the early fall months, but cases are sporadic and not thought to be spread from horse to horse. Potomac horse fever can cause severe diarrhea, fever, laminitis, and sometimes death, and it has been associated with causing abortions in mares. Mares experimentally infected with the organism typically aborted two months later. Mild and subclinical forms of the fever occur commonly, and it is conceivable that a mare might abort suddenly with no previously recognized illness. When clinical signs are present, veterinary treatment of the mare with oxytetracycline during the acute colitis might reduce the incidence of subsequent abortion. A vaccine against Potomac horse fever is available, but its effectiveness in preventing abortion is unknown. In endemic areas, it might be prudent to vaccinate broodmares before breeding.

The incidence of recognized equine abortions caused by leptospirosis has increased in recent years. There are different bacterial strains, or serovars, of the *Leptospira* organism that have been reported to cause equine abortion, but the most common one is *Leptospira pomona*. The source of the organism is any infected animal. White-tailed deer are thought to serve as a reservoir for

Leptospira in the Northeast. Horses are typically exposed when their mucous membranes or cut or abraded skin come into contact with the organism that has been shed, usually in the urine of an infected animal. Signs of urinary tract infection are seen, and some animals experience kidney failure. Other clinical manifestations of leptospirosis in horses include fever, jaundice (liver disease, hemolytic anemia), chronic uveitis (moon blindness or periodic ophthalmia), and abortion. Signs can be mild or severe, and abortion usually follows clinical illness by two weeks.

Mares that experience leptospiral abortions usually have very high titers to the offending organism in their bloodstream, and the organism can be isolated from their urine for as long as three months following the initial infection. Shedding mares need to be isolated from other horses, and all contaminated bedding, discharges, and aborted materials must be disposed of carefully and all contacting surfaces disinfected to ensure that the organism is not spread to another animal. A note of caution: Humans are susceptible to leptospiral infections as well, and extreme caution and sanitation should be employed when handling contaminated materials. Affected mares can be treated with penicillin, streptomycin, or oxytetracycline by a veterinarian, and treatment could decrease the shedder period and prevent infection of the fetus and subsequent abortion. There is no approved leptospirosis vaccine for horses. The best method of prevention is to eliminate exposure. This is best accomplished by keeping horses fenced away from wet areas and areas of runoff from other animals.

What To Do When Mares Abort

What should the mare's caretakers do in the event of an equine abortion? Many abortions occur unnoticed until a routine veterinary examination shows the mare to be open or her abdomen fails to enlarge as expected and the veterinarian confirms the owner's suspicions. Most commonly these mares were out at pasture and not closely observed. Mares that are monitored closely, however, are unlikely to abort without someone noticing, even if it is to only notice some discharge or blood on the mare's tail when she is led in from pasture.

All aborted materials should be saved in a plastic bag that will not leak and kept cool until a veterinarian can examine and sample them. Or they should be placed in a cooler with ice and taken to the nearest diagnostic lab. Gloves should be worn when handling all aborted tissues, and the person

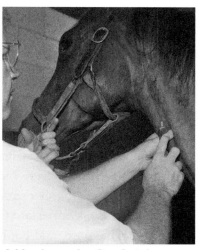

A blood sample often is taken after an abortion

should wash up thoroughly afterwards. Pregnant women, children, and immune-compromised individuals should not handle the aborted remains or discharging fluids. Any bedding should be carefully removed and disposed of and the ground surface on which the aborted remains lay should be disinfected.

The mare should be isolated immediately in a comfortable stall and closely monitored until the veterinarian can arrive. The veterinarian will give the mare a thorough physical examination, take blood and urine samples, and perform a culture and cytology of her uterus. The mare's reproductive tract will be assessed via rectal palpation and ultrasound and vaginal speculum and digital examinations for signs of infection or injury. Next, the veterinarian will carefully examine the aborted fetal remains to estimate fetal age and development and the degree of decomposition. The veterinarian also will examine the placenta for abnormalities and to make sure none of the placental membranes has been retained. Treatment will be initiated (antibiotics, anti-inflammatories, uterine lavage, etc.) depending on the exam findings. The veterinarian either will submit the entire fetal tissues on ice to a diagnostic laboratory or gather samples of the fetal heart, lungs, spleen, kidneys, liver, heart, blood, and stomach contents along with placental samples. The fixed tissues will be sectioned and examined microscopically for pathologic changes, and the fresh tissues will be cultured or otherwise processed in the laboratory to perform bacterial and viral isolations. Tissues not submitted for analysis should be burned or buried well away from any other horses.

The veterinarian might take blood samples from the mare's stable or pasture mates. The veterinarian also might perform follow-up examinations and a uterine biopsy, and take follow-up blood samples from the mare and her sampled pasture and barn mates. A thorough history also is important to solving the diagnostic dilemma that many abortions pose, and complete records on the mare and histories concerning any recent illnesses or arrivals on the farm should be made known and available to the examining veterinarian. It is important that the mare who aborted be kept isolated from her (pregnant) horse companions until the veterinarian indicates that the risk of the mare shedding offending organisms has passed. It pays to be vigilant and cautious.

Any pregnant mares that are injured, colicking, or showing signs of depression, fever, decreased appetite, vaginal discharge, premature mammary development, or any other abnormal sign should be examined by a veterinarian as soon as possible. Early detection and treatment of sick mares might save pregnancies in some cases.

Pre-Foaling Management

A mare should be brought inside at night beginning 30 to 45 days before her due date. This is done for two reasons. The first is so she can become comfortable with the surroundings and feel that the foaling stall is a safe, private place. Mares that are not at ease might delay foaling and prolong their labor until they feel more secure. Such a delay can lead to complications.

The second reason is to introduce the mare to all the local pathogens, giving her time to build immunity and concentrate this immunity in her first milk, or colostrum. The foal receives all its immunity for the first three or so months of its life via the antibodies absorbed from the mare's colostrum during the first 24 hours of life. By introducing the mare to the local organisms ahead of time, you are, in effect, protecting the foal.

Get a mare accustomed to the foaling stall

The foaling stall

should be a minimum of 14 x 14 feet, have solid walls that rise at least three feet from the floor, be free of any sharp edges, and be well ventilated but draft-free. The stall should be kept clean, dry, and well bedded at all times. The mare should be isolated from transient horses (show and sale horses) and young horses (weanlings and yearlings) to avoid exposing her or her unborn foal to any new and/or particularly virulent pathogen (rhinopneumonitis in particular). Ideally, foaling mares live in a separate barn and get turned out during the day in small compatible groups of five or six.

Normal mares in the late stages of pregnancy benefit greatly from daily exercise and should have ample opportunity to get out and move around freely in good weather. Daily walking helps decrease the buildup of pitting edema in a mare's legs and abdomen during late gestation. It also helps her maintain good muscle tone, an advantage when it comes time for delivery.

The mare ideally has a clean, grassy paddock or field where she can readily be observed in case she decides to foal during the day. A grassy location, free of manure buildup and cleaned by the elements, is a fine place for a mare to foal provided the weather is dry and not too cold. This probably offers a much cleaner environment than her stall. If the

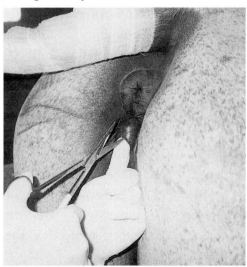

mare does foal in a field, it is important for her and the foal to be safe from other horses and to deliver where she will not hurt herself or lose her foal under a fence or into a body of water (tank or pond).

When mares are first brought into their stalls a month or so before foaling, they should be

Open the Caslick's two weeks in advance checked for the presence of a Caslick's in the vulva. Mares that have had a Caslick's procedure to prevent pneumovagina need to have them opened before delivery. Because mares can foal unexpectedly, open a mare's Caslick's when she begins to show signs of increasing udder development or two weeks before her due date, whichever comes first. A mare that attempts to foal through a closed

Caslick's in all likelihood will deliver the foal but will tear her perineum severely.

Make sure the mare has up-to-date vaccinations at this time. As already stated, the mare concentrates antibodies in her colostrum for the immune protection of the foal. Vaccinations given 30 days before foaling should be tailored by a veterinarian to meet whatever disease problems are typically encountered in the area. Having said this, however, it is prudent to vaccinate all foaling mares for tetanus, Eastern and Western encephalitis, and influenza. (This regimen is in addition to the rhinopneumonitis prevention regimen of vaccinations for herpesvirus at three, five, seven, and nine months of the gestation.)

Continue deworming programs throughout pregnancy. Make sure to administer anthelmintics that are safe for pregnancy and avoid organophosphate and phenothiazine dewormers.

Signs of Approaching Foaling

The mare undergoes external body changes in preparation for foaling that the conscientious caretaker can use to help him or her determine when the mare will foal. Although many of the changes discussed here are considered classic signs, not every mare reads the book. She might show all, some, or in rare cases even none of the typical signs. Once again, observe your mare closely and keep complete records from year to year. Mares tend to repeat the same outward changes and behaviors at each foaling, and accurate records can help you to outfox her and avoid too many sleepless nights watching the mare watch you watching her not foaling.

About four weeks before foaling, the mare's udder will begin to develop. The mammary gland is divided into two halves. Each half has its own teat, with usually two (but sometimes more) openings for the milk to exit. The udder development begins with the increasing size of the two halves. This initial enlargement is frequently accompanied by localized pitting edema surrounding the udder, making it appear larger than it is at this early stage. As the development progresses, this edema decreases in most mares, and you can begin to appreciate the true enlargement of the glandular tissues. This enlargement continues until about 48 hours before foaling, when the udder will appear full and somewhat taut.

Up until this point, the teats have remained flat, but during the last 12 to 24 hours they usually begin to fill with colostrum, and a wax-like substance starts to form on the endings. "Waxing up," as it is known, is considered one of the classic signs of impending labor. Waxing can range from the formation of tiny beads of secretion right at the teat endings to large "candles" that project from the teat ends. Remember that not every mare produces this sign in the classic manner, and many mares might wax up days ahead of the actual delivery or never wax at all.

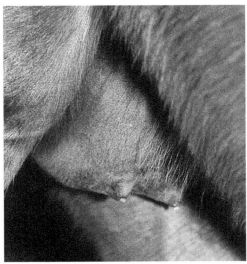

In addition to waxing, many mares also will begin to drip or even stream milk in the final one to four hours before delivery. Some mares will leak milk for days and even weeks prior to delivering, and these mares pose a special concern.

"Waxing up" signals impending labor

Mares that prematurely produce milk lose the valuable colostrum that has built up in their udders in preparation for their foals' needs at birth. The remaining milk frequently has poor antibody content by the time of the actual delivery. If this occurs, attempt to catch the leaking colostrum and save it in the freezer to be bottle or tube fed to the foal. Even better, identify a source of good-quality colostrum that has been banked for such an occasion (more on this later). This way, the foal can receive a colostrum supplement shortly after delivery (within the first one to four hours). In general, the mare that has a fully developed udder and full teats, that is waxed and dripping milk, likely is just hours away from foaling. Remember, though, many mares will foal without demonstrating all of these signs. Maiden mares, though enlarged, frequently will not have a great increase in the size of their udder halves when they first foal compared to the size increase seen in multiparous mares.

The appearance of the mammary gland secretions from the udder changes as foaling draws near. Initially difficult to squeeze out, thin and light straw- or serum-colored secretions become more copious and more like milk. As colostrum concentrates in the udder, the secretions become readily expressible and often thick with a honey-colored overtone. These changes can occur gradually or within the last hours before delivery.

Likewise, the concentrations of the electrolytes in the mammary secretions shift as the foal matures and delivery draws closer. Calcium (and magnesium) concentrations rise, and sodium and potassium levels fall and rise, respectively, in relation to one another. These changes serve as a subjective measure to help predict how close the mare is to foaling. Milk calcium concentrations of 40 milligrams per deciliter (mg/dL) or more have been associated with fetal maturity. Commercially available equine milk test kits and/or water quality hardness strips can be used to test the mammary secretions on a daily basis. Most mares demonstrate a rise in milk calcium levels above 40 mg/dL within 48 hours of delivering, although some might demonstrate this change for a considerably longer period before foaling. Therefore, milk calcium levels are a useful but not an absolute gauge for predicting foaling. A mare whose milk calcium is less than 40 mg/dL probably will not foal in the next 24 hours.

Daily laboratory milk analysis can be used to chart the shifts in milk sodium and potassium levels (as well as milk calcium concentrations) to detect when their inversion occurs. Scoring systems using absolute calcium, potassium, and sodium levels give a quantitative score by which the likelihood that a mare will foal within the next 24 hours can be assessed. As with the other indicative signs, measurement of milk electrolytes helps predict when a mare likely will foal but are not always absolute.

In preparation for delivery, the ligaments and connective tissues surrounding the mare's pelvis and perineum must become lax so the tissues can stretch and the pelvis widen to accommodate the foal's passage through the birth canal. Evidence of this change is seen in the softening and sinking of the ligaments surrounding the tailhead. This change becomes most pronounced just before delivery when the area over the muscular croup and the line between the tailhead and the point of the buttock become increasingly concave. This change appears more pronounced in mares that have foaled before. But almost every mare will exhibit an appreciable, progressive softening in this area that can be felt during the last week and especially during the few days just before delivery. The tissues of the vulva also become increasingly soft, lax, and filled with edema, a change most noticeable the day the mare delivers. In the final hours before delivery, the vulva lengthens dramatically. This sign can be subtle and easily missed.

Lastly, many mares will behave differently the last few days before delivery. Rather than staying with the group, many will keep to themselves when out at pasture. Some mares will pace the fence or hang back near the gait, anxious to return to the perceived security of their stall. When in their stall, some mares might act anxious or, conversely, become quiet, still, and almost reflective for long periods. Quite a few mares will stop eating in the hours just before labor, while others continue to eat right up to the point of delivery.

Taken together, the signs of mammary development, milk electrolyte changes, pelvic ligament softening, vulvar lengthening, and changes in behavior all indicate that a mare is close to foaling (i.e., within days or hours). But predicting the exact hour labor will commence is impossible.

Once it appears that a mare is close to foaling, monitor her around the clock to ensure that help is available if needed. Mares have a good deal of control over labor up to a point. It has been said that "the foal chooses the day of his birth, but the mare chooses the hour." Most mares foal at night. They can shut down stage I labor (provided it hasn't progressed too far) if they become frightened or insecure about their surroundings. They will delay the progression of labor for a few hours until the perceived danger has passed.

Office-to-stall observation windows, video cameras, and monitoring devices all aid in monitoring of the mare. A note of caution about electronic devices: They are useful adjuncts to a foal watch but should not be relied upon solely. Electronic mechanisms have a way of failing. Some of these devices are triggered by the events of a normal foaling but not an abnormal one and so fail just when their warning is needed most.

Ideally, night checks should be performed every 15 to 20 minutes with as little noise and light changes as possible. Begin these checks in

Some mares seek solitude before foaling

advance of the perceived due date so the watcher's presence during the night will become routine to the mare and not disturb her once her time arrives.

Normal Foaling

A working knowledge of the equine placenta is important to understand and recognize the events and progression of a normal foaling. The placenta consists of three membranes: the amnion, the allantois, and the chorion *(see placental illustration on page 178)*. The amnion is the white, glistening membrane that covers the foal. The umbilical cord exits the amnion and connects the foal to the allantois. The smooth, gray/white allantois contains the large placental blood vessels that carry the foal's circulating

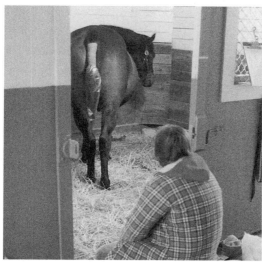

Preparing to foal

blood from the umbilical chord to the surface of the uterus then back to the foal via the umbilical chord. The chorion is a velvety red membrane that interlocks in a finger-like way with the entire endometrial surface (i.e., it covers the luminal surface of both uterine horns and the body). Millions of tiny villi covering the chorionic surface give it its characteristic appearance and large, effective surface area over which nutrient, oxygen, and waste exchange occur between the developing foal and the mare.

The allantois and chorion are fused, forming what appears to be a single membrane (the chorioallantois), with the chorion facing outward against the uterus, and the allantois facing inward toward the foal. Between the allantoic and amnionic surface is a large, fluid-filled space known as the allantoic cavity. There also is a small amount of fluid within the amnionic cavity surrounding the foal. In effect, the foal at term is contained in a sac (the amnion) within a sac (the chorioallantois) with a large amount of allantoic fluid between the two membranes.

Although parturition (delivery of the foal) is a continuous process, labor is divided into three stages:

Stage I Labor

Stage I labor typically lasts from one to six hours. As uterine contractions strengthen, the foal (which has been lying on its back within the uterus throughout mid-late gestation) is stimulated to rotate and spiral around from a curled up, upside down position to a right side up position with both forelegs and head and neck extended (diver's position). The foal's failure to achieve this normal delivery position could indicate a foal that is weak and compromised in some manner and that might require extra nursing care upon delivery.

As uterine contractions increase in strength and frequency, they cause the membranes and the foal to put increasing pressure on the ripened cervix, making it dilate. Inwardly these activities cause varying degrees of pain and discomfort to the mare, which she outwardly manifests. Many mares become restless and walk around their stall switching and elevating their tails. They might demonstrate mild colic signs: pawing, looking at their flanks, stretching out, getting up and down, Flehman (lip curling), etc. Many mares will break out in a light sweat, especially on their chest and behind their elbows and on their flanks. Some mares will demonstrate anorexia, but others will continue to eat small amounts of hay early on in between pacing, and some mares will defecate frequently.

As the cervix stretches, a neuroendocrine response releases the hormone oxytocin from the brain (Ferguson's Reflex). In addition to strengthening the uterine contractions, oxytocin also will cause milk to let down, and it is at this point that some mares begin to leak colostrum from their teats.

Closely observe the mare without disturbing her. Most mares would prefer to foal unobserved (and many do). Remember that the mare can and will delay stage I labor if she is upset about her environment. When a mare is suspected to be very close or actually in stage I labor, her stall should be quietly cleaned of any manure piles and rebedded with fresh straw. If it is not too disturbing to her, her tail can be wrapped and her perineum washed at this time. It might be less disruptive, however, if she is just maintained in a well-groomed condition each evening and only disturbed if she is

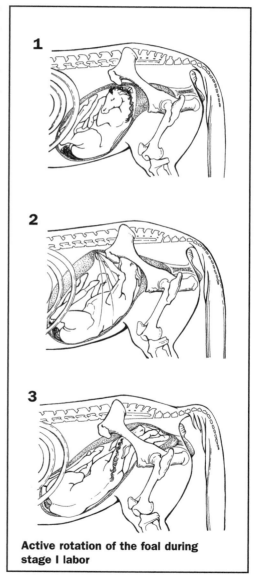

Active rotation of the foal during stage I labor

grossly contaminated or needs examination by knowledgeable attendants because of an abnormal progression of events.

As stage I progresses and the cervix becomes increasingly dilated,
the chorioallantois begins to bulge into the birth canal and finally
ruptures under the increasing pressure of the allantoic fluid and/or
the forelimbs of the foal. This fetal membrane rupture releases the
allantoic fluid. Normally amber colored and odorless, this fluid's
release can range from a sudden gush of fluid to a small, frequent
trickle. Again, the mare needs to be watched closely or this event can
be missed or mistaken for urination. Stage I labor ends with this
breaking of the water.

Stage II Labor

Stage II labor, the active expulsion of the foal, usually lasts between
five to 40 minutes. Within five minutes of the initial rupture of the
chorioallantois and release of the allantoic fluid, the glistening, white
amnion should appear at the vulvar lips. Delay or failure of the
amnion to appear indicates that the foal is malpositioned and that
the mare needs to be examined as quickly as possible. If the red
chorion appears instead of the white amnion, this indicates premature separation of the placental attachment to the uterus, endangering the foal's oxygen supply. If this red bag delivery is observed, it is
imperative to open the chorioallantois immediately so that the foal
in its amnion can be delivered rapidly through this opening. Once
delivered, the foal's head must be cleared of the amnion and its
breathing stimulated (receiving oxygen and resuscitation if needed)
as quickly as possible. Foals that have experienced premature separation of the placenta are in danger of becoming "dummy foals" and
require close monitoring.

In a normal foaling, the bubble of the amnion is followed quickly
by the appearance of one foot, then the second foot, and then the
nose of the foal. By presenting one foot at a time, the foal reduces the
diameter of its shoulders, making it easier for the mare to pass the
shoulders through her pelvis. The feet should be pointed heel side

down. Heel side up indicates either a backward delivery (i.e., hind feet first) or a foal that is upside down.

During stage I labor, the mare does not show signs of active straining, but as the foal engages the cervix and birth canal of the vagina and pelvis, the mare is stimulated to push. The hallmark of stage II labor is active abdominal contractions. Straining is intermittent with rest periods of two to four minutes between bursts of two to eight contractions. Progress should be made with each series of contractions. Lack of progress is cause for concern.

Most mares will get up and down once or twice and reposition themselves, then lie on their sides to deliver the foal. Occasionally a mare will remain standing, requiring her attendants to catch and hold the foal as it is delivered. The most forceful contractions frequently are those occurring with the passage of the head and then the shoulders, and the mare often will pause to rest after each becomes free of the vulva.

Once the foal's hips have passed through the vulva, the mare usually will lie quietly for several minutes with the foal's hind legs still in her. At this point it is important to make sure the foal's head is free of the amnion and that it is breathing. Note whether there is any meconium staining the foal within the amnion. A normal foal is clean, but stressed foals might defecate during delivery and be covered with meconium. This fetal diarrhea is also a sign that a foal will likely require assistance and medical care.

Disturb the mare as little as possible and allow her and the foal to have a few minutes to recover from the delivery and to lie quietly with the umbilical cord still attached. It has long been thought that a portion of the foal's blood supply (up to 20 percent) remained in the placenta after delivery. Leaving the umbilical attachment undisturbed was considered important so uterine contractions on the placenta would pump the remaining blood back into the foal. It is now unclear whether this actually occurs, but it is probably wise not to break the umbilical attachment prematurely. The magical moment of foaling occurs when the new foal takes its first look at the new world and is discovered by its dam. Frequently they will nicker at each other and the mare will reach around to touch her foal muzzle to muzzle.

Allow the mare the chance to lick her foal; intervene to help dry the foal only if it is extremely cold. The mare and foal need to bond, and any interference, no matter how well intentioned, can damage the pairing and potentially lead to the mare rejecting her foal (especially if the mare is a maiden). Resist the urge to participate in this moment. Once the foal begins to struggle, the mare usually will get to her feet and come around to inspect her baby more thoroughly. The umbilical cord will be broken naturally at this time.

Stage III Labor

Stage III labor is the passage of the fetal membranes. Expulsion usually occurs within an hour, but the placenta is not considered retained until three hours after the foal's birth. After the foal is delivered, the uterus continues to have contractions. The microvilli on the chorionic surface of the placenta release or unlock from their connection with the endometrium, and the placenta is expelled from the uterus. The chorioallantois usually is turned inside out as it is dropped. Some mares will become crampy during this process and show signs of colic; others will lie down quietly as they work on passing the membranes. Still others are busy taking care of their foals and show no outward sign of discomfort.

Some mares might become uncomfortable enough during this process to require walking or low-dose analgesics to help them through it. Remember to view any mare showing abnormal signs of discomfort after foaling with concern, and to consult with a veterinarian. Until the mare passes the membranes, tie up the placenta to itself carefully to keep the mare from inadvertently stepping on it. Never apply traction to the placenta because you can severely damage the mare's uterus. Just let gravity and the mare work on it. The placenta will slide out of the mare once it has released from the uterus, and there should be no straining on the mare's part. (A mare that continues to strain after delivering her foal should be examined immediately as she might have a previously undetected twin or might be trying to prolapse her uterus.) Once the placenta has been passed, it should be examined for abnormalities and to make sure it is intact. The chorioallantois most likely will be turned inside out, with the gray-white

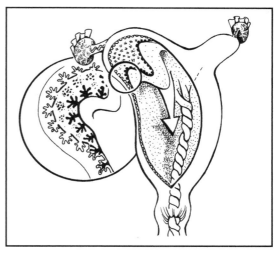

The placenta is actively expelled after the foal is delivered. First, the uterus continues to contract, causing microvilli and endometrium to unlock from one another. Then waves of contractions roll and push the placenta out.

allantoic surface with its large vessels facing outward.

Carefully check to see that both horns of the placenta are complete and that there are no missing portions on the placenta. Take especially good care to examine the tips of each horn, where the placenta is most likely to be retained. The only opening in the chorioallatois should be at the base of the body (bottom of the "T"). This is where the foal exited.

While handling the placenta and checking the horns, you frequently will encounter a soft, tan-gray mass of tissue that is free within the allantoic cavity. This is the Hippomane, a solid mass of cells that is a normal finding and not cause for alarm. As you examine the allantoic surface, the umbilical cord and amnion will be fully visible as well.

Next, turn the placenta right side out so that the red chorion is facing outward and check the entire surface to ensure that it is complete. At this time, you also are looking for any gross discolorations or abnormal thickenings. The chorion should appear a rich red. The only normal exceptions to this are the normal avillous pale areas that correspond to where the placenta was in contact with the cervix and the tiny openings of the oviducts at the tips of each horn. The cervical star will appear as pale striations radiating from the opening in the base of the body of the placenta. There frequently also will be pale linear areas (particularly close to the base of the horns) that correspond to where the chorion was folded on itself. Lastly, the placenta should be weighed. The normal placenta is about 10 percent of the foal's birth weight (10 to 12 pounds for an average 100-pound foal). Any abnormalities should be brought to a veterinarian's attention. Heavy or discolored placentas could indicate a placentitis, which might require medical treatment for the foal and mare. An incomplete placenta or one that has been retained for more than three hours is a medical emergency, and a veterinarian should be contacted at once.

Complications of Late Pregnancy and Delivery

In general, most late-term mares will accumulate some degree of edema on their abdomens and stock up in their hind limbs in much the same manner as a pregnant woman whose ankles swell. The weight of the developing foal and its surrounding fluids increase pressure on the veins that drain the ventral abdomen, which in turn causes fluid to pool in the tissues, resulting in a pitting edema that can be felt and, in many cases, seen. Typically, this edema is most obvious at the lowest point of the belly and around the udder, but it can extend all the way from the flanks to the elbows and become quite thick.

In some instances, the edema can become extreme. Any condition that increases the weight on the mare's abdomen beyond what is normally encountered during late gestation (i.e., twin pregnancy, fetal hydrops, etc.) will exacerbate this condition. Sometimes older mares will accumulate an impressive degree of edema without any discernable predisposing reason. Mares that are confined also frequently develop excessive edema. The concern in these extreme conditions is that the weight will exceed the abdominal tissues' ability to support it and the mare will rupture her prepubic tendon or other abdominal musculature. Prepubic tendon ruptures occur rarely in all breeds, but draft breed mares seem more prone to it.

Mares with impending rupture have abdominal pain, are reluctant to move, and have increased abdominal edema and swelling, especially around damaged tissue. Attempts to manage the condition and prevent rupture via anti-inflammatories, belly wraps, limiting exertional stress to the tissues, and decreasing dietary roughage have limited success and should only be tried if the foal is more valuable than the mare. Mares that have ruptured their prepubic tendon have a characteristic appearance. As the tendon gives way, the belly drops and the mare's udder pulls forward. Loss of the abdominal musculature attachments destabilizes the pelvis and it assumes an abnormal angle.

Once rupture occurs, the mare's chances are grim. Attempts at surgical repair seldom succeed, and the mare usually faces euthanasia. Therapy to save the mare before the rupture or in cases of partial rupture is aimed at removing the stress on the abdomen. This means terminating the pregnancy by inducing parturition and delivering the foal regardless of its state of development. If the foal is viable after delivery, a decision can be made to institute veterinary care or to euthanize, depending on the foal's condition and value. In many cases the mare needs help during delivery as she cannot generate enough abdominal press. A mare that has had a near or partial rupture should not be bred back.

Uterine Torsion

Uterine torsion (a twisting of the uterus around its long axis) sometimes is seen in mares during the last trimester, usually before but sometimes at term. The twist can be anywhere from 180 to 540 degrees in either direction and is thought to result from the foal bouncing inside the uterus, the dam rolling, or an unfortunate combination of the two. The uterus and the foal become increasingly compromised depending on how badly twisted the tissues are. The tighter the twist, the more cut off the uterine blood supply becomes. Death of the foal and uterine rupture could occur in cases that are severe, longstanding, or both. Initially the mare might show only signs of mild colic that persist and/or reappear after medication. A gastrointestinal (GI) source for the pain has to be ruled out, but frequently mares with a uterine torsion will continue to pass feces. Mares that have more severe twists and/or a piece of bowel caught up in the twist might exhibit severe and violent colic signs initially. As the foal and the uterine tissues begin to die, the mare could become depressed and "shocky" as her condition likewise deteriorates and peritonitis sets in.

AT A GLANCE

◆ Late-term mares showing signs of colic could have a uterine torsion.

◆ Rapid recognition and correction of dystocia is critical.

◆ A retained placenta can lead to laminitis.

◆ Uterine artery rupture is a potential foaling complication in older mares.

Any late-term mare exhibiting signs of colic is suspect for this condition and should be examined by a veterinarian. Diagnosis is made on rectal examination. Early diagnosis is key to saving the mare and the foal. The torsion can be corrected by rolling an anesthetized mare or performing standing flank surgery in cooperative individuals. If the condition is corrected early and care is initiated before tissue compromise occurs, the pregnancy frequently will progress normally.

Dystocia

Dystocia is an abnormal delivery. Any foaling that injuries the dam or compromises the foal and/or requires assistance is a dystocia. Rapid recognition and correction of dystocia are critical for two major reasons. First, delivery is an explosive event. The mare musters tremendous force in her abdominal press and delivery is rapid. Therefore, the potential for self injury to the mare is high if there is any fetal malpositioning. The mare literally will push the foal through any obstructing tissues (uterus, vagina, rectum) in her effort to deliver it, damaging herself, and compromising her reproductive capabilities. Secondly, the mare's placenta rapidly begins to detach during the delivery process. Normally, stage II labor (expulsion of the foal) is accomplished in 20 to 40 minutes. Any delay in delivery beyond this frequently results in compromise or loss of the foal as the placenta detaches partially or fully and the foal's oxygen supply is cut off inside the mare.

Never discount the importance of being present and able to recognize when a foaling is abnormal. Any delay in the normal sequence of events, deviations from the foal's normal positioning, or failure of the mare to make steady progress toward delivery with each effort is cause for concern and warrants immediate veterinary attention.

Examples of when to be concerned and call for help include (but are not limited to):

1) A mare that has been demonstrating signs of stage I labor for more than an hour but does not show any sign of progressing to stage II.

2) A mare that begins to exert abdominal straining without "breaking her water" — beware of premature separation of the allanto-chorion and a "red bag" delivery.

3) Failure of the white amnion to appear at the vulva within five minutes of the water breaking.

4) Failure of both front feet and the nose to appear in the expected fashion, the appearance of more than two feet, or the front feet being upside down or the hind feet presented.

5) Failure of the mare to make progress delivering the foal even if the foal's outward positioning appears normal.

6) Failure of the mare to make any abdominal effort even though the foal appears properly presented.

7) Appearance of the foal's head or a limb through the anus instead of the vulva.

8) Meconium staining of the amnionic fluid noticeable through the white membrane as the amnion presents. (Again, facilitating rapid delivery is indicated.)

9) Frank hemorrhage from the mare's vulva.

The constant rule is, if in doubt call for experienced help. In the meantime, the most important thing you can do to help your mare and foal is to remain calm. Your calm demeanor will reassure the mare, and she is more likely to let you help her. If the foal is obviously malpositioned (i.e., leg back, failure to make progress) the best thing you can do is try to keep the mare from straining further. This is best accomplished by getting the mare up and keeping her walking in an open area until the veterinarian arrives. This sometimes is easier said than done as the mare will want to lie down with each contraction and push with the stimulus of the foal in the birth canal. Some mares occasionally will become violent with the pain, so use caution to avoid placing yourself or anyone else in a dangerous position.

Once the veterinarian arrives, he or she will perform a brief, pointed physical on the mare to assess her vital signs and overall condition, then will move quickly to examine the reproductive tract. The tail is wrapped and the perineum thoroughly cleaned before the vaginal exam begins. The mare will require some restraint during this exam. Most mares respond better with a minimal amount of restraint in the form of a halter and shank and sometimes a twitch.

The use of sedatives and epidural anesthesia is at the discretion of the attending veterinarian and will likely be employed only if the mare is extremely fractious or straining too hard to permit examination and manipulation. (Sedation of the mare also means sedation of a possibly compromised foal. A mare that has had an epidural might not be able to push effectively and, therefore, will be of little to no help when the foal is in a correct position for expulsion.)

The veterinarian will assess the mare carefully to discern stage of labor, degree of cervical dilation,

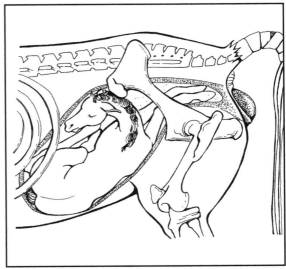

Dystocia due to a malpositioned foal with a head back

membrane rupture, the presence of any injuries to the mare's tract, size of the birth canal/bony pelvis relative to the size of the foal, position of the foal, and whether the foal is still alive. Fetal malposition is the most common reason for dystocia in the mare. A malformed foal also might be difficult to deliver. Unlike cattle, equine dystocias rarely are caused by a foal that is too large to pass through the mare's pelvis (exception: miniature horses) unless a previous injury has decreased the mare's pelvic diameter.

Once the veterinarian has examined the mare and identified the cause of the problem, he or she then will determine how best to proceed. Depending on the cause of the dystocia, this could range from simply adding lubrication and repositioning a limb to administering general anesthesia and elevating the mare's hindquarters to allow more extensive manipulations. Severe cases of malpositioning and a live foal might mandate a Caesarean section. If the foal is already dead, a fetotomy (dismemberment of the dead foal within the mare and delivery piecemeal) might be performed.

Mares requiring anesthesia, a fetotomy, and/or surgery are frequently better served by referral to a clinic that handles such emergencies. Fortunately, many dystocias are resolved on the farm. Anyone assisting the veterinarian with a dystocia must remember that all manipulations must be performed as quickly as possible and that all equipment and lubricants must be kept clean of contaminants (bedding, manure, etc.) to minimize the contamination inevitable during manipulations within the mare's tract. If traction is required to deliver the foal after any malposition is corrected, it is important not to use excessive force. Too much force can injure the foal and/or the mare's tract. (Traction should not exceed a maximum of two to three adults using obstetrical ropes or chains on the foal's head and limbs or direct grasping of the legs on the cannons above the fetlocks.)

When in doubt, use more lubrication and massage and stretch the vulva, allowing a little time for the mare's soft tissues to stretch as the foal's head and shoulders are passed. Pull when the mare strains (her pelvic diameter is at its widest then) and maintain tension when she rests so the foal does not slip back. Initially pull straight back and as the shoulders and ribs clear the vulva, direct the pulling force downward toward the mare's hocks. Pulling in this fashion works with the bend of the foal's body and the curve of the mare's birth canal. Once the foal's hips have cleared, traction on the foal can cease. Everyone can rest provided the foal does not require resuscitation, its head is free of the amnion, and it is breathing normally. To quote Dr. Robert Hillman, the most important points when assisting a foaling are, "Be clean, be gentle, and use lots of lube."

Retained Placenta

Retention of the placenta after foaling is a medical emergency in the mare. Retention of even a tiny piece of the chorioallantois, or even a patch of chorionic microvilli, is enough to cause delayed uterine involution and form a nidus for bacterial endometritis.

The exact mechanism by which the placenta detaches from the uterus is not fully understood. But it is thought that separation occurs when blood flow through the umbilical vessels ceases, which collapses the chorionic villi. Uterine contractions continue during stage III labor. These contractions effectively decrease uterine size and further unlock the chorionic villi from their interdigitation with the uterine crypts. In addition, the uterine contractions act to push the detaching placenta out of the uterine lumen in a propulsive fashion. The waves start at the tips of the horns and flow into the body, ending at the cervix. In this manner the chorioallantois is released beginning at the tip of the horns and is rolled inside out (or allantoic surface outward) as it is expelled. As the placenta passes through the cervix, the mare once again might be stimulated to push but seldom shows outward signs of concerted straining. As the placenta passes through the lips of the vulva, gravity also begins to work on the weight of the dangling portion, adding mild traction to the process. Once the placenta fully detaches, it usually slips to the ground in a sudden rush, seemingly unnoticed by the mare.

The placenta has not fully detached

Placentas are retained in approximately 2 percent to 10 percent of foaling mares. While not fully understood, possible causes of retained placentas include any swelling in the microvilli (uterine or placental) that locks them together, poor or absent uterine contractions perhaps caused by hormonal imbalances, and/or low blood calcium at the time of foaling. In many cases of retained placenta, the chorioallantois remains at or near the tip of the non-pregnant horn and either the whole placenta will hang partially from the mare with the rest remaining inside the mare's tract or the attached portion will be torn away as the placenta tears free. This tearing will leave an abnormal hole in the membranes that is discovered during examination of the placenta. Retention of chorionic villi could be a subtle finding during a placental examination.

Leaving behind a small piece is just as bad as having the whole placenta inside the mare. Potential complications include toxemia (a release of cellular and/or bacterial endotoxins into the mare's bloodstream), septicemia (bacterial infection spreading to the generalized circulation), laminitis, permanent damage to the uterine lining (endometrium), and even death. Prompt medical therapy can improve the chances for the mare's long-term reproductive health, soundness, and overall survival. Veterinary attention should be sought if there is any question that the placenta might have been retained. Treatment is aimed at causing the retained membranes to be expelled by improving uterine contractility (oxytocin), protecting the mare from bacterial infection (broad spectrum antibiotics) and endotoxemia (Banamine®), overall systemic support (IV fluids), and protecting and addressing the feet for any possible development of laminitis (frog support, IV DMSO, vasodilators that are not counter-productive to uterine tone).

The veterinarian might recommend cleansing the uterus with sterile saline before and after expulsion of the placenta. Manual removal of the placenta is not recommended because of the potential for causing hemorrhage and thrombosis, damaging the endometrium, and leaving chorionic villi behind. Use extreme care when handling the dangling portion of the placenta while tying it to avoid placing sudden, forceful traction on it. Never pull on the retained placenta. Great potential exists for doing permanent damage to the mare's uterus and compromising her future fertility. Most retained placentas respond to therapy within a few hours and are released, but some will remain attached for days before finally letting go.

Untreated, a mare's condition will deteriorate over 24 to 48 hours. She will become depressed and febrile, back off eating, and stop caring for her foal. As she becomes increasingly toxic, her gums will redden and darken and laminitis will set in. Early signs of laminitis include increased heat in the feet, a palpable bounding digital pulse, and lameness. Foundering horses usually will become lame first in their front feet and characteristically will rock their weight back onto their hind feet. When walking, they will land heel first with their front feet to avoid weight on their toes. They often will be reluctant to move or pick up their feet when asked and prefer to lie down rather than stand. Any mare demonstrating any of these signs after foaling requires immediate attention.

How rapidly these signs set in and how severe they become is determined in large part by the virulence of the organism residing in the uterus. While one mare may be only mildly affected by a placenta that was retained 24 hours, another mare may literally sink out of her hoof walls within 24 hours of foaling. Once it appears that the mare has retained her placenta, seek veterinary assistance immediately. Delaying treatment poses a risk because it is difficult to predict how the condition might affect the mare.

With good, supportive care and immediate therapy to control the infection, endotoxemia, and possible laminitis, most mares recover fully and are reproductively sound even if their placenta is retained over several days.

Perineal Lacerations

The tremendous force of uterine contractions and abdominal press during foaling poses great potential for damage to the soft tissues of the mare's reproductive tract. Nature has provided some protection to the mare's delicate structures in the form of thick tissue pads that cover the soles and sharp edges of the unborn foal's hooves ("angels' slippers"). Further, the slippery amnion and allantoic fluid lubricate the foal and the birth canal, respectively, and facilitate the foal's passage. Even so, failure of the mare's tract to stretch and dilate adequately, or malpositioning of the foal's head and/or limbs, could bruise and tear the mare's uterus, cervix, vagina, rectum, vulva, and perineum. Also any potential ridge of tissue (i.e., an incompletely opened Caslick's, tight vestibulo-vaginal junction, or partial hymen) creates an edge on which a foal's foot might catch and cause a tear as the mare pushes the foal through the soft tissue obstruction. Maiden foaling mares seem particularly prone to lacerations of the vagina, rectum, and perineum, as these tissues never have stretched before. Tight vestibulo-vaginal junctions also increase this risk.

Perineal lacerations are divided into three categories based on their severity. First-degree perineal lacerations involve only the skin and mucosa at the top edge of the vulvar opening (the dorsal commissure). These tears result from a failure of the tissues to stretch adequately to permit passage of the foal's poll and shoulders, and the dorsal commissure instead tears during the delivery.

Second-degree perineal lacerations are a tearing through the mucosa of the roof of the vestibule/caudal vagina into the perineal body and out through the dorsal commissure of the vulva, creating a tear that dissects up to but not into the anal ring. Second-degree perineal lacerations occur as the foal's feet become hooked on the vestibulo-vaginal junction and plow through the tissues as the mare pushes out the foal. This can occur even though the foal is in the normal "diver's position" for delivery, but it is even more likely to occur if the foal has hooked one or both of its feet up behind its ears and over its head.

Third-degree perineal lacerations occur in the same manner as second-degree lacerations, but instead of the foal's foot merely raking the roof of the

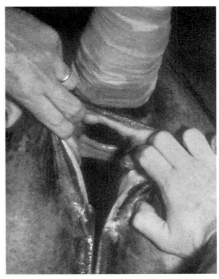

Third-degree laceration

vestibule, it is pushed up through the roof and into the mare's rectum. If the foal is able to retract its foot back into the birth canal before the mare's next effort to push it out, then a recto-vaginal fistula is formed by the hole created between the mare's rectum and vestibule/caudal vagina. If, however, the foal does not retract its limb from the rectum, the foot (and/or sometimes the head) then will exit through the anus. As the rest of the foal is passed, all of the tissue between the opening of the anus and the dorsal commissure of the vulva will be torn out.

Minor tears that might predispose the mare to pneumovagina can be sewn and the mare's vulva sutured right after she foals and before tissue swelling has had a chance to form. In the case of second- and third-degree perineal lacerations and recto-vaginal fistulas, tissue damage, bruising, and swelling usually are severe enough at the time of injury that repair has to wait. Bruised and swollen tissue will not hold suture well, and any attempt to repair the tissues will break down. Elective surgery to repair these injuries usually is performed four to eight weeks after foaling.

Bruising and tears to the mare's cervix likely occur when the foal passes through an incompletely dilated cervix, or a dilated cervix that must open even farther to allow passage of a large foal. Again, the tissues are asked to stretch beyond their limits and tear. This situation also can be caused by overzealous and hasty attendants who apply traction to deliver the foal rapidly before the cervix has had a chance to dilate completely.

The major concern over cervical tears concerns the damaged cervix's ability to form an adequate seal during subsequent diestrous periods. Destruction of the diestrous cervical barrier severely compromises the mare's fertility, as her cervical lumen and uterus are more vulnerable to contamination and resultant inflammation and ascending infections. Cervical tears usually are identified at the mare's postpartum check. The torn cervix is re-examined once the mare is in diestrus and assessed for the seal's competency. If the cervix can form a tight seal, no further repair is warranted. If the seal is judged inadequate, surgical repair can be attempted once all swelling and bruising of the tissues have resolved. Once torn, a cervix is likely to tear again at subsequent foalings because the scar tissue is not as resilient as normal tissue.

Uterine tears can occur because of a malpositioned foal, obstetrical manipulations, injury to the uterus during uterine lavage, as a result of a uterine torsion, or in the course of an otherwise apparently normal foaling. This is a life-threatening injury to the mare because of the potential complications of herniation of bowel through the torn uterus, resultant peritonitis, and/or hemorrhage. Mares that tear during stage II labor might abruptly stop pushing and become rapidly shocky (they are cold to the touch, sweaty, etc.). Conversely, mares may deliver their foal, then go on to show signs ranging from acute to gradually developing colic, no vulvar discharge to frank vulvar hemorrhage, severe depression, or possibly no outward signs for 12 to 24 hours.

Any mare not acting normally during the postpartum period should be examined by a veterinarian as soon as possible. Uterine body tears might be identified by direct palpation of the uterine wall via the vagina, but tears elsewhere in the uterus most likely will be unreachable in the immediately post-partum uterus. In that event, your veterinarian will be able to make a presumptive diagnosis based on the mare's clinical signs and examination of contaminated peritoneal fluid. This fluid is obtained by placing a needle or teat canula through the mare's ventral body wall and into her abdomen to collect the fluid (abdominocentesis). Immediate abdominal surgical repair of the uterine laceration (along with good supportive care, anti-inflammatories and antibiotics) is indicated to give the best chance of saving the mare's life and future fertility.

Complications in Older Mares

As broodmares age, the potential for complications associated with pregnancy and labor naturally increases. A common problem encountered in the aged broodmare is a sometimes fatal rupture and hemorrhage of one of the arteries supplying the uterus (frequently it is the right middle uterine artery). Rupture can occur anytime during late gestation — especially if the mare is excited or stressed — and into the early post-partum period, but it typically occurs at foaling. As the pregnancy progresses, stress increases on the walls of the uterine arteries as blood flow through the arteries increases.

During labor the internal blood pressure acutely increases, adding more strain on internal vessel walls. There is additional pressure on the outside of the vessel walls as the vessels (which course along on either side of the uterus within the broad ligaments) are stretched and compressed between the foal and the pelvis during the birthing process.

Possible reasons why these arteries rupture in some mares include: 1) Degenerative old age changes within the arteries themselves; 2) Low relative serum copper levels. (Adequate copper levels are necessary for normal vessel elasticity. Older mares in general and mares that rupture their uterine arteries in particular have been shown in one study to have lower copper levels overall when compared to young mares or age matched unaffected mares.); 3) Increased broad ligament and uterine artery tension due to left-sided uterine displacement caused by a full cecum.

Rupture of the uterine artery could result in rapid, extensive blood loss and death if hemorrhage occurs directly into the abdominal cavity. If bleeding is contained within the broad ligament and under the adjacent uterine serosa, a hematoma and subsequent clot could form, containing and stopping the hemorrhage. Mares that bleed directly into their abdomens demonstrate signs of rapidly developing shock: pale mucous membranes (gums), rapid heart rates, rapid respiratory rates, and cold sweat. They might exhibit signs of colic as well and die fairly quickly.

Mares whose bleeding is contained within the broad ligament experience pain and act colicky as tension and stretch is applied to the tissues by the dissecting and enlarging hematoma and resultant clot. Pain increases the heart and respiratory rates. Signs of colic caused by hematoma formation might be subtle, start off mildly, and be mistaken for foaling "after cramps." Any mare that becomes colicky during or after foaling needs close monitoring. If the colic fails to subside or increases in severity, the mare should be examined by a veterinarian as quickly as possible.

Little can be done to save mares that have rapid bleeding into their abdomens. In general, mares that die do so within the first 24 hours of foaling, but death can occur up to several weeks afterward if the clot is disturbed and bleeding recurs. Fatalities occur most typically in mares 18 years or older, whereas non-fatal clot formation is more typical in affected mares 11 to 15 years of age.

A veterinarian will make the diagnosis based on the mare's clinical signs, by direct rectal palpation of the hematoma in the broad ligament, and sometimes by abdominocentesis. For mares that have survived the initial bleeding, treatment is aimed at keeping them as calm as possible. The attending veterinarian might choose to administer sedative drugs. If the mare's blood count becomes severely low, the veterinarian might administer IV fluids, plasma, or blood transfusions. In general, though, transfusions do not seem to alter the final outcome in these cases and actually can be harmful if they excite or agitate the mare during their administration. Surgery usually is a last-ditch effort to save a valuable mare that is already at a veterinary hospital. If the mare survives, it is recommended that she not be bred back.

Mares that have bled before likely will do so again with subsequent

Older mares can have complications

pregnancies. The likelihood that they will die also increases. Management practices that might decrease the risk of uterine artery rupture in older broodmares include feeding less dry roughage (e.g., hay) in the days just before foaling in an effort to decrease the size of the cecum by decreasing gut fill. Avoiding stressful situations (floating teeth, vanning, strenuous exercise) in late gestation or just after foaling also can help. It might help to monitor copper levels in at risk older mares (especially those 15 years and older) and adjust dietary minerals accordingly with the help of an equine nutritionist and your veterinarian so that the diet meets an individual mare's needs and remains balanced. Checking for low blood copper levels, especially in the last month of gestation, also might help identify at-risk mares that warrant especially close monitoring at foaling time. Lining up a nurse mare might not be a bad idea in case the dam has a problem.

Gastrointestinal Problems

A gastrointestinal cause of abdominal pain needs to be ruled out in all horses demonstrating signs of colic (flank watching, kicking at belly, rolling, depression, decreased appetite, wringing/elevating the tailhead, etc.). Foaling mares are susceptible to a number of labor-related GI complications. These include cecal and large colon ruptures, large colon volvulus (twisted gut), small colon contusions and ruptures, herniated small bowel secondary to uterine or cranial vaginal tears, impactions, and rectal constipation.

The force generated during stage II labor is strong enough to contuse and/or rupture the mare's large or small bowel if it becomes caught between the mare's pelvis and uterus containing the foal while she strains. Contusions can cause mild colic that subsides as the intestine heals, or they can result in portions of badly devitalized bowel that cause peritonitis and increasing signs of depression, pain, and toxemia. Ruptured bowel causes severe peritonitis and septic shock within four to six hours. Surgery can save horses with devitalized bowel if the lesion is accessible, not too extensive, and operated on early enough.

Mares that have already ruptured their bowel have little hope of survival because horses cannot cope with the resultant peritonitis. The humane recourse is to euthanize these mares as soon as the presumptive diagnosis is confirmed via abdominal tap and evaluation of the peritoneal fluid or through exploratory surgery.

Although the reason(s) remains unclear, broodmares seem susceptible to developing large colon torsions during the first 100 days after foaling. A twisted colon compromises its blood supply, and the intestines distend with gas over time. These horses usually are in a lot of pain and want to lie down. They often will be quite bloated, increasing the chance of a rupture, and they rapidly succumb to shock.

Uterine tears already have been discussed. When an opening in the uterus exists, there is potential for small bowel to herniate through it. Herniated bowel might become severely constricted and devitalized. Herniated bowel also might become grossly contaminated with bacteria when exposed to the uterine or vaginal lumens or the outside air if it exits the vulva.

Impactions in post-foaling mares can result from abnormal peristalsis or ilius in a portion of bowel that may have been contused (small colon impactions secondary to contusions especially). Impactions also can be a result of consuming too much roughage and/or dehydration around the time of foaling.

Decreased manure production is an early and significant sign of a problem in these cases.

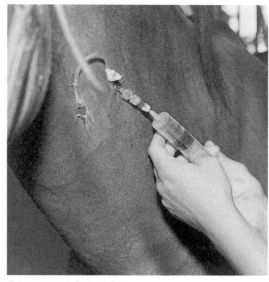

Treatment after colic

Most mares voluntarily decrease their own hay consumption in the days before foaling, but as previously discussed, it is a good management practice to feed less hay at this time. Laxative feeds such as grass and bran mashes also can help prevent post-foaling impactions. Mildly salting the feed to encourage water consumption also can help, and providing plenty of clean, fresh water at a palatable temperature is vital. Having a veterinarian administer mineral oil in an impaction-prone mare before she foals is another good way to anticipate and ward off a problem. (This requires a judgment call to weigh the risk of upsetting the mare by the tubing process during late pregnancy.)

Post-foaling mares can experience simple constipation, especially if there has been a lot of bruising and hematoma formation in the tissues of the vagina and perineum. It is painful for these mares to defecate, so they resist and become constipated. Again, laxative feeds and cold compresses (initially) and topical use of ointments such as Preparation H® might help these mares become comfortable enough to continue to pass feces. Judicious and restrained use of anti-inflammatory drugs such as Banamine® (flunixin meglumine) and oral laxatives (mineral oil) and/or fluids at the discretion of a veterinarian also might help decrease the pain and inflammation in the perineal tissues in moderately to severely bruised mares.

Post-Foaling Management of the Mare

D uring the first 12 to 48 hours post foaling, the mare should be watched closely. As previously discussed, mares that appear colicky or depressed should receive immediate veterinary attention. The normal post-foaling mare will be bright, alert, and responsive to people and her surroundings. She will take an active interest in her foal and will nurse it frequently. The mare will be attentive and protective, standing with her head over the foal as it sleeps. (Stabled mares often continue to eat hay as they stand over the foal and end up half burying their sleeping foal under dropped wisps!) She will place herself between her foal and any perceived threat from other animals, horses, or people. She will be comfortable, and her vital signs (heart rate, respiratory rate, pulse quality, and mucous membrane color) will be stable and normal.

The normal post-foaling mare will take an active interest in her foal

Unless the mare shows signs of a serious problem, physical examination of her reproductive tract is limited to visually examining her
perineum for tears or abnormal discharge so as not to disturb the
course of early involution or introduce infection to the recovering
reproductive tract. Mares with serious perineal conformation flaws
that necessitate a Caslick's procedure to keep them from "wind sucking" may be resutured by a veterinarian in the immediate hour after
delivery unless the surrounding tissues is very swollen. Mares that
have swelling and/or are not severely afflicted by pneumovagina if
left unsutured may be repaired as needed at the seven-day post-foaling examination or later once tissue bruising and swelling have sub-
sided and the tissues will hold suture.

A complete placental examination should be performed to ensure
that there are no abnormalities and that the passed placenta is complete. Many postpartum mares are tired from the strain of carrying
the foal through the last days of gestation and the effort of delivery.
Many will lie down beside their foal after the first few hours and
sleep. This is normal, but any mare that spends long periods down
should be examined for any indication that her feet are becoming
sore (laminitis/founder) or for other abnormalities that would cause
her to be recumbent.

Normal postpartum mares have good appetites, and they frequently will begin eating within the first hour after foaling. (The
demands of lactation are higher than that of even late pregnancy and
represent the highest energy and nutrient requirements of any point
in the mare's life cycle.) Laxative feeds, such as bran-based mashes,
should be fed for the first few days postpartum as well as good-quality hay in moderation and pasture when available. Many people
think it is a good idea to worm the mare with Ivermectin or Strongid
in the first 12 to 72 hours after foaling because it can help lessen the
severity of the nursing foal's heat diarrhea. This idea is controversial,
but if the mare has not been on a regular deworming program, she
should be dewormed as soon as possible after foaling under a veterinarian's direction, then placed on a regular deworming schedule.

Likewise, if the mare's vaccination history is unknown, she should receive tetanus prophylaxis (both tetanus antitoxin and tetanus toxoid) as soon as possible after foaling.

Lastly, the mare's udder should be examined (this can be done initially while sampling the colostrum) at least twice a day to make sure she has milk, there is no mastitis, and the foal is nursing. One of the first signs that a foal is ill is that it will "go off the bag" and stop nursing. Many sick foals will continue to comfort nurse for short bouts and might appear still to be eating, but when the mare's udder is examined it is full of milk and distended. A normal foal will keep the mare nursed out and the udder will be somewhat slack.

AT A GLANCE
◆ Normal post-foaling mares are alert and responsive.
◆ Mares can go into heat five to 12 days after foaling.
◆ Mares should receive a complete examination seven days after foaling.
◆ Foal-heat breeding can help mares foal in a timely manner year to year.
◆ Limit grain and keep newly weaned mares under supervision at pasture to help with the "drying off" of their milk supply.

The mare has an amazing capacity to recover rapidly from foaling. Barring any complications or metritis, the mare returns to a fertile estrous period within five to 12 days, on average, and the first ovulation typically occurs eight to 12 days after parturition. As always, some mares might ovulate sooner than eight days and others will go longer than 12, and, in general, mares ovulate sooner relative to foaling if they foal later in the spring (closer to the physiological breeding season) as compared to earlier foaling mares.

To conceive on this foal heat and go on to establish and maintain a new pregnancy, the mare's postpartum uterus must return rapidly to its pre-pregnancy size and condition. During this post-foaling period, the uterus actively contracts almost continually. This causes the uterus to shrink rapidly and helps it to clear the normal fluid, lochia, and bacterial contamination present after foaling. The normally involuting uterus will shrink back into the mare's pelvis within about 10 days of foaling, and it will return completely to its pre-pregnancy size by 30 days.

Likewise, the uterine lining needs to transition from a pregnant to a non-pregnant state to be ready to support a new embryo. If uterine involution is normal (and the mare has not experienced any complications), the endometrium usually will be completely regenerated by 14 days after foaling. When conditions are right, therefore, it is possible for a mare to foal, return to estrus, be rebred, and establish a new pregnancy within two weeks of her foal's birth.

The normal foaling event itself can generate quite a bit of bacterial uterine contamination. It is very easy for bacteria to gain access into the uterus given that the cervix is wide open in the immediate post-foaling period and the vagina, vestibule, and vulva have been greatly stretched open. Cultures taken from the uterus during the postpartum/foal-heat periods invariably will be positive for a mix of contaminating organisms. One of the functions of the foal heat is to help the mare clear this bacterial contamination so she does not become persistently infected and develop a postpartum endometritis. Anything that interferes with and delays normal uterine involution (retained placenta, decreased uterine fluid clearance, foaling injuries that lead to chronic contamination) puts the mare at risk for developing an infection and damaging her reproductive capabilities. Management of the mare in the immediate postpartum period, therefore, is aimed at preventing problems and rapidly identifying abnormalities in order to correct them.

It is important that the mare get adequate exercise in the form of turnout in a paddock (weather permitting) or a clean arena with her young foal during the first days after foaling. Hand walking is also a good alternative if the mare tends to be silly when she is initially turned out with her young foal and endangers it by running excessively. Walking helps the mare's abdominal and pelvic tissues regain muscle tone and helps the uterus clear fluid. Confined mares, such as those whose foals are ill, are at risk of pooling excessive amounts of uterine fluid, which creates an inviting environment for bacteria. The mare's attitude should be monitored to make sure she is bright, eating, and interested in and caring for her foal. Mares that appear dull and depressed and/or develop a fever need to be examined by a veterinarian.

The quantity and character of the mare's vulvar discharge also should be monitored closely. Frank blood or pus are immediate cause for concern and veterinary examination.

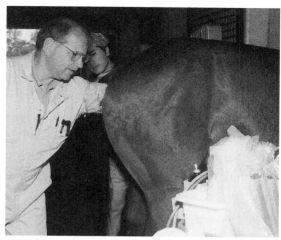

Examining the mare to determine her status

Normally a mare's discharge will appear serous and slightly bloody in the first few hours after foaling, then become more amber colored and mucoid. It should appear mucoid and clear within a week. At no point should the discharge become excessive, and it is a good idea to examine the underside of the mare's tail and the tail hairs for accumulated debris.

The mare's perineum should be cleaned once or twice daily with a mild soap and rinsed clean with water as needed. Cleansing decreases the likelihood of accumulated discharge causing skin irritation in the perineal region or the mare picking up a uterine infection because of the increased number of bacteria around her vulva. Cleaning also allows the observer to assess more accurately the amount the mare is discharging. Discharge that remains watery, copious, or blood- or pus-tinged warrants veterinary attention. Application of ointment such as Preparation H® to the outside skin of the perineum and vulva also might help reduce swelling in this region in mares that are excessively bruised and swollen.

Unless a problem exists, the mare's first thorough reproductive examination should be performed seven days after foaling. At this time, the cervix has had a chance to begin closing from its dilated state, making it harder for air to enter the uterus during a vaginal speculum examination. Also, the mare should be returning to her foal heat and estimations of when she might ovulate can begin to be made.

This examination includes: 1) An overall assessment of the mare's attitude and condition; 2) Visual and tactile examination of the mare's perineum to assess the amount of damage done at foaling and the degree of tissue healing up to that point; 3) A rectal palpation and ultrasound to assess the degree of uterine involution (tone and size of the uterus and quantity and quality of any inter-uterine fluid that might be present) and also to identify what structures might be on the ovary (i.e., Is there a dominant follicle present yet, and what size is it? Has she already had a post-foaling ovulation and now there is a CH or CL present on the ovary?); 4) A vaginal speculum examination to assess the vestibule, vagina, and cervix for bruising or tears, and to assess whether the mare is pooling any urine or exudate in her vagina. It is not uncommon for a mare to be pooling a small amount of urine in her vagina at this time, and in many cases the pooling will resolve once the pelvic tissues have tightened back up; and 5) A digital vaginal examination to feel for any tears in the vagina and especially the cervix. Many cervical tears can be detected only by feeling the external cervical os and the cervical lumen and internal os directly with a sterile, gloved hand.

Mares that are free of injury, involuting normally, have little to no accumulations of vaginal or uterine fluid, and have not ovulated at this point are potential candidates for foal-heat breeding. Most mares that are not foal-heat breeding candidates will be recovered and ready to be bred by their 30-day heat (the first ovulation, plus 21 days). Some of these mares might even be short cycled from their foal-heat ovulation with prostaglandin and bred sooner.

Breeding on the foal heat can be controversial. Conception rates from foal-heat breedings can be as much as 10 percent to 20 percent lower than those seen breeding later post-foaling cycles, and there is some question as to whether there is an increased incidence of early embryonic loss associated with these pregnancies. The lower success rates arise, of course, from attempting to breed mares that have delayed involution, post-foaling metritis, and/or unhealed foaling injuries. All these factors will decrease fertility. When foal-heat breeding candidates are chosen based on a strict set of criteria, the pregnancy rates can be comparable to those seen in mares bred at later cycles.

Lastly, a good candidate for foal-heat breeding should ovulate for the first

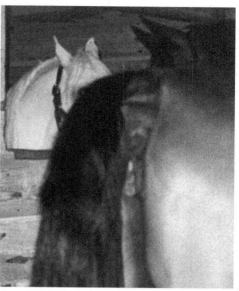

Breeding on the foal heat has advantages

time 10 or more days after foaling. As previously mentioned, it normally takes the uterine lining 14 days to regenerate and be ready to support and maintain a new embryo. The embryo does not reach the uterus until five to six days after ovulation (it is in the oviduct up until this time). Therefore, breeding only those mares that ovulate 10 or more days after foaling ensures that the endometrium will be ready to support a pregnancy by the time the new embryo reaches the uterus (i.e., at day 15-plus post foaling) and therefore decreases the likelihood of early embryonic loss.

The main advantage to achieving a pregnancy on a foal heat is to enable the mare to foal earlier the following season. In those breeds where a January, February, or March foal is preferred over a foal born later in the season, it is important to have the mare pregnant again by April. Successfully establishing a pregnancy on the foal heat means the mare will foal one month earlier the next season (i.e., if she foaled in May this year and becomes pregnant on the foal heat, she will foal sometime in April of the next year). When managed correctly, foal-heat breeding is a useful tool for helping mares to continue to foal in a timely manner from year to year and provides a means for "backing up" a late-foaling mare so she does not have to be left open for a year. It is important to remember, however, that only those mares meeting the criteria should be bred on foal heats. It will save time in the long run to wait to breed less-than-ideal candidates because the chance for success will increase when the mare is at her optimum condition.

FOAL CARE

by Christina S. Cable, DVM,
Diplomate ACVS

Understanding the Newborn Foal

F oals should be monitored closely during the first hours and days after foaling. The transition from apparently normal foal to critically ill foal can occur rapidly, and initially the signs can be subtle. A sick neonate should be identified as quickly as possible. Many of the conditions that can afflict the very young foal are life-threatening. They include septicemia, "joint ill," umbilical abscesses, pneumonia, neonatal isoerythrolysis (anemia and jaundice due to blood type incompatibility between foal and dam), meconium impaction, and ruptured bladder. Any of these conditions require immediate veterinarian intervention.

A number of management practices need to be performed to ensure that the foal gets off to a healthy start. Initially, the most important thing to ensure is that the foal's head is free of the amnion and that it is breathing. If the foal has not ruptured the white amnion during delivery, it needs to be torn open manually so the foal does not suffocate. (Attendants should remain calm and assist quietly and competently.) If the foal is not breathing, blunt stimulation with a fingertip or piece of straw applied to the inside of the nostril is often noxious enough to cause the foal to sneeze and take a breath. The nose should be stripped of fluids by stroking down the length of the nose on either side. Rubbing the foal vigorously along its ribs also can stimulate breathing. If needed, Dopram® (a respiratory stimulant provided at the veterinarian's discretion) can be given under the foal's tongue, and nose-to-mouth resuscitation can be initiated until the veterinarian arrives and administers more invasive resuscitation techniques. On large farms that foal many mares, a veterinarian can instruct attendants on how to provide oxygen to a newborn in critical condition.

Once it is clear that the foal is breathing and making the rapid adjustment to life outside the womb, the foal and mare should be left alone so they can rest and get acquainted. Bonding between the mare and foal begins once the foal is delivered and starts to move. It is important not to interrupt this process. Eager owners and friends who want to pet and cuddle the foal immediately after it is born risk the mare rejecting the foal because of the interruption in bonding. Loud noises or sudden movements that could startle the mare should be avoided, especially if the mare is a first-time mother.

After a short rest, the mare will nicker and nuzzle the foal. The mare will lick the foal and shortly afterward she will stand. As she stands, the umbilical cord will rupture at its natural break point, about one inch below the foal's abdomen. If the cord has not broken after about 30 minutes, it should be broken by hand. This is best left

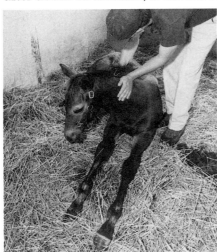

for your veterinarian, but if your veterinarian is not available, then someone else will have to break the cord. The cord should be grasped above and below the breaking point, then twisted and pulled. It is important not to pull too hard. The cord could be torn internally, leading to internal bleeding or the passing of urine (also called patent urachus). The cord should not be cut because cutting could result in bleeding

Call the vet if the foal does not seem normal

from the stump. After the cord is broken, it should be dipped in a diluted solution of Betadine® or chlorhexidine. For more detailed information on umbilical cords, please see the section on umbilical stump care on page 235.

AT A GLANCE

◆ It's important not to interfere in the bonding process between mare and foal.

◆ The foal should stand within one hour of birth and nurse within two hours.

◆ Call your veterinarian if the foal does not appear normal.

◆ Keep a supply of colostrum.

Standing and Nursing

The foal should show a suckle reflex (sticking out its tongue and making sucking noises) within 20 to 30 minutes of birth. Most foals can lift their heads and necks within the first few minutes. The foal will make several attempts to stand, usually taking several spills in the process. With each try, though, the foal should seem stronger. After the foal makes a few solo attempts to stand, offering a gentle helping hand to steady it is always acceptable. The foal should be able to stand unassisted within one hour of birth.

Although at first the foal will suckle everything but the mare's nipple, it should be nursing within two hours after birth. The foal should then continually nurse and lie down to rest. This pattern is perfectly normal. It is abnormal for a foal to lie down and stay down for several hours. Call a veterinarian if this occurs. The veterinarian will check for musculoskeletal problems, such as contracted tendons, that might prevent the foal from standing.

Foals suffering from neonatal maladjustment syndrome, called "dummy foals," might not be able to stand, or they might stand but wander the stall with little interest in the mare. These foals will not have a suckle reflex. You can check the suckle reflex by placing your clean fingers in the foal's mouth, which should stimulate sucking action. If there is no reflex, have your veterinarian examine the foal.

Colostrum or "First Milk"

A foal must receive colostrum, or "first milk," within six to eight hours of birth because the foal's gastrointestinal tract can only absorb the immunoglobulins (antibodies) present within the colostrum during a short window of time — usually within 12 hours of birth. Remember, the foal cannot obtain antibodies from its dam before birth due to the impermeable placenta. In many species the permeable placenta allows for a transfer of disease-fighting antibodies from the mother to her fetus. The foal is born with virtually no ability to fight infection other than the antibodies it absorbs from the colostrum. Without adequate colostrum, a foal could succumb rapidly to overwhelming infection. Although there might be some nutritional concern when a foal has not ingested colostrum, the temptation to feed it milk, or anything else, during the first few hours should be resisted. Such feeding will hasten the closure of the intestinal cells, preventing adequate antibody transfer. If the foal needs nutritional support, it should be administered intravenously until after 36 hours of age. This support should be directed at keeping blood glucose levels normal until milk is ingested. The postpartum mare will produce colostrum for 24 to 36 hours; then the milk will return to a more normal consistency and appearance.

Every farm should have a banked supply of colostrum. The colostrum can be saved from mares that drip colostrum early (prematurely lactate), then administered to their foals after birth, either by bottle or naso-gastric tube. Colostrum also can be saved from a mare with a healthy foal. The milk can be frozen and kept for nearly two years. Frozen colostrum can be used when the mare does not produce any colostrum of her own (agalactia) due to illness or fescue toxicity.

If you have a source of frozen colostrum, thaw it in a warm water bath. Microwaving the colostrum on a normal or high setting will destroy the beneficial immunoglobulins within the milk. Thawing it in a warm water bath takes more time (up to an hour) but is safe and effective.

Routine Care of the Neonatal Foal

R outine care of the foal in its first two weeks of life, the early neonatal period, should begin with a thorough veterinary examination within 24 hours of birth. After that, it is good management to monitor the foal's basic parameters daily. This means taking its heart and respiratory rate and its rectal temperature and observing its activity level and behavior. Obviously, if the foal appears weak or sick, call your veterinarian immediately.

Care of the Umbilical Stump

The care of the foal's umbilical stump is a key aspect of neonatal management. A foal's umbilical stump can be likened to a freeway — the potential for rapid transit of bacteria into the foal's bloodstream. This potential for bacteria to use the umbilicus as a portal into the foal is the reason keeping the mare and foal in a clean stall is so important.

The foal's umbilical stump should be dipped in a dilute solution of povidone iodine (0.1 percent to 1 percent) or chlorhexidine (0.5 percent) two to three times a day for two to three days. It has been traditional to treat the umbilical stump with tincture of iodine, an alcohol-based solution. In the right strength, tincture of iodine is very effective because it dries the stump while disinfecting it. Three to 4

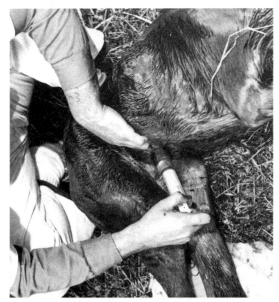

Care of the umbilical cord is extremely important

percent solutions will accomplish the objectives while stronger tincture (7 percent) and the strongest water-based solution (Lugol's solution) could cause excessive inflammation and, in some cases, predispose the tissues to infection.

You can use many different kinds of containers to dip the umbilical cord in, including a cleaned baby food jar or a large, plastic syringe case. Just pour the antiseptic into the container, place it over the umbilical stump, covering it completely, and hold it there for a few seconds.

During the first few weeks of the foal's life, the umbilical cord should be monitored at least once a day for any abnormal swelling, moistness, purulent discharge, or the passage of urine (patent urachus). If you notice any of these problems, have your veterinarian examine the foal immediately. These abnormalities could indicate a serious infection.

Meconium

The meconium is the first manure produced by a foal. Unlike the looser "milk feces" that it will pass later, the meconium is sticky, hard, and pelleted. The meconium is made up of amniotic fluid and other material that the foal has swallowed while in the uterus. Most foals will strain to some extent to pass their meconium. Colts more than fillies tend to have a problem passing meconium. This phenomenon is thought to be related to the smaller diameter of the colt's narrow pelvis compared to a filly's. Usually a foal will begin to pass the meconium within a few hours of birth, to be replaced by the softer, yellow milk feces by 24 hours of age. Some foals will not strain at all and pass their meconium with no problems; others will strain and strain and may show signs of colic.

AT A GLANCE

♦ A foal should have a thorough veterinary exam within 24 hours of birth.

♦ A foal should pass meconium within a few hours of birth.

♦ Administer an enema if the foal does not produce any meconium within a few hours of birth or is straining to defecate.

♦ A foal's umbilical cord should be cleaned and monitored.

Signs of Meconium Impaction

A foal assumes a distinctive posture when it strains to defecate. It arches its back and holds its tail up in the air. A foal also might wag its tail back and forth if it is having trouble passing the meconium.

Standard operating procedure on many breeding farms calls for giving every neonatal foal a warm, soapy water enema or a commercial enema, like a child-size Fleet's enema, to help ease the passage of meconium. Use a dose syringe to administer the enema through a soft rubber tube. This allows for a gravity flow enema and a larger volume of fluid. If you do not have a commercial enema available, make one by mixing several drops of liquid Ivory hand soap in a quart of warm water, combined with one cup of mineral oil. (If you do not have mineral oil, substitute one cup of general lubricant.) The mineral oil will coat the meconium balls so they will pass more easily.

Administration of an Enema

Giving an enema to a newborn foal should be performed with care. The foal must be properly restrained to lessen the risk of perforating its delicate rectum. Furthermore, the fluid's temperature must be checked very carefully to avoid scalding the rectum. The temperature should be warm but not uncomfortable on your hand.

When your supplies are ready, the foal should be restrained in a standing position. Put lots of lubricant, such as K-Y jelly, on the nozzle of the enema (or the end of the rubber tubing). Insert the enema nozzle (or tubing) gently. Then squeeze the enema bottle (or begin pouring the soapy water through the tubing).

After you administer the enema, step out of the stall and leave the foal to pass the meconium. Keep watching the foal closely. If it does not produce any meconium or produces meconium but then resumes straining after 30 minutes or so, it is likely that more meconium remains to be passed.

If administering a second enema does not produce more meconium or alleviate the signs of distress, call your veterinarian. Some foals develop large meconium impactions and need further treatment, such as mineral oil administered through a naso-gastric tube or intravenous fluids.

Meconium impaction is not necessarily life-threatening. But it does require prompt treatment because the meconium can act like a cork in the foal's rectum so that gas and fluids accumulate in the intestines, leading to severe bloat. The bloating can be extremely uncomfortable for the foal. A distressed foal will not nurse properly, and the bloating may also compromise the foal's ability to breathe normally.

Unfortunately, after the foal reaches the severely bloated stage, medical treatment with intravenous fluids and mineral oil will not work fast enough to clear the blockage. Sometimes the young foal will require surgery. Don't wait until it is too late. If your foal has not passed meconium within the first 24 hours, call the veterinarian immediately.

Healthy Foal Check

The healthy foal check is a routine examination of a newborn foal before it is 24 hours old. Many veterinarians prefer to examine foals at around 12 hours old. This exam is performed, even in an otherwise healthy appearing foal, for a variety of reasons but most importantly to determine if the foal has acquired enough immunoglobulin (IgG).

During the healthy foal check, your veterinarian will perform a complete physical examination on the foal. This will include taking its temperature, listening to (ausculting) its heart and lungs with a stethoscope to determine if there are any abnormalities that might signal a congenital heart defect or disorders of the lungs, The veterinarian should also examine its chest for fractured ribs, which can happen during the delivery. In addition, the veterinarian will look for other congenital problems such as a cleft palate, wry nose (crooked nose), or entropion (rolling in of the eyelids).

The foal's musculoskeletal system will be evaluated for angular or flexural deformities (both will be discussed in a later chapter). The veterinarian will take a medical history by talking to the caregiver who has watched over the foal's first few hours of life. The vet will want to make sure the foal has passed its meconium and is defecating and nursing normally. By evaluating the IgG level, the vet can make sure that the foal has absorbed an adequate amount of immunoglobulins, which can be performed on the farm using portable test kits. Depending on your geographic area, the foal may require an injection of vitamin E and selenium to help prevent white muscle disease.

Vaccination of the foal is usually recom-

Examining the healthy foal

mended at this time. Hopefully, no abnormalities will be found, and your foal will receive a clean bill of health.

Later chapters will describe problems your veterinarian might find on the first day or in the first few weeks of the foal's life.

The First Week

The first week of life is one of the most exciting for an owner and for the foal, or so it seems. During the first week the foal will continue to explore its new environment as it gains strength. The owner or handler can lay the groundwork for training by getting the foal accustomed to being handled, wearing a halter, and following the mare. Handling the foal in the early stages of its life could prevent the anxieties and potential injuries that might occur when handling is attempted later. Monitoring the foal for any signs of disease should occur throughout the first week as neonates remain at risk for infection. Monitor the foal's basic parameters (temperature, heart rate, and respiratory rate) once a day if possible during the first week. This will allow you to become familiar with your foal's vital signs and get the foal used to being handled. It also can alert you to early signs of illness. If your foal is sick, your veterinarian can begin treatment early. The rest of this chapter will cover basic management concerns of the newborn foal.

Turn-out

Mares and foals enjoy being turned out, and it is an excellent source of exercise for both of them. However, it is wise to leave the mare and foal confined to a box stall for 24 hours until the foal is strong enough to follow the mare at a trot or gallop. This can take

Mares and foals benefit from turn-out

two or three days if the foal has been ill or has musculoskeletal problems which preclude exercise. Once the foal is strong enough, it and the mare should be turned out alone, at least for the first few days. Keeping the pair separated from other horses can prevent injury in the event of an overly protective mare or overly curious foal.

The paddock should be free of objects that could hurt the foal, such as farm equipment, hardware, or other debris. The other factor in turn-out is the weather. Young foals should not be turned out if it is cold and wet. The neonate cannot keep its body warm for long periods in adverse weather, and frostbite is a real concern. If it is rainy and cold, keep your foals inside. However, foals do well on sunny days in the snow. Snow offers a better footing than mud, so turn-out is fine for an hour or so. If you live in a warmer part of the world, turn-out in a dry paddock is always good. Many people in colder climates turn out their mares and foals individually in small indoor rings or covered round pens. With the soft footing, they make an excellent alternative to outdoor paddocks.

Foals in the first week of life need to be monitored while outside to make sure they do not become tired and lie down in the mud or snow. One hour of turn-out per day often suffices for foals of this age.

Haltering and Handling

The best time to begin handling a foal is when it is small. Gentle handling during this stage can save hours of frustration later. The newborn can begin wearing a halter within the first few days of life.

Just make sure the halter fits properly. A foal wearing a loose halter runs the risk of getting its foot caught in it. With a properly fitting halter, you should be able to place two fingers underneath the jaw comfortably. Remember, the halter will need to be adjusted or replaced with a larger halter on a weekly basis as the foal grows or rub sores can occur. Leather halters are preferable to nylon halters if the halter is to be left on all the time. If the foal becomes caught, leather halters will break much more easily than nylon halters. Foals can injure themselves quite severely if left to struggle in a caught halter.

> **AT A GLANCE**
>
> ◆ One hour of turn-out per day is sufficient for young foals.
>
> ◆ Early handling makes working with foals easier in the long run.
>
> ◆ Use milk supplements if the mare does not produce enough milk.
>
> ◆ Foal heat diarrhea usually occurs within the first six to 10 days.

Handling can begin with gently restraining the foal by placing your arms around it. One arm should go across the foal's chest and the other should gently lift the tail in the air. Do not pull on the tail — just lift upward from the base. This usually will immobilize a newborn foal so that a physical examination can be performed, blood drawn, or bandages applied. Older foals also might need to be placed against a wall to be restrained in this manner.

While restraining foals younger than two weeks, never pull against the halter or attempt to restrain a foal by the halter. Furthermore, never attach a lead shank and attempt to restrain a foal of this age by the lead. This could result in disaster. Healthy foals often will pull or rear against this type of restraint, sometimes flipping over backward. Flipping can

Start handling foals early

have disastrous consequences — from blindness to broken cervical vertebrae (necks) to any other number of broken bones in the legs or skull.

When the foal becomes accustomed to following its mother to and from the turn-out area (this should only take one or two days), it is a good idea to begin using a butt rope. A butt rope is some type of soft cotton lead that goes around the foal's butt and is held at the withers. Pressure on the rope will encourage the foal to move forward. Moving the mare away from the foal usually will prompt the foal to move forward as well, so this in combination with the butt rope should help the foal learn quickly. The cotton lead can be attached to the halter and still used as a butt rope, offering an early lesson in leading. The handler should always remain patient during this process.

Feeding

Feeding a foal during the first week only becomes a concern if the foal is an orphan or if the mare is not producing enough milk. If you have an orphan foal, please read the chapter about orphans. If the mother is producing enough milk, then the foal can acquire all its nutrition from mother's milk during this time. Foals usually become curious and within the first few weeks of life begin to eat hay and share their mother's grain, but milk delivers all their nutritional needs. How do you know if your mare is producing enough milk? Excellent question. I think the best way to tell whether a foal is receiving enough milk is to watch the foal and check the mother's udder for milk production. Let me explain. First, a neonate will nurse up to seven times an hour. Foals need frequent small meals. As they approach their mother's udder to nurse, they often "butt the bag" or knock the udder with their heads to stimulate milk let down in the mare.

After the foal nurses, it will lie down and nap. Then the foal will wake up and nurse and play a bit before sleeping again. If a foal is not receiving adequate milk, it will constantly butt its mother's udder. The foal might nurse but will not lie down and sleep and will act restless.

The other parameter to monitor is the mother's udder. A mare producing adequate milk often will stream milk after the foal butts the udder. You actually can milk the mare to gauge how much milk she is producing. If you can milk only a few ounces from the mare, she might not be producing enough for the foal. However, if you can milk several pints in one milking, she has plenty of milk. Ultimately, the foal's condition will tell you if the foal is receiving enough milk, but you don't want to wait until you notice that your foal is quite skinny to begin supplementing.

Supplementing milk is necessary if the mare is not producing enough milk, either due to illness or fescue toxicity. Supplementing the foal can be done by using the pail feeding method with any of a number of good quality equine milk replacers.

Training the foal to drink is usually quite simple, especially if the foal is hungry. Place milk on your fingers and have the foal suck on your fingers; then guide the foal to the milk pail and place your fingers in the milk while the foal is sucking on them. Foals can receive milk replacer two to four times per day, depending on how much supplementation is necessary. Your veterinarian can help make that determination. The beauty of this type of feeding program is that it is simple and requires very little of your time.

This was best exemplified on a visit to a farm in northern Georgia where a mare had produced very little milk following her foal's birth because of fescue grass ingestion. The foal was three weeks old at the time of our follow-up visit. The mare and foal were in a large paddock when we arrived at the farm. The owners wanted us to see how they were feeding the foal. After one owner had mixed up the milk replacer and walked out to the gate, the foal came running toward them, stopped, drank the replacer, and ran back to join his mother. The foal was growing normally and was very healthy, but it had required multiple plasma transfusions and antibiotics shortly after birth due to the lack of colostrum production.

Most foals not getting enough to eat will require milk supplementation until they are six to eight weeks old, at which time they can be weaned onto solid feeds. If you have a question about your mare's milk production, have your veterinarian examine your mare and foal as soon as possible.

Foal Heat Diarrhea

Foal heat diarrhea usually occurs at six to 10 days of age, and corresponds to the same time as when the mare is experiencing her first heat cycle after delivery. The foal will have loose feces (diarrhea or scours), but will remain bright, nurse well, and show no ill effects from the diarrhea. The diarrhea usually resolves in a few days. Veterinarians think the cause of this diarrhea is a change in the flora (normal bacteria) within the gastrointestinal tract and not related to the heat cycle of the mare as orphan foals also experience "foal heat diarrhea." Foals of this age also are susceptible to other causes of diarrhea, so the foal must be monitored carefully. Diarrhea from other causes often will result in a fever, and the foal will become depressed, lose interest in nursing, and/or become dehydrated. If any of these signs are present, have your veterinarian examine the foal immediately as these are not typical of foal heat diarrhea. The diarrhea can result in feces scalding the foal's hindquarters, so cleaning the backside once or twice a day with a gentle soap, then applying petroleum jelly, Desitin, or Vitamin A and D cream will help prevent hair loss and irritation.

The First Month and Beyond

The early months in a foal's life are critical. Once a foal has made it through the delicate newborn period, it's time for you to consider other aspects of foal management. For example, when a foal reaches four weeks of age, you should decide whether to start the youngster on its own solid feed and how to handle any problems, such as persistent angular limb deformities or persistent hernias (scrotal/inguinal or umbilical).

Feeding

Many foals, even while nursing, will sample their mother's hay and grain within the first few weeks. Once foals have reached the end of the first month, you may give them their own solid food. Though this change to solid food can begin at the end of the first month, some owners or caretakers prefer to wait until the foal is three months old. Talk to your veterinarian. Feeding grain might be necessary for a foal whose mother does not produce enough milk to sustain it at this age. If the mother's milk is very rich and profuse, then the foal might benefit from waiting until it is older to receive grain as too much protein can induce acquired flexural deformities, physitis, or other developmental orthopedic diseases. Remember, the general guidelines for feeding: one pound of grain daily per month of age until six months.

After your foal has been eating grain for a couple of weeks, have your veterinarian determine whether the foal is receiving an adequate amount. Clean, mold-free hay is always good for mares and foals, and if you feed alfalfa, much less grain will be required. As for the broodmares, if you live in a selenium-deficient area, then a daily supplement of vitamin E/selenium might be necessary.

The feed can be placed within a "creep feeder" or feed tub that has bars across it to prevent the mare from being able to gain access to the foal's feed. Otherwise, the mare often will eat the foal's grain in addition to her own.

Angular Limb Deformities

All foals should be evaluated at four weeks of age by an experienced veterinarian to determine if corrective measures need to be taken. Foals with angular limb deformities might need only hoof trimming or corrective shoeing to resolve the problem. Others might need surgery.

One type of surgery is periosteal stripping, which involves making

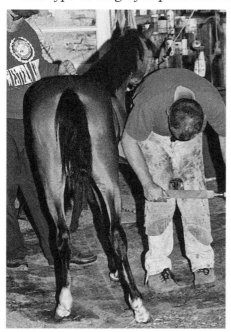

Good hoof care is crucial

an incision on one side of the periosteum of the affected long bone. One of the theories about how this procedure works is that the release of the periosteum stimulates bony growth. This surgery is minor, quick, and comes with very little risk. A more invasive procedure for severe angular deformities or for foals with little growth potential left is transphyseal bridging. This procedure involves implanting orthopedic staples, lag screws, or screws and wires to close one side of the growth plate (the area of the long bone from which the bone grows), enabling the other side of the leg to "catch up" and straighten.

Transphyseal bridging increases the risk of infection and can leave cosmetic blemishes. This type of procedure also requires two surgeries: one to place the implants and one to remove them. The foal also must be monitored diligently for when the affected leg is straight; then the implants must be removed or overcorrection can occur.

Hoof Care

Another aspect of foal management that too often goes ignored is good hoof care. Some people overlook hoof care because foals are usually not forced to exercise (riding, lunging, etc.). Foals that spend a lot of time outdoors will keep their hooves worn down to a certain extent. But all foals need to have their hooves trimmed regularly. Foals with abnormally shaped hooves or those with rotational or angular limb deformities require trimming every three to four weeks to correct their problems.

If you are unsure, ask your veterinarian and farrier. Furthermore, teaching the foal to stand for a hoof trim will only make future farrier work less stressful.

Normal Behavior

Throughout the first month the foal will continue to remain very close to its mother. During the first week, foals will nurse as often as seven times per hour. By the end of the month, the nursing frequency will decrease significantly to three to four times per hour as the foal begins to consume feed from other sources.

Foals also might eat their mother's feces. Known as coprophagy, this behavior is quite normal and cannot be prevented. Many veterinarians think that foals acquire nutrients and/or bacteria necessary for their gastrointestinal tract by eating their mother's fresh feces.

Second Month and Beyond

The next step in raising a healthy foal is preventing diseases through a regularly scheduled vaccination program. Other management concerns at this time are deworming and hoof care, often overlooked in youngsters.

Vaccinations

Vaccinating the foal is an important part of its health management. The maternal antibodies acquired from the colostrum will protect the foal for the first eight to 12 weeks of life, then begin to fade. At this time, it is important to begin stimulating the foal's immune system with vaccines. However, some veterinarians have noticed recently that vaccinating foals early is not beneficial and can give a very false sense of security. The problems arise when foals receive vaccinations while they still have maternal antibodies present. The maternal antibodies will interfere with the vaccination and prevent a proper

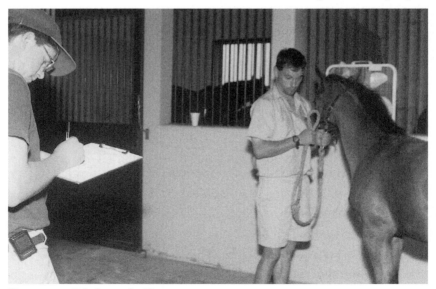

Keep a record of vaccinations

immune response. Therefore, new recommendations for foal vaccination strategies are being initiated to ensure a proper response. Vaccinations recommended to be administered to foals include tetanus, influenza virus, Eastern and Western encephalitis, rhinopneumonitis (EHV-I and EHV-4), West Nile virus, and in some areas rabies and Potomac horse fever. The American Association of Equine Practitioners recommends that foals not receive vaccinations until they are three to four months of age, then get monthly boosters for two months. The exception to this is influenza. Foals should wait to be vaccinated against this disease until they are six months old.

The vaccination schedule for your horse(s) should always be discussed with your veterinarian as every farm will have a different situation. Furthermore, the vaccination status of the mare will also dictate when the foal will require vaccination. Hopefully, these vaccination schedules will minimize infectious disease outbreak on your farm. Remember, however, that vaccines alone cannot prevent disease. Isolating new and infected horses and sanitizing areas exposed to infectious organisms are important as well.

Deworming

Deworming programs are just as important for foals as for adult horses. Start a deworming program when the foal is four weeks old and continue deworming every four to six weeks. All of the commercially available dewormers (paste dewormers) are quite effective, but the rotation of major classes of

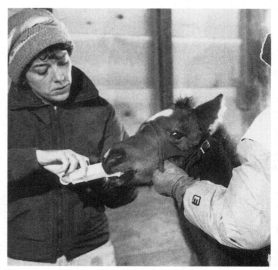

Place foals on a deworming program

dewormers (not just brand names) every other month is still advis-able. One exception is that foals should not be dewormed using the drug moxidectin (ex. Quest). The label on the box states that this dewormer is not safe for use in foals less than six months old. Please always read drug labels carefully. The printed information is useful, not just decorative.

Furthermore, as with adult horses, young horses should be dewormed against tapeworms once a year (usually after weaning). These worms have been associated with intussusceptions (when one section of bowel telescopes into another section). Veterinarians think that the tapeworms might alter normal motility of the bowel, pre-disposing intussusceptions. Always consult your veterinarian on what deworming program is appropriate for your situation.

Foal Rejection

M ares that reject their foals usually do so right after giving birth. As the foal moves toward the mare looking for milk, the mare runs away. Most of the time the mare is afraid of the foal and does not try to harm it, but sometimes the mare will attack. Some mares will reject their foals after a prolonged separation.

In one particular instance a mare was sent in for colic surgery. The farm manager kept the six-week-old foal at the farm to prevent the pain-stricken, thrashing mare from injuring her baby during transport. The owners were not pleased that the mare and foal had been separated, so the farm manager brought the foal to the hospital three days after the mare's surgery. When the foal was put in the stall with the mare, she tried to remove a large section of the foal's neck as the foal attempted to nurse. Fortunately, the mare had a lead shank attached to her halter and her head was pulled away just as her teeth snapped!

This chapter will focus primarily on the major causes and remedies for foal rejection following delivery and the different manifestations and degrees of foal rejection, such as the one mentioned above.

To understand why foal rejection occurs and how to prevent it, you first must understand normal post-foaling maternal behavior.

A mare begins to form the bond with her foal during the early stages of labor. At the end of stage I labor, the mare's water breaks and the allantoic fluid surrounding the foal is expelled. The mare usually spends a fair amount of time sniffing and smelling the fluid. After the mare gives birth, she again will smell the fluid along with the placenta. Initially, she might show more interest in the fluids and placenta than in her foal. The mare also might show flehmen (curling her upper lip) after she smells the fluid. This is considered normal behavior. Some people believe this is how the mare recognizes the foal as hers. The mare will identify the foal with both the allantoic and amniotic fluid because the foal will smell like the fluids.

After she has investigated the placenta and fluid fully, she will turn her attention to the foal. First, she will smell the foal, then start to lick it, beginning at the head and moving to the hindquarters. The mare will continue to lick the foal on and off during the first few hours of its life. Other species of animals, including cats, dogs, and cattle, lick their offspring for several days or weeks after birth. This initial touching and smelling experience is crucial for establishing a strong bond between the mare and her foal.

Because the first hour of a foal's life is the most important one in

A mare will smell then lick her foal

establishing this bond, human contact with the pair should be kept minimal unless the mare or foal needs veterinary care. As the mother licks the foal, the youngster tries to stand. This scenario should occur within one hour of delivery. Foals should begin to nurse from the mare within two to three hours. The mare's first milk, or colostrum, is of the utmost importance because it contains the immunoglobulins (antibodies) that will help prevent infection in the young foal.

Remember, foals are born with little to no antibodies. If the foal does not ingest the colostrum within three hours of birth, for whatever reason, including the mare's unwillingness to permit nursing, it's an emergency.

AT A GLANCE

◆ Foal rejection rarely occurs but requires immediate human intervention.

◆ Some mares show aggression toward their foals but not necessarily rejection behavior.

◆ Fear motivates some mares to reject their foals.

◆ Sedation, stocks, or hobbles sometimes can help a mare learn to accept her foal.

Normal Mare Nursing Behavior

Chapter 21 describes a foal's normal nursing behavior of the foal. What is normal behavior for the mare? As the foal nurses, the mare can show a range of normal, even normal aggressive behavior. Mares might pin their ears, squeal, swish their tails, push the foal away, make smacking noises, and bite or kick at their foals during nursing. These behaviors do not necessarily indicate rejection but may be a response to pain as the foal bumps against her udder or bites a teat. Although normal, this type of aggressive behavior occurs more frequently when the foal reaches several months of age rather than when the foal is newly born.

Another normal post-foaling behavior that many people erroneously consider abnormal is aggression of the mare toward humans and/or other horses. This behavior is totally unpredictable until the foal's birth. Even the nicest mare can show dangerous aggression toward humans after the birth of her foal. This behavior is thought to occur instinctively in mares because very young foals instinctively follow any large moving body. So if the mare does not bond properly with the foal, the foal might begin to follow humans or other horses. In the wild, a foal that follows another horse most likely will starve or be attacked by a stallion. Remember to approach new mothers with caution and common sense. Aggression toward humans or other horses usually will subside in a few days to one week after birth.

Foal Recognition

How does a mare recognize her own foal? It is not by vision or smell alone, but through a combination of vision (appearance), smell, and sound. If any one of these senses is obstructed (naturally or artificially), the mare will take longer to identify her foal from other foals. People sometimes use smell to fool a mare and help an orphan foal. For example, if a mare loses her foal and is given an orphan to nurse, the dead foal's placenta can be draped over the orphan foal so the mare will recognize the scent. Placing a product such as Vicks VapoRub ointment in the mare's nostrils and on the orphan foal also will disguise its scent. This can help in the acceptance process.

Maternal Behavior

Maternal behavior is a complex, instinctive process in most animals. Researchers believe that hormonal influences, genetics, and some learned behaviors can trigger the onset of maternal behavior. Other factors that contribute to maternal behavior include the sight, sounds, and smells of the foal itself. All of these factors come together to induce normal, motherly behavior.

Foal Rejection

Foal rejection can be divided into three categories: avoidance of the foal, rejection of nursing, and aggression toward the foal. The first type of abnormal behavior is foal avoidance. This usually involves first-time mothers, otherwise known as primiparous mares. It seems to be a fear-based reaction. The mare will run away from the approaching foal. She usually will not hurt the foal intentionally. However, if they are confined in a small area, such as a small box stall, the mare might accidentally run over the foal or step on it.

A mare that refuses to allow her foal to nurse is an example of the

Stallions benefit from exercise, both for mental well being and in the production of sperm (above). Sturdy fencing is a must for stallion turn-out (below).

A mechanical walker is one option for ensuring adequate exercise (above). Daily grooming should be a routine part of stallion care (below).

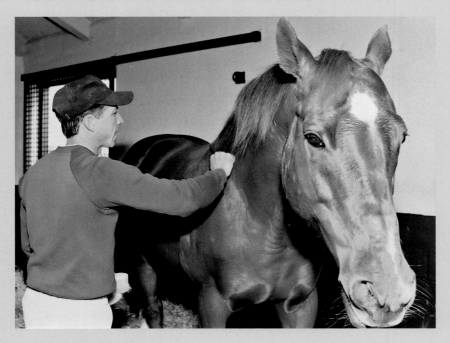

Stallions always should be led with a shank (above) at least 12 feet long and by a handler who is not fearful. A stallion demonstrating the flehmen response (below).

Preparing a mare for breeding includes wrapping her tail (above).
Hobbles (below) prevent a mare from kicking the stallion as he mounts.

A controlled breeding in which the stallion is presented to the mare, then allowed to mount. The mare wears a protective covering and is twitched. An outdoor breeding requires fewer handlers (below).

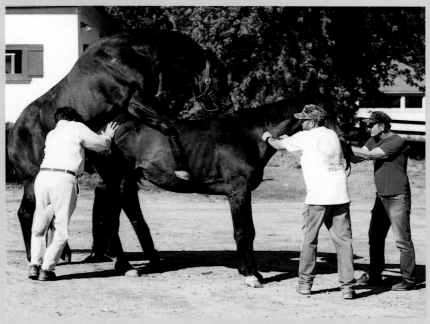

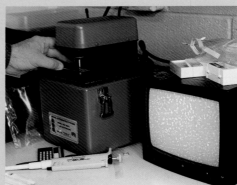

Putting a semen specimen on a slide (above); checking motility and morphology on a video microscope (right); and putting a specimen in the sperm counter (below).

Adjusting the phantom mount to fit the stallion (above); a stallion mounts the phantom and his semen is collected (below).

A pipette (above) is used to inseminate a mare with transported semen. The inseminator inserts the pipette with a gloved arm and hand (below).

most common maternal behavior problem, according to Katherine A. Houpt, VMD, PhD, a behavior specialist at Cornell University. This problem typically occurs with first-time mothers. Udder problems such as mastitis (inflammation or infection of the udder), which causes swelling and pain in the udder, can lead to this type of behavior. Sometimes, the mare will allow a human to milk her but will not allow her foal to nurse. Showing no sign of pain as she is being milked indicates it is just the foal's nursing to which she objects.

The third type of abnormal behavior is aggression by the mare toward the foal, which is the least common but the most serious. This kind of abnormal behavior is characterized by the mare attacking the foal by kicking or biting its neck and back. The attacks usually come when the foal is standing up and often start when the foal moves close to the mare's food. Most aggressive mares will not attack their foals while the foals are lying down. The cause of unprovoked aggression, more prevalent in some breeds, is unknown. There is some speculation that this behavior actually might be genetic in origin. Arabians are the breed whose mares are most commonly reported to demonstrate foal rejection, a study by Houpt reports.

Horsemen know that some mares act aggressively toward their first foal, then settle down to become good mothers in following years. However, aggressive behavior can recur with every new foal. Although the mares that show this types of aggression are usually primiparous, those that have rejected two or more foals will probably give a repeat performance the following year.

Treatment of Foal Rejection

Prompt human intervention and treatment of any type of foal rejection offer the best chance of reversing the behavior and, most importantly, allowing the foal to ingest colostrum. If the mare will not allow the foal to nurse, she should be milked and the colostrum administered to the foal either by bottle feeding or through a nasogastric tube. Your veterinarian will have to do the latter and should be alerted if the mare shows rejection behavior.

A mare frightened of her foal might require sedation to learn to accept it. The veterinarian sedates the mare, which is either placed against a wall in stocks or is hobbled to reduce the possibility of her hurting the foal. The foal is allowed to approach and to nurse. The mare usually learns that the nursing relieves the pressure of her full udder and will soon accept the foal. This method also is used to treat mares that object to nursing.

First, your veterinarian should examine the mare to determine if she has any problems that cause her udder pain, such as mastitis. If the mare's udder is not painful, she should be sedated and walked into stocks or restrained using hobbles so she cannot hurt the foal. At this stage an experienced horse handler should be present to prevent injury to the foal as the mare becomes accustomed to it. The mare that is aggressive toward her foal will need to be restrained at all times to prevent injury to her foal. Some useful restraints include cross ties, hobbles, or a bar creating a straight stall to prevent the mare from being able to kick the foal or turn sideways. The mare is often sedated just before the foal is first introduced.

Punishment and reward also are used to help the mare overcome her aggressive behavior, but only after the nature of rejection is understood. Obviously, a frightened mare or one displaying rejection due to pain should not be punished. Grain or treats can be fed to the mare while the foal nurses. If she shows any aggression toward the foal, a whip can be used, but punishment must be given immediately every time she shows aggression or other behavior problems will arise.

Dealing with a case of foal rejection requires a great deal of time and effort on the owner's part because the foal will need to nurse every half-hour around the clock, especially in the first week of life. Furthermore, some mares will not accept their foals, no matter what method is tried.

Returning to Instincts

Maternal behavior is in part instinctive, so if all else fails, give nature a chance. Mares have a strong instinct to protect their foals, especially in the first few days of life. Hence, some mares will exhibit normal maternal behavior when the foal is threatened. For example, if the mare and foal are turned out with other horses and another horse shows interest in the foal or the foal approaches another horse, the mare's maternal instincts might be stimulated to guard the foal. If none of these methods work and the mare will not accept the foal, the foal will have to be raised as an orphan or placed with a nurse mare.

Prevention of Foal Rejection

Following a few simple rules can help decrease the chances of foal rejection. 1) Keep interruptions of the new mare and foal to a minimum unless there is an obvious problem, especially in the first few hours after birth. 2) Avoid introducing strange horses or other unfamiliar animals to the mare's environment for the first few days after foaling. Anxiety over new animals can lead to poor bonding of the mare and foal and possible rejection. For example, do not place a newly arrived horse in the stall next to a mare and new foal or in the same paddock. The new horse might be

Mares have a strong instinct to protect their foals

carrying diseases that could make the foal sick. Also, if the new horse and the mare do not get along, the aggression the mare feels toward the new horse could become directed at her own foal. 3) If the mare has rejected previous foals, do not re-bed the stall immediately after the delivery. Leave the placenta there for an hour or so. Monitor the mare and make sure she does not try and eat the placenta. If she tries, remove it from the stall and save it. Mares do this occasionally, perhaps as an instinctive reaction to the dangers posed by equine predators in the wild.

In the case of a foal that had to be separated from its colicky mother, the mare was moved after surgery into a split stall where she could see her foal all the time. She was examined for any udder problems. Then she was sedated and twitched to allow the foal to nurse. The foal nursed every hour for the first several days. After a few days, the mare did not need sedation or the twitch and was just held with a lead line. But if left in the stall together, the mare would bite the foal, especially at feeding time. In an attempt to appeal to her maternal instincts, the mare and foal were turned out with another mare and foal. It worked like magic. She protected her foal and that ended the problem.

In most cases, mares deliver their foals and accept them without hesitation. However, in the unlucky few cases, rejection poses a serious problem, possibly leading to foal injury or illness. If your mare shows signs of rejection, notify your veterinarian at once.

Orphan Foals and Twins

People new to the breeding and raising of horses probably have never experienced the challenge of raising an orphan foal or feeding a foal whose mother is producing little or no milk. The solutions to both problems can be time consuming and somewhat of an ordeal. A foal can become an orphan after losing its mother to sickness such as colic or uterine hemorrhage. Also, the mother might reject her foal. Other problems can occur that result in the mare's inability to produce adequate milk for the foal, such as mastitis, metritis (infection of the uterus), and other serious illnesses. If the mare eats certain kinds of fescue in late pregnancy, her milk production can be blocked if the grass harbors a fungus called *Acremonium coenophialum*. Although her foal is not technically an orphan, another source of milk must be found immediately.

This chapter will address raising and feeding orphan foals. It also will discuss the supplemental feeding of foals whose mothers cannot produce enough milk to meet a foal's nutritional needs.

Newborn Orphans

Newborn foals rely entirely on their mothers' milk for nutrition. If a foal is orphaned at birth, it is critical to find another source not only of milk but of colostrum, too. It is imperative that the colostrum be administered as soon as possible because, as stated before, a foal can only absorb the immunoglobulins from the colostrum for approximately 18 hours.

If colostrum is not available, the foal will require intravenous plasma within the first 24 hours of life. Equine plasma contains immunoglobulins to help protect the foal from infection. However, it is expensive, costing about $250 per liter. A 100-pound foal needs between one to two liters of plasma if it has not received any colostrum. If colostrum is available, the newborn foal needs about 250 ml of colostrum every hour for the first six hours, then free choice (but not more than one pint, or 16 ounces) every one to two hours.

A nurse mare provides the best source of milk for an orphaned foal

Your veterinarian should test the foal at 12 to 24 hours of age to determine if it has absorbed adequate levels of immunoglobulins. If its absorption is low, the foal should be given additional colostrum or intravenous plasma as a booster. Otherwise, it will be susceptible to life-threatening infection. Now comes the next problem — getting the foal to drink.

Nurse Mares

If a foal has been orphaned, a nurse mare provides the best source of milk. The orphaned foal is placed with another mare that has lost her foal or one whose foal has been weaned. Some farms raise mares specifically for this purpose. Commercial mares can be expensive, costing $2,000 or more to lease a mare until the foal is weaned. Also, many nurse mare suppliers require that you have the mare bred before returning her. Secondly, the fostering process can take a lot of time. However, the successful placement of a foal with a nurse mare guarantees the foal a constant food source and ensures proper socialization.

Do not attempt fostering without an experienced person to supervise the introduction process because the mare often requires sedation and/or

restraints to prevent her from injuring the foal. The mare should be placed into stocks or hobbled to prevent her from kicking the foal. Even so, two people are needed at all times while introducing the mare and foal: one to restrain the mare and one to guide and protect the foal. The mare and foal should not be left alone until the mare has fully accepted the foal.

Signs of acceptance include the mare nickering to the foal when the foal is led away and allowing the foal to nurse without resistance. Acceptance of the foal can take several days or as little as a few hours with a good foster mare.

Foster Mares

Another option that has recently become more widely used is a foster mare. This is a mare that has given birth at least once before, has hormonally been brought into lactation, and then been fostered onto the orphan foal. Older unbred or barren mares are perfect candidates for this job. The only disadvantage is that the process takes eight days to bring a mare into lactation. The cost of the drugs necessary to bring a mare into lactation is far less than the cost of a nurse mare, and after 14 days or so the mare will not require any further drugs to keep her producing milk.

For purposes of fostering, it is important to choose a mare that is gentle and that potentially has shown interest in or at least tolerance of other foals. Introducing the foal to the foster mare is very similar to introducing the foal to a nurse mare and should be done with an experienced person available, if not a veterinarian present.

Bottle or Pail Feeding

If a nurse mare is not an option or if the mare rejects the foal, an alternative is bottle or pail feeding the foal. If the foal has never nursed from the mare, it usually will nurse from the bottle willingly. Lamb nipples are excellent as they most resemble a mare's teat. If these are not available, Gerber NUK® nipples, which are designed for human babies, may be used. Calf nipples are usually too big for foals to nurse effectively. Whichever type is used, make sure the hole in the nipple is not too large. When the bottle is turned upside down, milk should not flow out of the nipple; otherwise, it flows too fast and the foal could aspirate milk (inhaling the milk into the windpipe).

A foal should be placed in an upright position to nurse from a bottle. This lessens the chance of milk traveling down the foal's windpipe instead of the esophagus, which can lead to pneumonia. To simulate a natural position for nursing, stand with your back to the foal and hold the foal's nose underneath your arm; then gently insert the nipple into the foal's mouth (make sure the nipple is over the tongue). The foal may bump your arm with its head. That is how the foal would stimulate the mare to "let down" her milk. Do not hold the bottle above the foal's head as this position can make it very easy for foals to aspirate milk. Healthy foals usually drink only until they are full, so the foal

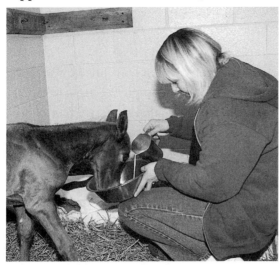

Pail feeding can be an alternative

should be allowed to drink free choice to consume enough colostrum in the first 24 hours.

It is a good idea to record the amount of milk the foal consumes at every feeding, especially in the first few weeks of its life because this can help alert you to a decreasing appetite or developing illness. Remember to clean the bottles and nipples after each use.

If the foal has been nursing a mare, getting it to nurse from a bottle can be quite difficult. These foals might be more likely to drink from a pail or bucket. Pail feeding is definitely less time consuming and has an advantage as the foal can drink free choice.

Foals usually can be taught fairly easily to drink from a pail. Place milk on your fingers and insert them into the foal's mouth to stimulate the suckle reflex. With your fingers still in the foal's mouth, lower your fingers into a pail of warm milk. Eventually, the foal will get the idea. With this method of feeding, a bucket of mare's milk or milk replacer can be left in the foal's stall or paddock. To avoid the problem of the milk curdling, the milk in the pail should be dumped and replaced with fresh milk every six to 12 hours. The bucket or pail should be hung at chest level for the foal to drink and cleaned every time the milk is changed. Remember, the foal must have access to fresh water at all times.

What To Feed

The next question is what type of milk should be fed to the foal. Mare's milk is the perfect solution because it alone matches the nutritional needs of the foal exactly. However, few breeding farms or even equine hospitals have enough milk stored to feed a foal for more than a few weeks. If mare's milk is available, it is the first choice. Otherwise, milk from other animals can be used. Cow or goat milk is usually readily available, although neither is the perfect substitute. Cow and goat milk both contain more fat, and cow's milk does not contain enough dextrose (sugar). Therefore, if cow's milk is used, one teaspoon of honey should be added per pint of milk. Goat's milk can be fed without alteration, but it is more expensive than cow's milk. Some foals prefer the taste of goat's milk.

Commercial milk replacers also are available. They are convenient and very acceptable alternatives. Several brands specifically formulated to supply the complete nutritional needs of a foal are now available. Whichever brand is used, the replacer should contain approximately 15 percent fat and 22 percent crude protein, so check the label before purchasing. Some commonly used milk replacers for foals are Mare's Match®, Foal-Lac®, Foal Life, and NutriFoal. These by no means represent a complete list, and other foal milk replacers are perfectly acceptable.

Calf milk replacers also have been used to raise foals successfully. However, many calf milk replacers contain antibiotics, which should never be used in foals. Furthermore, calf milk replacers historically have not contained enough protein for normal growth of the foal. Though newer brands of milk replacers are more acceptable, read the product label carefully or talk to your veterinarian before purchasing. Goat or lamb replacers are also alternatives. But the nutritional requirements for foals are quite different than those supplied by these replacers, especially the ratio of calcium to phosphorus.

Milk replacers also can cause gastrointestinal upset. Some foals will develop loose stools when the replacers are first used. This is normal, but if the foal develops diarrhea, then the milk replacer should be diluted with water or changed to another brand or type. If the diarrhea persists for more than one day, your veterinarian should evaluate the foal and institute proper treatment. Sometimes, foals can develop mild bloat (gas) from the milk replacer. If this occurs, discontinue feeding for a few hours then try a more diluted formulation. While using these kinds of replacers, make sure your veterinarian monitors the foal's growth rate and finds it acceptable.

Once foals reach one month of age, most are ready for solid feed. A foal will mimic the mare's eating habits and begin to eat grass, hay, or grain with the mare as early as two to three weeks of age. These foals usually are introduced to a creep feed by one month of age.

Orphaned foals also should be introduced to grain at this time as well. Feeding milk replacer pellets also can be tried at an earlier age. The pellets usually have to be placed gently into the foal's mouth. Often, the foal will spit them out until it gets the idea.

Starting at one month of age, the foal may be fed small amounts of grain. Newer recommendations for feeding foals include not feeding a high percent protein feed as a creep feed, but instead use the same feed that a weanling would receive (12 percent or 14 percent). A good rule of thumb for feeding young horses is one pound of grain per day, per month of age, not giving more than six pounds per day, so a three-month-old foal would receive three pounds of grain per day. Splitting the total amount of grain into two to three feedings also is recommended. This is a guideline only; have your veterinarian check your foal for proper growth and size as some foals will need more grain and others less. Remember, more is not better. Excessive amounts of grain can result in any number of developmental orthopedic diseases in foals such as physitis (abnormal activity in the growth plates), osteochondrosis (including OCD lesions), and flexural deformities.

Foals generally can be weaned from milk replacers by three or four months of age if adequate grass or grass hay and grain are available.

How Much and How Often To Feed

A healthy newborn foal will nurse from its dam about seven times in one hour. As the foal gets older, this number decreases. As a result, frequent feedings are most compatible with the foal's digestive system. Although calves often are fed only two to three times per day with large volumes at each feeding, this method is not acceptable for foals ingesting only milk. Foals also require anywhere from 21 percent to 25 percent of their body weight in milk per day.

The ideal approach is free-choice feeding of milk to ensure meeting the foal's requirements. This is quite easy with the bucket or pail feeding method. However, with bottle feeding, the newborn foal will need to nurse every hour for the first few days to one week, then can decrease to every two to three. As you can see, the bucket feeding method has its advantages. The problems arise when the foal is ill and does not consume enough milk. If this happens, your veterinarian should be notified and forced feeding (via a naso-gastric tube) must be instituted.

Sometimes the foal will need to be taken to an equine hospital for intensive care to ensure adequate nutritional support as well as treatment for the underlying illness. In severe cases, intravenous fluids must be administered to correct and prevent dehydration.

But how will you know when your foal is consuming enough milk? Newborn foals should drink about five to seven liters per day in colostrum and milk. Remember, healthy foals need to ingest between 21 percent to 25 percent of their body weight in milk per day, so a 75 kilogram foal will need about 19 pints of milk per day. Foals should gain about one to two kilograms of body weight per day. Contact your veterinarian if you are unsure whether your foal is consuming enough milk or not growing properly.

Special Problems of Orphans

Raising a foal is a time-consuming job. One main problem with humans raising foals is that the foal will identify with the human species not the equine species. This might be cute when the foal is a newborn but presents its own set of problems as the foal gets older. Foals raised by people without contact with other horses have been known to show fear of and avoid other horses later in life. One study even showed that foals raised by humans did not learn how to graze properly. Orphaned foals also will try to nurse themselves, other foals, or other horses — male or female. These problems can be eliminated by raising the foal with another horse or pony to use as a role model.

Raising an orphan foal can be challenging, but it also can result in a healthy, well-adjusted foal. The loss of a mare is not a death sentence for the foal. Raising an orphan foal, however, should not be attempted without your veterinarian's guidance.

Twins

Twin embryos are an unusual and very undesirable phenomenon. Many other species (cows, sheep, goats) frequently produce healthy twins. But a mare can rarely support twins and carry them to term because of her unique placental attachment to the uterus.

Mares develop twins due to a double ovulation. Both eggs are fertilized and develop into embryos. Twins are a leading cause of abortion in the mare. For those twins born alive, one is usually weaker and dies within a few days. Mares that abort twin pregnancies have a higher incidence of retained placentas and are often difficult to rebreed during that season. For all of these reasons, veterinarians do not recommend allowing mares to carry twin pregnancies. Mares are examined early in pregnancy (usually around day 14 and 29 post-ovulation) to determine if twins are present. If they are, the veterinarian will determine which procedure to use to eliminate one so as to prevent loss of both of the embryos later.

Despite the awareness, sometimes twin pregnancies are missed and the mare miraculously carries both fetuses to term. Twin pregnancies should be detected before the mare foals as the birth can be difficult and require veterinary assistance. Furthermore, mares usually cannot produce enough milk to support both foals, and preparations should be made to help care for them.

Mares carrying twin foals will be much larger than mares carrying one foal and they often will deliver the foals early, so monitoring should begin before the last month of gesta-

Twins are rare

tion. Monitoring the mare for early udder development and lactation is crucial. If the mare was not evaluated by ultrasound early in the pregnancy, your veterinarian can perform trans-abdominal ultrasound in an attempt to determine if twin fetuses are present.

If both foals are born alive, they will need special attention. Twins are usually born smaller than single foals and often do not survive the first few days. Your veterinarian should be summoned immediately to determine if they are healthy or if either requires treatment to help the chances of both surviving. If the foals are premature or dysmature, they might need intensive care.

Twins foals also will require nutritional support in the form of supplemental feedings. Most mares will not be able to produce enough milk for both foals, so after the colostrum is ingested, institute pail feeding with milk replacer to give the foals adequate nutrition. Twins also should be evaluated for adequate absorption of immunoglobulins, and supplemental colostrum or intravenous plasma administered if needed. Many twin foals will have musculoskeletal problems in the form of angular or flexural deformities.

Twin foals can be raised successfully, but it usually takes cooperation and hard work between the veterinarian and owner or caregiver.

CHAPTER 27

Neonatal Problems

Remember, just because your foal was born healthy does not mean you are out of the woods. Raising a foal requires close daily observation. This section will describe what the problems look like, what they mean, and what to do about them.

IgG (Antibody) Determination

The main antibody or immunoglobulin produced in the mare's colostrum is the gamma globulin or IgG. The mare concentrates IgG within her colostrum, and, as the foal's intestines selectively absorb this molecule for the first 18 to 24 hours of life, this is a very important immunoglobulin. The transfer of IgG from mare's colostrum to the foal is called the passive transfer of antibodies. After this first 24 hours of life, these specialized cells are replaced and the foal can no longer absorb the gamma globulin. Peak absorption of IgG often occurs around eight hours of life, as long as the foal in nursing normally. Peak blood concentration of IgG often occurs around 18 hours of life. One of the greatest developments in foal care has been the stall-side tests for measuring IgG. These portable tests allow veterinarians to estimate the quantity of gamma globulins absorbed by the foal. These tests can be performed on the farm during the healthy foal check and take, at most, 10 minutes to complete.

Because of the time limit of absorption of IgG, many veterinarians prefer to perform the healthy foal check when the foal is 12 to 18 hours old. By testing the foal's blood at this time, if the IgG level is low, then banked colostrum or colostrum substitute can be administered via stomach tube. However, if the available colostrum is poor quality or if no colostrum is available, then plasma can be administered intravenously. Harvested from donor horses, plasma has concentrated immunoglobulins and can protect the foal from infection.

Many different types of tests can estimate the level of immunoglobulins within the blood stream. Some of the tests can be performed at the farm; others require laboratory analysis. Several on-site tests have a fairly high accuracy level and are an important part of the physical examination of the newborn, as low levels of immunoglobulins can mean the foal is at risk of developing infection.

Failure of Passive Transfer

Failure of passive transfer is a syndrome in which foals fail to absorb adequate colostrum. This can result from 1) the foal failing to ingest an adequate quantity of colostrum; 2) the mare producing poor quality colostrum; 3) the mare producing normal colostrum but prematurely lactating, thereby losing the colostrum; 4) the mare failing to produce any colostrum or milk of any kind (agalactia). Regardless of the cause, this syndrome is thought to be the most common predisposing factor of infection (sepsis) in neonates.

Failure of passive transfer can be classified as complete failure (no detectable IgG) or, more commonly, partial failure. In the latter case, some degree of immunoglobulins is transferred from the mare to the foal, but not enough to protect the foal from infection. If the foal is found to have a very low level of immunoglobulins and is older than 18 hours, your veterinarian will recommend a plasma transfusion. Although it's a bit expensive (about $250 per liter), its contents can save a foal's life.

Just because a foal has a low immunoglobulin level does not automatically mean that it will develop septicemia (a disease caused by infectious microorganisms in the blood). However, the chances are greater than with a foal that has a "normal" amount of immunoglobulins. No one knows exactly what level of immunoglobulins is necessary to protect a foal from septicemia — it varies with the individual

AT A GLANCE

◆ Have your veterinarian check the foal's main immunoglobulin within the first 24 hours.

◆ A foal might need extra colostrum or plasma if it fails to absorb enough colostrum.

◆ A foal might need tetanus anti-toxin if the mare has not been vaccinated.

animal. However, your vet knows what test range comprises an adequate level. Be aware that it is not uncommon for a foal to be tested at 24 hours of age and found to have a high level of immunoglobulins and still succumb to an infection within the first two weeks of its life. If the bacterial numbers or challenge is great, the foal is more likely to develop septicemia. Therefore, a clean and healthy environment is so important. Keep the stalls or paddocks clean and free of manure as much as possible, and keep all sick horses separated from the foals. This will help reduce bacterial numbers and consequently lower the infection rates on your farm.

Vaccinations

Neonates do not require many vaccinations. The routine gamut of vaccinations — influenza, Eastern and Western encephalitis, tetanus toxoid — is not required until the foal is four to six months old. The newborn foal, however, might require tetanus anti-toxin if the mare was not vaccinated with a tetanus toxoid booster during the

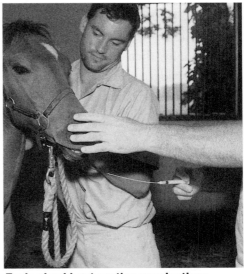

Foals should get routine vaccinations

last few months of gestation. An unvaccinated mare cannot transfer tetanus antibodies to the foal. Consequently, the foal needs protection immediately from the tetanus organism which is found everywhere in the environment.

The vet will probably give the newborn a combination injection of vitamin E and selenium, especially if the mare and foal live in an area that is selenium deficient and particularly if the mare did not receive supplements during pregnancy. Failure to supplement the mare during pregnancy and failure to administer vitamin E/selenium to the newborn could result in the development of White Muscle Disease. The disease could strike the foal at any time up to one year of age. White Muscle Disease is most commonly associated with a deficiency in selenium. Please find out from your veterinarian whether you live in a selenium-deficient area. The levels of both substances within the horse can be measured using a blood test, but getting the lab results takes up to one week.

Hypoxic Ischemic Encephalopathy (HIE)

HIE, previously known as neonatal maladjustment syndrome, is a term used to describe foals that suffer a decrease of oxygen (hypoxia) during birth. This syndrome has many names, the most common being "dummy foal." For a short time after being born, these foals act normally, then "forget" how to nurse, appear blind and weak, and then progress to seizures. The decrease (or lack) of oxygen for a short period of time may occur from dystocia (fetal malposition), premature separation of the placenta, or obstruction of the umbilical cord during delivery. Although the causes can be myriad, the result of the hypoxia is thought to be the same — swelling of the brain (cerebral edema). The degree of damage to the brain can produce a variety of clinical signs, including a lack of interest in the mare, wandering the stall or paddock, or a very deep sleep from which it is difficult to rouse the foal. More severely affected foals will have convulsions or seizures. The onset of these signs also can vary from immediately after birth to a few days later, when a seemingly normal foal suddenly begins to display abnormal behavior.

Foals with this syndrome often require intensive care, especially those with seizures. Even foals without seizures might require intensive care to ensure that they receive appropriate nutrition. Because most of these foals will not nurse adequately, they often need to be tube-fed. Treatment is aimed at reducing the cerebral edema and protecting the foal against infection. Many foals recover and do not appear to suffer any long-term effects. Mildly affected foals can recover with minimal care. If your foal displays any abnormal behavior, please notify your veterinarian as soon as possible, as early detection and therapy can improve the outcome.

Neonatal Isoerythrolysis

Neonatal isoerythrolysis, often referred to as NI, is a condition that affects neonatal foals within the first few days of life. The foals are born normal, then begin to show signs of the disease after ingesting colostrum. NI results in anemia, which occurs when the foal ingests maternal antibodies primed to attack the foal's red blood cells and destroy them. The mare develops these antibodies and concentrates them within the colostrum. This happens when the mare is sensitized to a red blood cell group, usually from a previous delivery. One example is if the foal's blood mixes with the mother's blood during the birth process. The mother, if exposed to a red blood cell group from the foal's blood, which she does not possess, will develop antibodies to those red cells. The next foal born to that mare is at risk of being affected. These foals are born healthy, then can develop sometimes-fatal anemia if not treated appropriately.

The clinical signs of NI are lethargy (weakness), decreased appetite, and icterus (yellow color to the mucous membranes). The foal also will have a rapid heart rate because as the red blood cells are progressively destroyed, then the blood loses its ability to carry oxygen. The heart must pump blood faster and faster to keep up with the body's oxygen demand. A cross match between the foal and mare's blood will determine if the foal has neonatal isoerythrolysis.

Your veterinarian also can do a field test by mixing the mare's colostrum with the foal's blood to look for a reaction. If positive, the foal will require a blood transfusion to replace the red blood cells that were lost. Also, the foal should have no more access to the mare's colostrum.

How To Prevent NI

The incidence of NI in Thoroughbred mares is about 1 percent, so it is not a terribly common disease, but it can be devastating. Tests can be performed before the foal is born to reduce the risk. If a mare has had an NI foal, then she should be tested one to two months before she foals to allow enough time to arrange for another source of colostrum. Usually, if the mare is delivering her first foal, this disease is not a concern.

Prevention is the best treatment. Talk to your veterinarian about testing your mare against the stallion's blood. Another way is comparing blood typing of the mare and stallion.

If your veterinarian determines the foal is at risk, then the foal will need to have another source of colostrum. In these cases, the delivery must be attended and the foal often muzzled to prevent it from ingesting the mother's colostrum. Colostrum that has been banked from another mare that is negative for the offending antibodies (determined from a blood test) or plasma transfusions can be used to achieve normal immunoglobulins levels. After the mare stops producing the colostrum (at about 24 to 48 hours), the foal can be allowed to nurse. If plasma is used, the foal must receive equine milk replacer or another source of equine milk from a bottle or pail or tube fed by your veterinarian until the foal can begin normal nursing. See the section on feeding the orphan foal in Chapter 26 for an idea of how much milk the newborn requires. Always consult with your veterinarian as well.

Entropion

Entropion is a condition of the newborn's eyelid that often goes unnoticed until the foal begins tearing from the affected eye. This is considered a congenital defect but also could be caused by dehydration and/or trauma during birth. Entropion usually occurs in the lower lid, which rolls inward and touches the surface of the eye (the cornea). The eyelashes soon start to scratch the cornea, which could result in a painful corneal

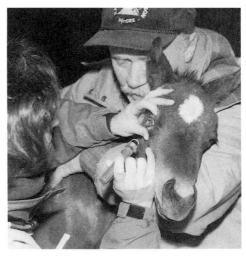

Checking for entropion

ulcer. You might be able to correct the problem by rolling the lid outward with your thumb. If the lid immediately goes back to touching the eye, your veterinarian will need to suture or staple the lid to keep it from touching the eye. If a corneal ulcer has formed, the eye will need treatment with topical ophthalmic ointment. The staples or sutures will remain in place (usually two weeks) until the lid no longer rolls inward. Entropion is not an emergency but should be corrected at the 24-hour healthy foal check.

Patent Urachus

The urachus is the structure that connects the foal's bladder to the allantoic space. The urachus travels within the umbilical cord along with other structures such as the umbilical veins and arteries. During gestation the foal's urine collects in the allantois. After the foal is born, the urachus should close as soon as the umbilical cord is severed. If at any time, you see urine dribbling or streaming from the urachus, it is considered patent. A patent urachus is easily determined in fillies but is harder to spot in colts. It can be difficult to tell whether the colt just sprayed urine from the urethra onto the end of the umbilicus or whether the urachus is truly patent. It can often take several close looks.

The urachus can be patent for one of two reasons: 1) the urachus never closed after the umbilical cord broke, a condition known as a congenital patent urachus; or 2) the urachus can open back up after having been closed, usually due to infection of the urachus or infection elsewhere in the body. If you notice that your foal is urinating through the urachus, call your veterinarian. An examination will determine infection within the umbilical stump/urachus or elsewhere in the body, such as in the lungs or gastrointestinal tract.

Treatment of a patent urachus is controversial. Most veterinarians agree that if there is evidence of an abscess or infection within the urachus or umbilical stump, it should be surgically removed to prevent spread of the infection. The controversy begins when discussing whether a patent urachus without signs of infection should be removed. Many veterinarians believe that an open (patent) urachus is just a portal for more bacteria to enter the blood stream. Others believe that an acquired patent urachus — one which has opened due to infection elsewhere in the body — is not the source or even potential source of infection and will close on its own as soon as the foal recovers from the infection. In the meantime, the foal is often treated with umbilical dips and/or cauterization of the urachus to encourage it to close.

As an owner, you should be aware that surgery to remove the urachus can have complications. The anesthesia itself is stressful on the foal, especially if pneumonia is present. Surgery can lead to excessive scar tissue formation within the abdomen (called adhesions), which can cause obstruction of the intestines. Sometimes, a second surgery is needed to correct the adhesions. This complication is rare, but you need to discuss the options with your veterinarian and reach a decision that satisfies you both.

Umbilical Hernia

An umbilical hernia, an outward swelling or mass in the umbilical area, results from a defect in the abdominal wall involving the portion of body wall through which the umbilical structures pass. When the vet palpates the area, the swelling should be soft and non-painful and it should be possible to push the bulge back gently into the abdomen (reducing the hernia). Umbilical hernias are usually surgically corrected for cosmetic reasons. Also, they could entrap a section of intestine, which will cause colic. A severe entrapment could lead to loss of blood supply to the segment of bowel, necessitating resection of that segment. A hernia also might result from the umbilical structures becoming infected. If so, it should be corrected.

Hernias less than a few centimeters in length often close spontaneously and usually do not require surgery. Larger hernias are usually corrected surgically when the foal is weaned, unless they are very large (greater than 10 cm) and those should be corrected early in life. If your foal does have a hernia, then monitor it for swelling, pain, and reducibility. If the hernia ever becomes non-reducible, it means the contents are entrapped and surgery should be performed as soon as possible.

Scrotal Hernia

A scrotal hernia is also a hernia, but the herniated intestines have gone through a natural slit in the body wall, the one through which the spermatic cord travels. Needless to say, scrotal hernias only occur in male foals. The natural opening is the inguinal (vaginal) ring and in these foals or adults, the ring is abnormally large and allows the intestines to slip down into the scrotum. The herniated intestine often slips down next to the descended testicle. You will notice this type of hernia as a soft swelling in the scrotum. With congenital scrotal hernias, the intestine usually does not become entrapped and you can easily push the intestines back into the abdomen.

Your vet may recommend that the hernia be reduced (pushed in) multiple times a day. Eventually, the enlarged ring will close on its own without surgery. However, the herniated intestine can become entrapped, making the hernia non-reducible, or the intestines will

Non-reducible hernias usually require surgery

burst out of the scrotum. When this happens, it is called a "ruptured" scrotal hernia. In such a case, the intestines are just underneath the skin and the hernia looks quite large. This type of scrotal hernia needs surgery immediately. You should also know that because this type of hernia is congenital, most veterinarians will insist that the colt be gelded at the time of surgery in order to prevent passing on the trait.

Flexural and Angular Limb Deformities

lexural or angular deformities (crooked legs) can be very shocking and even disturbing in severe cases. Luckily, these are rare; the mild deformities are more common. Flexural deformities can be classified into two categories. The first is flexor tendon laxity, which causes the newborn foal's fetlocks being dropped. The second type is flexural contractures, which result in flexion of any of the lower limb joints.

Flexor Tendon Laxity

Flexor tendon laxity usually occurs in newborn foals but can occur in slightly older foals. This laxity can range from a slight drop in the fetlock to the extreme where the fetlock(s) actually touch the ground. Flexor tendon laxity is common in premature or dysmature foals. This doesn't necessarily mean if your foal has lax tendons that he/she is pre-

Every owner wants a foal with good legs

A foal with severe deformity

mature/dysmature. Mild laxity usually resolves on its own as the foal gets stronger and exercises — often within a few days to one week. If the laxity is more pronounced, then hoof trimming to create a flat, weight-bearing surface is very beneficial.

Cases of severe laxity require more care, and the foal should be evaluated by your veterinarian. First, the foal's lower limb (heel, pastern, and fetlock) must be protected when it moves or bruising and wounds can develop. Bandaging the lower leg before turn out or hand walking is imperative because sores can develop even on a soft surface. When in a stall, make sure the foal is kept in a well-bedded environment (clean wheat straw is ideal). Second, if hoof trimming is not adequate to raise the foal's heels off the ground, then special shoes are required. These special shoes are usually some form of glue-on shoe with a heel extension. These shoes stay on well even when the foal exercises. Foals should not wear these shoes for more than two weeks at a time or hoof contracture could develop. Other options include gluing small pieces of wood to the hoof. Miniature horse foals can be treated with tongue depressors glued together, then taped or glued to the hoof. Even for mild cases of tendon laxity, foals will continue to weight bear on their heels, and the glue-on shoes are very helpful in correcting this problem.

Flexural Contractures

Flexural contractures are often referred to as "contracted tendons" because when the affected foal stands, it appears that the tendons are tense and too short. However, this isn't a complete explanation of the problem. This deformity can be present at birth (congenital) or develop in the older foal (acquired). The source of this problem in the newborn is not completely understood but is thought to be caused by malposition of the foal within the uterus. However, nutritional abnormalities and even genetics have been implicated as some mares produce multiple foals with flexural deformities.

Flexural contracture results in the flexion of the joints of the lower limb(s).

The joints most commonly affected are the carpus, fetlock, and coffin joint. One or multiple joints or legs can be affected. Flexural deformities also can occur in older foals, known as an acquired flexural deformity. Treating this type of deformity depends on the severity. Mild cases of flexural deformities can resolve on their own with light bandages and exercise. Moderate cases might need splinting and/or casting with the hoof exposed (tube casting).

Treatment with oxytetracycline (an antibiotic) has been used with some success in relaxing the tendons, but its use requires caution because of the potential toxic effects to the kidney. Surgery also might be necessary to help the foal's legs return to normal. Severely affected foals, especially those that cannot stand because of the severity of the contracture, often require intensive care in a hospital, and euthanasia can be the best alternative in some cases.

Flexural Contractures — Acquired

These types of contractures occur in older foals and in fairly specific locations. Young foals (one to six months) might develop contracture at the coffin joint. Older foals (at least three months) as well as yearlings and, occasionally, two-year-olds might develop contracture at the fetlock joint. These contractures occur in the forelegs, usually in both (bilateral), except for cases where the contracture in one leg is due to lack of use because of pain. The cause is not completely understood and is thought to be related to overnutrition (excessive carbohydrate and/or protein content) and/or mineral imbalances. Treatment depends on the severity of the disease; however, early treatment is imperative for the best outcome.

Clubfoot

Acquired flexural deformity of the coffin joint is often referred to as "clubfoot." The foot's appearance can vary from dished with the heel raised to a boxy shape with the hoof wall nearly perpendicular to the ground. In very severe cases the foal or horse might walk on the front (dorsal) aspect of the hoof or fetlock. Mild cases might require only a decrease in nutrition; in young foals, weaning might work. Hoof trimming, along with a shoe with an extended toe, might be necessary.

If this conservative therapy does not work, surgery to cut the inferior check ligament is warranted and often very successful. Severe cases often do not respond well to treatment, including surgery, unless the entire deep digital flexor tendon is cut, which is a salvage procedure only. The prognosis for athleticism in these cases is guarded. The key is beginning treatment early. A delay in treatment or diagnosis can lead to undesirable results. Young foals should be evaluated daily to ensure they are not beginning to develop contracture or other developmental orthopedic diseases.

Angular Limb Deformities

Angular limb deformities are those deviations that occur from a side to side plane, as the leg deviates from the carpus, tarsus, or fetlock to the outside (laterally) or inside (medially). A lateral deviation is called a valgus deformity and a medial deviation is called a varus deformity. These deviations are extremely common and can be congenital or acquired. There are several primary reasons angular deformities occur:

• Unossified carpal and tarsal bones due to prematurity or dysmaturity

- Laxity in the soft tissues surrounding a joint
- Abnormal uterine positioning
- Uneven growth at the physis (growth plate) of long bones
- Rapid growth
- Trauma

A veterinarian must determine the cause and the joints involved by performing a physical exam and taking radiographs. X-rays allow for evaluation of the bones to ensure that they are formed completely. X-rays also allow for documentation of the degree of angulation. Many foals, especially Thoroughbreds, are born with a mild angulation to both carpi and this usually will correct spontaneously during the first month of life. But what about more severe deformities?

Treatment

Soft tissue laxity can lead to some very severe deformities. These types of deformities are corrected most easily with tube casting. This type of casting leaves the foot exposed. These casts keep the affected joints in a normal position until the soft tissue structures become stronger and can support the joint.

Unossified carpal or tarsal (hock) bones also are treated by tube casting. Without cast support, the incompletely formed bones cannot bear the weight of the foal and literally can become crushed, which is referred to as carpal crush or tarsal crush syndrome.

Surgical Treatment

If the angular deformity does not correct on its own within a few weeks or is moderate to severe, surgical therapy should be attempted. Surgery to treat these deformities involves one of two procedures. Periosteal elevation helps stimulate growth. This procedure is used when one side of a long bone grows faster than the other, leading to an angular limb deformity. This procedure involves making an incision in the periosteum (the covering of the bone) on one side of the bone. This is a rather simple surgery, involves little risk, and yields good cosmetic results. Many times this procedure will be performed early in a foal's life, even on those with only mild deformities, just to ensure that the leg(s) become straight.

The second type of procedure is transphyseal bridging. This involves placing screws and wires, orthopedic staples, or, more recently, lag screws across one side of a growth plate. to slow growth on that side of a growth plate. This is for moderate to severe deformities. The procedure's disadvantage is that a second operation is required to remove the implants.

The foal requires close monitoring as the implants, if left in place too long, actually can cause the foal to overcorrect, leading to an angular deformity in the opposite direction. The implants must be removed as soon as the leg is straight.

The trick with angular limb deformities is timing. Angular limb deformities, even severe ones, can be corrected, but the foal must be treated at the appropriate time for that joint. Improper timing can result in a residual deformity, which might decrease the foal's value as a sale yearling or lead to early joint degeneration due to abnormal loading. Deformities of the carpus and hock should be corrected within four months of life. However, most corrective surgeries are performed between two and four weeks of age to ensure correct conformation.

Deformities of the fetlock are much more critical given that the rapid growth phase is much shorter in this area, therefore not allowing as much time for correction as in the carpus or tarsus. These deformities should be addressed by one month of age. It is always tragic to see a beautiful yearling whose conformation was ignored until preparations got under way for sale. By then, it is just too late. Have your veterinarian evaluate your foals early. Correct conformation goes a long way in preserving soundness in any discipline.

Foal Pneumonia, Septicemia, and Diarrhea

F oals can be particularly prone to developing pneumonia, which makes it a major concern on most breeding farms with large populations of horses. Foals are susceptible at all ages, so the disease poses a constant threat. Pneumonia can develop insidiously with no obvious outward signs until it has reached the advance and terminal stages.

What Is Pneumonia?

Pneumonia is inflammation of the lungs and can be due to a multitude of factors: bacterial pneumonia, viral pneumonia, etc. A Texas A&M University study found pneumonia to be the major cause of illness and death in foals from one to six months of age. A Canadian report found that 75 percent of foals on Thoroughbred breeding farms in that area developed pneumonia. Many foals develop pneumonia that goes undetected and resolves on its own but is unknowingly transmitted to other foals on the farm. That's the danger with pneumonia in foals; certain bacteria can cause huge outbreaks on farms and affect the majority of the foal population.

Foals in the early stages of pneumonia might show no obvious signs of disease. The more subtle signs of pneumonia include an increased respiratory rate (tachypnea) and/or increased respiratory effort. Foals with more advanced pneumonia might have a fever, nasal discharge (purulent material or pus coming from both nostrils), and/or coughing. Unfortunately, these obvious signs are not always present, even in very sick foals. Nasal discharge might not be present as the discharge often is swallowed. Foals with severe pneumonia will have marked respiratory effort — the foal might be breathing as if he has just finished a race. Foals that are this sick often are misinterpreted as having colic because they are in such a state of distress.

Other signs of illness (not just pneumonia) in foals can include lethargy (not as active or playful as normal). Sick foals also might not eat or nurse as much as they should. You might notice that the foal's head is covered in milk due to its weak attempts at nursing. A sick foal will go to the udder and bump the mare's bag, stimulating milk letdown, then just stand under the udder while the milk streams all over its face. Monitoring the mare's udder also is a telltale sign of foal well-being. If the mare's udder is engorged, and occasionally streaming milk, the foal is not nursing. A healthy foal will nurse from the mare six to seven times an hour, keeping the udder small.

The best way to monitor your foal is to watch for any signs of coughing or nasal discharge — these are the hallmark signs of pneumonia. You also should become familiar with the normal resting respiratory rate and character of breathing for your foals. Neonates (foals less than two weeks of age) often have resting respiratory rates of 30 breaths per minute. Older foals (one to six months) often have respiratory rates much lower at 12 to 24 bpm. These rates can change if the weather is very hot and humid or if the foals have just been running or playing. But, if your foal's respiratory rate is high for no reason, have your veterinarian examine the foal.

Being able to detect subtle changes in your foal's breathing requires skill. Watch for flaring of the nostrils and increased movement of the rib cage. If your foal is displaying these signs while resting, there is a problem. So, keep a close eye on your foal, and if you notice an increased respiratory rate or even if you are suspicious, have your veterinarian examine your foal.

What About Defense?

Horses have several defense mechanisms in their lungs to help prevent infection. The horses' normal defense mechanisms of the lung include the mucociliary clearance system, by which tiny cilia move mucus, bacteria, and foreign material (particles of dirt, shavings, hay, etc.) out of the lung and up the trachea. The particles usually are swallowed. Other defense mechanisms include special killer cells that engulf bacteria and other foreign debris that reach the deep lung tissue, and two different types of immune systems (cellular and humoral) to protect the lungs from infection.

AT A GLANCE
◆ Pneumonia is a common and sometimes fatal disease.
◆ Pneumonia can be so subtle that it might go undetected until it is too late.
◆ Weak foals could be suffering from septicemia.
◆ Diarrhea can have many causes and be contagious.

What Causes Pneumonia?

Pneumonia in the foal can be caused by multiple organisms — viruses, bacteria, and even internal parasites, either working alone or together to wreak havoc in the lung. The immune status of the foal — especially in the neonate — also is a factor in the development of pneumonia. In foals less than one month of age in particular, veterinarians are very concerned about the degree of immunity the foal has acquired from its dam's colostrum. A foal's failure to receive adequate colostrum (failure of passive transfer) results in an inadequate supply of immunoglobulins. Therefore, the foal is very susceptible to infection. Remember, at this age, foals have no other defense mechanisms to fight infection. These foals can develop pneumonia from an infection that originally occurred in another part of their body, such as diarrhea or an umbilical infection.

The most common organisms that cause pneumonia in the foal are bacteria. Bacterial pneumonia generally is caused by the same bacteria that normally inhabits the upper respiratory tract (pharynx, larynx, nasal passages), and gastrointestinal tract of horses, such as *Streptococcus sp.*, especially *S. zooepidemicus*. Bacteria usually found in the gastrointestinal tract, such as *Salmonella* species, *Klebsiella* species, and *E. coli*, are much more commonly implicated in causing pneumonia in neonatal foals. In these cases, bacteria gain access to the blood stream and spread throughout the body, leading to sepsis (generalized infection) and, subsequently, pneumonia.

Older foals develop pneumonia usually not from the bloodstream (hematogenously) but from inhaling the bacteria. The bacteria are inhaled and implant themselves in the lungs. If low numbers of bacteria are inhaled, the foal's body can destroy the bacteria and head off infection. If, however, an overwhelming number of bacteria are inhaled or if the foal's defense mechanisms are down from stress, concurrent or recent viral infection, or poor ventilation, the bacteria can take over and lead to pneumonia.

However, most pneumonia in foals occurs between the ages of four weeks and six months. The bacteria are thought to be inhaled. They then attach to the respiratory tract, and if the defenses of the respiratory system are down or the sheer numbers of bacteria inhaled are great, the bacteria will multiply and eventually cause disease.

What About Rhodococcus?

Another bacterium that causes pneumonia in foals (one to six months of age) is *Rhodococcus equi*, commonly just referred to as *Rhodococcus*. This bacterium, which lives in the soil, can cause disease in the lungs as well as in other areas of the foal's body, such as in the gastrointestinal tract, where it can lead to colitis (diarrhea) or affect the musculoskeletal system, where it can cause septic joints. *Rhodococcus* is not a simple infection that cures itself. Treatment can be intensive. Overwhelming infection is not uncommon and can lead to death or a recommendation of euthanasia due to a hopeless prognosis.

This bacterium leads to pneumonia and abscesses within the lungs or other areas of the body in foals that are less than six months of age. The problem with *Rhodococcus* is that it is often not recognized until the disease is well advanced and very difficult to treat.

Rhodococcus typically affects only foals. There are only a few reports of the disease occurring in adults, and these horses either were immunocompromised or had other simultaneous diseases that made them susceptible. *Rhodococcus* also has been reported to cause disease in humans who are immunocompromised, such as people infected with the HIV virus.

How Do Foals Become Infected?

The *Rhodococcus* bacterium is thought to gain access to the lungs from being inhaled with dust particles. The bacteria live in the soil, and when the ground becomes dusty in the summer from over-crowding or lack of rainfall, they easily gain entrance to the foal's lungs. The bacteria also enjoy warm temperatures, so they can multiply tremendously during summer, leading to exposure and possible infection for more and more foals. The bacteria are endemic on some farms and become a chronic problem every summer.

Preventing Rhodococcus Infection

There are several methods for controlling *Rhodococcus* on farms known to have the disease. Because the environment is a contributing factor to the disease's development, Steve Giguere, DVM, from the Ontario Veterinary College, recommended housing foals in well-ventilated, dust-free areas. Both dusty paddocks and aisles can be hosed or sprinkled with water to help keep the dust under control. Overcrowding also contributes to this disease. Housing sick foals in the next stall or same paddock is playing Russian roulette with the spread of this disease — it only will be a matter of time. Foals from another farm that are coming in with their mares to be bred should be kept separate from resident foals. Mixing foals from different farms is a sure way to spread respiratory viruses and bacteria.

Rotation of pastures also is an ideal way to prevent dust formation and therefore inhalation of the bacteria. This helps decrease the amount or concentration of bacteria to which a foal might be exposed and, thus, decrease the chance that a foal will develop the disease.

Other Types of Pneumonia

Bacteria also can be inhaled along with food particles. This is known as aspiration pneumonia. It is not as common as other types of pneumonia but can occur if a foal or horse develops choke (esophageal obstruction). This also can occur if there is a communication between the nasal passages and the oral cavity through a defect in the soft palate. When the foal nurses, milk can travel from the palate into the nasal passages and be inadvertently inhaled. Most people have had that occasional bit of food or drink travel down the wrong pipe — a mouthful of food gets inhaled into the trachea or windpipe instead of being swallowed. We hopefully just cough it back up and no big deal. When this happens over and over due to choke or other problems that allow for aspiration of food, the sheer number of bacteria eventually overwhelms the natural defense mechanisms of the lungs, and, in short order, the foal has pneumonia.

What About CID?

In combined immunodeficiency (CID), which is a hereditary disease usually seen only in purebred Arabians, the foal is born without the ability to develop a normal immune system. More specifically, the foal is unable to produce a type of white blood cell that helps fight off infection. So, the foal is usually born normal and healthy, but after six weeks or so, as the antibodies from the mother's colostrum wane, the foal cannot fight off infection. Many of these foals develop life-threatening pneumonia, and although antibiotics can be used to help kill the bacteria, without a functional immune system to take over where the maternal antibodies have left off, the bacteria overwhelm the animal, and pneumonia often results.

Diagnosing and Treating Pneumonia

If your foal is showing any of the clinical signs of pneumonia that were discussed, have your veterinarian examine the foal. Your veterinarian will perform a physical examination that includes listening to the lungs with the aid of the stethoscope. If the lungs are diseased, they will have abnormal sounds called crackles and/or wheezes. Or the lungs might be too quiet and not have normal breath sounds. To make an accurate diagnosis of pneumonia, a tracheal wash can be performed one of two ways. One way is to perform the "wash" from the underside of the horse's neck. The "wash" can be performed by placing a needle through the skin, then into the trachea, and advancing a small plastic catheter deep into the trachea. A small amount of sterile water is injected into the trachea; then the water, along with mucus, phlegm, and, hopefully, bacteria, will be aspirated back into a syringe and evaluated under the microscope. The veterinarian will look for the type of cells present, such as bacteria and white blood cells. He or she also will look for food particles to determine if the animal is aspirating food.

The second way to perform a tracheal wash involves placing an endoscope (a small fiberoptic camera) into the horse's trachea. A long plastic catheter then can be advanced into the trachea through the endoscope and the sterile water can be injected into the trachea. The rest of the procedure is exactly the same. Regardless of the method, a tracheal wash allows the veterinarian to acquire a sample of material from the lungs that contains bacteria that will be grown in culture to determine what type of bacteria is causing the infection. Furthermore, the bacteria can be tested (called a sensitivity test) to see what antibiotics will be most effective to treat the infection. This procedure often is necessary for successful treatment of pneumonia.

Other diagnostics used to help evaluate the severity of pneumonia are ultrasound examinations and radiographic (X-ray) studies of the chest. An ultrasound examination easily can be performed at the farm to help your veterinarian determine if there is fluid between the chest wall and the lung, which indicates pleuropneumonia. Using ultrasound, the veterinarian also can evaluate the health of the lung that is outermost in the chest. Radiographs of the chest are very useful in foals as they can detect abscesses, such as seen with *Rhodococcus* infection, or deep lung disease that simple auscultation and ultrasound examinations cannot detect. Radiographs are difficult to obtain on the farm, and your foal might need to be referred to a clinic for the X-rays to be performed.

Having diagnosed pneumonia, your veterinarian will place the foal on antibiotics to help fight the infection. The choice of antibiotics is dictated by the results of a culture and sensitivity. The foal will be placed on an antibiotic that has been effective in killing the bacteria that are present from the tracheal wash. If necessary, foals will be placed on intravenous antibiotics.

In very severe cases of pneumonia, the foal will need intensive care in a hospital. In these situations, an air-conditioned stall helps to decrease cooling demands on a young animal. In intensive care, oxygen also can be used. Nasal oxygen is often used in cases where the pneumonia is so advanced that a proper oxygen supply cannot be delivered from the diseased lungs. A small tube can be sutured into place in the foal's nostril and 100 percent oxygen supplied until the lungs recover the ability to transport oxygen effectively from room air, which is only about 20 percent oxygen.

Other treatments used as an adjunct in treating foals with pneumonia include nebulization of saline with antibiotics and brochodilators. Nebulization is the process of aerosolizing saline into very small particles. The saline can be used to loosen very sticky secretions, allowing the foal to have a more productive cough. The saline also is used as a carrier to transport antibiotics directly into the lung. Bronchodilators can be added to the solution to open airways and allow for easier breathing. This can be performed several times a day. Nebulization also is used in adults for the treatment of pneumonia and heaves (chronic obstructive pulmonary disease). A commercial mask such as the Aeromask can be used or a home-made one using half-gallon to gallon jugs can be used to deliver the aerosol.

Prevent is the best treatment. So, if you have had a problem with foal pneumonia on your farm, discuss with your veterinarian ways to prevent it in the future — such as keeping foals from different farms separated, so as not to expose them to new bacteria and/or viruses to which they have no immunity. Monitor closely for early signs of infection. Make sure the mares are well vaccinated to help prevent viral respiratory outbreaks that can lead to bacterial pneumonia. Furthermore, if you have had a problem with *Rhodococcus* in particular, discuss with your veterinarian the possibility of administering intravenous hyperimmune plasma within the first week of life, to help foals develop resistance to this particular infection.

Weak Foals (Septicemia)

Weak foals, those that do not stand and nurse within the normal time frame, are probably born sick. These foals most likely developed an infection in utero, usually the result of placentitis (infection within the placenta). Although these foals usually nurse, they tend to sleep excessively and are "easy to handle." Not all foals with infection will have a fever, so this is not a reliable indicator. This is the reason the 24-hour check is so important as your veterinarian can evaluate the foal for any other signs of septicemia. However, if your foal is weak and does not stand and nurse readily, you should call your veterinarian early rather than waiting until the foal is 18 to 24 hours old.

Foals also can develop septicemia later — within two to four weeks of age. Bacteria can enter the body through the umbilicus as well as through the gastrointestinal tract or respiratory system. Septicemia also can lead to septic arthritis, with the bacteria setting up infection within one or multiple joints in a foal's leg(s). This will lead to signs of lameness (limping) and swollen joints. The most common complaint from owners is that they think the foal is limping because the mare stepped on it. This rarely happens. Limping usually indicates joint infection. Treatment must be prompt and aggressive or the foal's joint can suffer permanent damage.

Foal Diarrhea

Diarrhea diseases of foals are some of the most dreaded diseases on a horse farm as many of the causes are not only infectious, but contagious as well. This means that you not only must be concerned about the foal that is sick, but also prevent the spread of the disease to other foals. Diarrhea is not simply loose manure but is an increase in the frequency and amount of feces produced, which are usually watery in character.

Diarrhea in the foal can be caused by numerous factors, including overnutrition, antimicrobials, bacteria, or even viruses, so there is a wide range of causes your veterinarian has to investigate once diarrhea has developed.

Foal heat diarrhea was discussed previously, as was diarrhea caused by a foal being fed milk replacer. If the replacer is too concentrated, then the foal might develop diarrhea. The foal might be depressed, but it should not be febrile (feverish). Once the replacer is eliminated, the diarrhea should resolve. If overnutrition is suspected, the replacer can be eliminated from the diet for 24 hours and an electrolyte solution can be fed. Feeding of milk replacer can resume once the diarrhea has resolved. When reintroducing feed, use Lactaid® and administer oral products containing live cultures (such as yogurt) to promote normal, healthy bacteria within the gastrointestinal (GI) tract. The Lactaid® is added to the milk to help the foal digest the milk and thus help reduce the risk of continuing diarrhea. Some of these foals might have a transitory problem with digesting the milk and benefit from the Lactaid®.

Antimicrobials

Antibiotics, especially those administered orally, often are implicated in causing diarrhea not only in foals, but also in adults. The antibiotics meant to kill "bad" bacteria that are causing disease, often also kill the normal bacteria within the GI tract. The normal bacteria are necessary for a well-functioning GI tract. Without these normal bacteria, diarrhea results. So, if your foals are being administered antibiotics either prophylactically or to treat an infection and diarrhea develops, notify your veterinarian immediately. Stop administering the antibiotics until an examination can be performed.

Rotavirus

Another very common cause of diarrhea in foals is rotavirus. There are other viral causes of diarrhea in foals, but they are not as prevalent as rotavirus and will not be discussed here. Rotavirus can affect a wide range of ages in foals and can cause profuse diarrhea. The foals can be febrile, but this is not consistent. The foals usually are depressed and do not nurse well. Rotavirus diarrhea can lead to huge outbreaks on breeding farms as the organism is shed in the feces for days to months post-infection. The diagnosis can be made by testing the feces — two lab tests are available. Depending on the severity of the diarrhea, many foals can be treated with yogurt or other agents to repopulate the GI tract with normal, healthy bacteria. Neonates that have a fever often are treated with antibiotics to prevent a secondary bacterial infection. More severely affected foals are treated with intravenous fluids to combat dehydration, as fluid loss from the diarrhea can be large. These foals also are treated with anti-ulcer medication as sick foals are more prone to develop gastric ulcers. Another concern with rotavirus is preventing the spread of the infection to other foals. Handlers should wear disposable shoe covers or rubber boots that are easily disinfected. Hands should be washed thoroughly after contact with these foals. Thermometers or other instruments used on a foal with diarrhea ideally should be committed to that foal. Otherwise, they should not be used on another horse until properly disinfected. Prevention of rotavirus diarrhea has been focused on containing outbreaks by the above methods. There is a vaccine available that is administered to the mare in the latter part of her gestation. If you have had a problem with rotavirus in the past, please talk with your vet about this vaccine.

Bacteria

Bacterial causes of foal diarrhea include *Salmonella*, *Clostridium*, and others such as *Rhodococcus*, which is a less common cause. *Salmonella* is the most common bacterial cause of foal diarrhea and also can cause septicemia with or without diarrhea in neonates.

These foals usually are very sick, with fever, depression, and a decreased or lack of appetite. The diarrhea can be profuse and can take several fecal cultures to prove infection. *Salmonella* must be treated aggressively with intravenous antibiotics, and usually treatment at an equine clinic is necessary due to the round the clock care. These foals usually must be treated with intravenous fluids as well to combat dehydration and other electrolyte imbalances. Needless to say, this organism is a particular cause for concern as it is potentially contagious not only to other horses but also to humans. Care should be taken to prevent exposure and spread of the disease by using coveralls, disposable/rubber boots, gloves, etc. Of course, isolation of these foals is imperative. *Salmonella* is a very serious illness, and death of the affected foal is not uncommon. The organism is often spread from other horses that can shed the bacteria in their feces. Horses also can be silent carriers of *Salmonella*, meaning they shed the organism intermittently in their feces but have never developed clinical signs of the disease. Of course, if affected with *Salmonella*, recovered horses also can shed the bacteria. If *Salmonella* has been isolated from any of your horses, discuss with your veterinarian about a protocol for fecal cultures and disinfection of stalls, paddocks, and barns. Unfortunately, there is no vaccine available to prevent this disease.

Clostridial diarrhea caused by *Cl. perfringens* and *Cl. difficile* usually affects the very young neonate and also can be a fatal infection. It can lead to a very rapid course of diarrhea and subsequent death, so it must be treated aggressively and immediately. The diarrhea often is bloody, but not always. It also can be accompanied by signs of colic, more severe than if seen with other diarrheas. The organism is found in the environment and often is shed in the feces of normal adults. The disease is treated with aggressive antibiotics (intravenous and oral) and intravenous fluids. A vaccine is available for prevention against the disease, but it is made for ruminants, not horses. However, it has been administered to pregnant mares to prevent diarrhea in foals.

Weaning

Your foal has made it through the fragile neonatal period, has adapted well to life with its dam, and now is ready to be weaned. But when is the best time? How can you make the transition as stress-free as possible? And after weaning, when should you castrate or have other elective procedures performed?

The weaning process is recognized as one of the most stressful times for a foal. Foals recently weaned usually lose some weight due to anxiety and inappetence. Many people will delay weaning because of this problem until the foal is six months old or even later, so the foal is older and hopefully less dependent on and less attached to the dam. But there are some things you can do to help reduce stress. We'll discuss strategies for weaning and decreasing the weight loss during the weaning period.

There are as many strategies for weaning foals as there are breeding farms and managers. Your particular circumstances (one mare vs. 100 mares) and the available space at your farm will dictate, to some degree, how you wean your foal(s). If you have had little to no experience with weaning, you might want to discuss the process with your veterinarian to decide what works best for you and your horses. The most important aspect of weaning is safety. The process should be performed carefully and the mare and foal monitored in the early weaning period so that they do not harm themselves.

Options include sudden, complete weaning by moving the mare to a separate location out of hearing range. Gradual weaning involves separating the mare and foal by placing them in adjoining stalls or in separate paddocks where they can see and hear each other and even have some contact. One factor that can help reduce panic during the weaning process is to place foals with other foals or older horses to act as foal sitters. Many large farms will wean several foals at one time and place them in a paddock together for comfort. If you are going to place a recently weaned foal with an older horse, make sure that the horse is gentle and will not attack the foal or kick at it too much if the foal tries to nurse.

When To Wean

Mares and foals often let you know when they are ready to be weaned. The mare and foal will begin to spend less and less time together as the foal gets older. The mare might become irritated when the foal is nursing. The foal will become more independent as well, not staying close to the mother when turned out with other horses. Mares in the wild usually wean their own foals, but there have been wild and domesticated horses that have allowed their foals to nurse until they are two-year-olds.

The occupations of your mare and foal often dictate when you wean. Most breeding farms wean their foals between the ages of five and seven months. However, foals can be weaned much earlier with no adverse consequences. For example, if your mare is a show horse,

Weaning can be a stressful time

the foal might need to be weaned earlier (at three to four months) so the mare can get back in shape to perform.

If you have only one mare and foal with a small farm, you may decide to wean gradually. First separate the mare and foal by placing them in different stalls where they still can see and touch each other but the foal cannot nurse. Turn them out in separate paddocks or in shifts so the foal cannot nurse. This is a "low stress" method of weaning but more time consuming. Foals intended for sale as weanlings often need to be separated completely (out of sight and hearing range) from the mare, but they can be separated by a stall or paddock first.

Pay attention to the environment you move your mare and foal to, keeping an eye out for broken rails on fences, nails sticking out of boards, etc. If the mare or foal becomes panicked, then what is usually a safe area could become a trap.

AT A GLANCE

◆ Weaning usually occurs between five and seven months but sometimes earlier.

◆ Weaning can take place gradually to reduce stress to mare and foal.

◆ A foal should be accustomed to eating grain before weaning to minimize the weight loss that can accompany weaning.

◆ Male foals can be castrated at weaning or earlier.

Feeding the Weanling

Feeding a newly weaned foal can pose problems. Too much protein can result in developmental orthopedic diseases, such as acquired flexural deformities, while feeding a foal too little could result in a stunted foal. Feeding an adequate amount requires a balanced approach and careful scrutiny of the foal's growth. An equine nutrition specialist working with your veterinarian can help tremendously with feeding questions.

The weight loss that occurs in foals during the weaning period can be decreased if the foal is used to eating grain before weaning takes place. Foals often eat their mothers' grain, but it is important to begin feeding the foal separately early in its life, usually at one month of age. This helps ensure that when the foal is weaned, it will eat appropriately.

Feeding a high protein, creep-type feed once was advocated. But nutritional researchers such as Dr. Skip Hintz at Cornell University now recommend feeding a lower protein feed of 12 or 14 percent. The higher protein feed could predispose a foal to developmental orthopedic diseases. A foal accustomed to eating grain should not go through an adjustment period during weaning or lose much weight.

Many people want to know how much grain to feed. One rule of thumb is one pound of grain per day per month of life. So, a three-month-old foal should receive about three pounds of feed per day. This ratio is intended as a guideline and could be too much or too little for individual foals, so consult with your veterinarian. Foals should have free access to clean, fresh water and grass or grass/alfalfa mix hay. If you are feeding an alfalfa mix hay, less grain should be fed.

When To Castrate

Many owners want to know when to castrate their colts. Colts should be castrated as soon as possible, perhaps at weaning time or even earlier.

Many people think that if a colt is gelded before he is one or two years old, he will not develop properly. This has been proved completely false. Colts will grow to the same potential even if they are gelded within the first few weeks of life. Castrating is one of the most common surgical procedures a veterinarian performs. However, this procedure is fraught with complications, especially in the mature horse (two-year-olds or older). Gelding a horse early in life not only makes for a simple surgical procedure with a vastly reduced rate of complications, but also helps eliminate behavioral problems that can occur because the horse is intact. Many people do not understand that as the horse develops large testicles, he also develops an even larger blood supply, and hemorrhage is one of the most common complications following castration. Furthermore, castrating a horse that has bred a few mares does not guarantee elimination of stud-like behavior. So if you have a young colt, please talk to your veterinarian about castration.

STALLION CARE

by E. L. Squires, PhD

CHAPTER **31**

Reproductive Physiology of Stallions

To manage stallions properly, stud managers and veterinarians must understand the basic structure and function of the stallion's reproductive organs. In simple terms, the male reproductive system consists of a factory (testis), finishing school for spermatozoa (head and body of the epididymis), warehouse for the sperm (tail of the epididymis), and a delivery system (penis).

Testes

The testes of the stallion have two main functions: to produce sperm and to produce testosterone and other hormones. In normal stallions the testes descend into the scrotum shortly before birth or within two weeks after birth. The scrotum protects the testes and serves as a

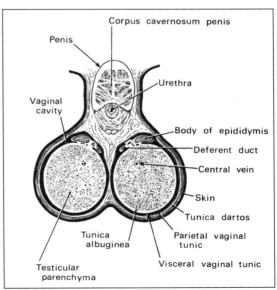

The penis, scrotum, and testes of the stallion as seen in a vertical cross-section

thermoregulatory mechanism. For spermatogenesis to proceed normally, the testicles must be exposed to a temperature several degrees below that of the horse's body. Underlying the scrotum skin is the tunica dartos, a layer of smooth muscle fibers intermingled with connective tissue. This body of muscles helps lower and raise the testicle, depending upon environmental temperature. The external cremaster muscle also assists in regulating the testicles' position.

The spermatic cord extends from the abdomen to its attachment on the testes. It suspends the testes in the scrotum and acts as a passageway for the deferent ducts, nerves, and blood vessels associated with the testes. The spermatic cord includes the highly coiled testicular artery. The veins draining the testes form a network of small veins around the highly coiled artery. This network is the pampiniform plexus, which cools the blood entering the testicle.

All of these thermoregulatory mechanisms are extremely important to maintain proper sperm production. Any temperature increase of the testes, due to elevation of body temperature or insulation of the scrotum due to swelling, will disrupt normal sperm production. Thus, stallions should be monitored closely for any sign of elevated body temperature or scrotum swelling.

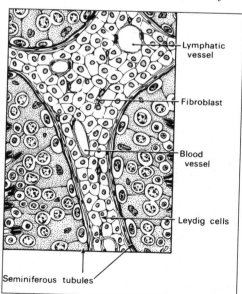

This drawing shows the relationship among the blood vessels, lymphatic vessels, and Leydig cells

The testicular tissue minus the capsule, termed parenchyma, consists of two components: seminiferous tubules and interstitial tissue. The seminiferous tubules are lined by seminiferous epitheliums that consist of different types of germ cells and the Sertoli cells. Leydig cells, which produce testosterone, comprise most of the interstitial tissue. The most immature form of germ cells (spermatogonia) line the basement membrane of the seminiferous tubules, and Sertoli cells extend toward the lumen in a radial pattern. The Sertoli cells are termed "nurse" cells in that they are essential in providing nutrients to the developing germ cells. Convoluted seminiferous tubules lead to the straight portion of the seminiferous tubules. The straight tubules converge in the cranial two-thirds of the testis — an area termed the rete tubule. Each rete testis fuses with one of the 13 to 15 efferent ducts that lead to the epididymal duct. The epididymal duct then leads to the proximal part of the epididymis.

> ## AT A GLANCE
>
> ◆ Sperm production occurs year-round and requires approximately 57 days.
>
> ◆ Elevated body and/or scrotum temperature can disrupt sperm production.
>
> ◆ It can take up to two months for normal sperm production to resume after trauma to the testes.
>
> ◆ Sperm production in a normal stallion decreases nearly 50% during the non-breeding season.

Leydig cells, within the interstitial tissue, produce a variety of steroid hormones, of which testosterone is a major hormone secreted by the stallion's testis. Other steroid hormones include androgens and estrogens. Concentration of testosterone at the level of the testicle is approximately 45 to 55 times higher than that in the jugular vein.

Epididymis

The epididymis is divided into the head or caput, body or corpus, and tail or cauda. The head curves around the testis and the spermatic cord and continues as the body of the epididymis. The head is rather flat, whereas the body of the epididymis is cylindrical and the tail of the epididymis is a large, bulbous structure attached to the caudal pole of the testis. Efferent ducts plus the initial head of the epididymis are involved in resorption of fluid and possibly secretion of compounds. In the body of the epididymis, sperm maturation occurs and spermatozoa gain the ability to be fertile and motile. The tail of the epididymis stores approximately two-thirds of the spermatozoa. The tail contains sufficient number of spermatozoa for several ejaculates.

Spermatozoa move through the epididymis by peristaltic contraction. Ejaculation does not alter the time required to move spermatozoa through the head and body of the epididymis. In contrast, ejaculation does alter the number of sperm stored in the tail of the epididymis. Stallions that are sexually rested for several days have more spermatozoa stored in the tail of the epididymis. One misconception is that frequent use of a stallion will result in ejaculation of immature spermatozoa. Spermatozoa are produced continuously, regardless of ejaculation frequency. Sperm that are not ejaculated are eliminated during urination.

Sperm travel from the tail of the epididymis through the deferent ducts and into the urethra. The deferent ducts widen in the pelvic area to form structures called the ampullae. The ampulla also is a storage area for spermatozoa. However, since the ampulla is contained within the body cavity, sperm stored in the ampulla are exposed to higher temperatures and usually are of lower motility with higher morphological abnormalities. Some stallions do not routinely void excess spermatozoa in the urine and thus accumulate large numbers of spermatozoa in the epididymis, deferent ducts, and ampullae. Generally, ejaculates from these stallions contain large numbers of spermatozoa that are morphologically abnormal. These stallions must be ejaculated several times to obtain good-quality semen.

Accessory Sex Glands

The accessory sex glands of the stallion include the vesicular glands (previously termed seminal vesicles), prostate gland, and bulbourethral gland. The vesicular glands are paired glands that contribute the gelatinous (gel) material contained in the ejaculate. The amount of gel produced varies with the season and the individual stallion. More gel is produced from April to July. In addition, the amount of gel in the ejaculate depends upon the sexual stimulation of the stallion. Those stallions used to tease several mares prior to ejaculation will produce large amounts of gelatinous material. The gel's function in the ejaculate is not truly known.

For artificial insemination, generally the gel is separated from the gel-free fraction and is not used for insemination. The prostate gland is a single, firm nodular gland surrounding the urethra. The secretion of the prostate gland is thin and watery and possibly serves to cleanse the urethra during ejaculation and contributes to seminal plasma. The two bulbourethral glands are positioned on each side of the pelvic urethra. These glands contribute to the seminal plasma. Collectively, these glands contribute most of the fluid to the ejaculate.

Penis

The urethra is a long, mucous-secreting tube that extends from the bladder to the free end of the penis. The pelvic portion of the urethra is covered by thick muscle that contracts vigorously during ejaculation. The urethra terminates in a free extension called the urethral process. The urethral process protrudes beyond the end of the glans penis and sometimes becomes irritated during collection or breeding. It is important when washing the stallion before breeding to examine the urethral process for trauma or laceration.

The penis is termed a muscular cavernosus type that becomes engorged with blood during erection. The major component of the penis is termed the corpus cavernosum, and the minor component is a bulbospongiosus muscle. Both of these muscles become engorged with blood during the erection process. Ejaculation in a stallion involves movement and deposition of the spermatozoa from the deferent ducts and tail of the epididymis, as well as fluid from the accessory sex glands into the pelvic urethra. Ejaculation is the actual expulsion of semen through the urethra. In a stallion, ejaculation occurs in a series of strong, pulsatile contractions (three to six), which have been termed "jets" of semen. The majority of spermatozoa are contained in the first three to four jets.

Sperm Production (Spermatogenesis)

Stud managers and veterinarians must have a thorough knowledge of the events of spermatogenesis. Production of sperm is a continuous process throughout the year and requires approximately 57 days. Spermatogenesis is the sum of cell divisions and cellular changes that result in formation of spermatozoa from the most immature sperm cells, spermatogonia. The different types of germ cells are spermatogonia, primary spermatocytes, secondary spermatocytes, and spermatids. If one looks at a cross-section of a normal seminiferous tubule, four or five generations of developing germ cells are arranged in a well-defined cellular association. Formation of a spermatozoon starts near the basement membrane where spermatogonia divide to form other spermatogonia and, ultimately, primary spermatocytes that are moved to a position from the basement membrane. A junctional complex between adjacent Sertoli cells forms a blood-testis barrier, which divides the seminiferous epitheliums into two functional components: a basal (lower) compartment and an upper compartment. Primary spermatocytes are moved from the basal compartment through the junctional complexes into the upper compartment, where they eventually divide to form secondary spermatocytes and spherical spermatids. The spermatids elongate and are eventually released into the lumen of the seminiferous tubules as spermatozoa. When released as spermatozoa, a major portion of the cytoplasm of each spermatid remains as a residual body, termed a cytoplasmic droplet. These droplets generally are extruded during passage through the head and body of the epididymis.

Knowledge of the time required to produce a spermatozoon is essential for understanding the course of events after drug injection or trauma to the testes. At least two months could be required for restoration of normal spermatogenesis after trauma to the testes. For example, if a stallion's temperature is elevated for several hours, quality of the spermatozoa in the ejaculate might be altered within a few days. This is attributed to damage of sperm within the epididymis. If the number and quality of spermatozoa in the ejaculate continue to be altered, this could reflect damage to the developing germ cells. If damage occurs at the level of the spermatogonia, then at least two months will be required before the quality and quantity of sperm in the ejaculate improve.

Daily sperm production is the number of spermatozoa produced per day by a testis or the testes of a stallion. Efficiency of sperm production is the number of sperm produced per gram of testicular tissue. During the breeding season, efficiency of sperm production is reasonably similar for normal stallions although testicular size can differ greatly among stallions. Consequently, sperm production can be estimated with fair accuracy by measuring testis size. Because testis size increases as the stallion grows from two and three years of age to a sexually mature stallion, daily sperm output also increases.

Daily sperm production also is affected by season, with nearly a 50 percent decline during the non-breeding season in mature stallions. Efficiency of sperm production in a stallion decreases during the non-breeding season. This is especially true of 13- to 20-year-old stallions. In the non-breeding season, the number of spermatogonia decreases, as well as the number of Leydig cells and Sertoli cells. Daily sperm production in the breeding season is approximately 19 million sperm per day per gram of testicular tissue and only 15 million sperm per day per gram of testicular tissue in the non-breeding season.

Hormonal Control of Reproductive Function

Proper functioning of the testicles and maintenance of sex drive is governed by hormonal secretion from the hypothalamus, pituitary, and testes. Gonadotropin-releasing hormone (GnRH) from the hypothalamus (a portion of the brain) travels through the portal vessels that link the hypothalamus and anterior lobe of the pituitary and stimulates release of luteinizing hormone (LH) and follicle-stimulating hormone (FSH) from the anterior pituitary. Luteinizing hormone stimulates the Leydig cells of the testes to produce testosterone. The four major functions of testosterone are to provide a hormonal environment for germ cells; to travel back to the pituitary and hypothalamus and inhibit through a negative feedback any further LH secretion; to maintain the function of the accessory sex glands; and to induce normal sexual behavior. Some of the testosterone is also converted to estradiol, which also has some role in maintaining sexual behavior in the stallion. Furthermore, testosterone stimulates the formation of androgen-binding protein (ABP), which is involved in transporting testosterone to the germ cells.

Follicle-stimulating hormone stimulates function of the Sertoli cells to provide nutrients to germ cells. The hormone also stimulates the carrier protein, ABP. FSH action on the Sertoli cells also includes the stimulation of the hormone inhibin, which travels back to the pituitary gland and inhibits further FSH secretion. A second hormone produced by the Sertoli cells, activin, is involved in regulating FSH secretion by stimulating the pituitary to produce and release FSH. As noted, this delicate balance in hormonal secretion between the hypothalamus, pituitary, and testes depends upon the balance of hormones in the stallion's blood. Therefore, any alteration in hormonal levels in the stallion's blood may, in fact, upset the delicate balance and inhibit sex drive or sperm production. It is important to determine a stallion's hormonal profile prior to injecting any hormone.

Breeding Soundness Examination

E very stallion should undergo a breeding soundness exam. These examinations test the stallion's physical and mental ability to breed mares. The tests include assessing the quality and quantity of semen, as well as the libido and mating of the stallion. Furthermore, this examination could uncover any possible congenital defects and infectious diseases and could be used to estimate the number of mares that can be booked to the stallion. Breeding soundness exams should be done any time the stallion is:

- being purchased or sold
- entering a breeding program for the first time
- experiencing a reproductive problem
- starting a breeding season (to establish an estimate of the number of covers or artificial inseminations that can be conducted)
- suspected of having lower fertility
- being bred to a larger number of mares
- suspected of harboring a pathogenic bacteria
- displaying abnormal sexual behavior (to determine if the stallion's breeding potential has changed from the previous year).

Breeding Soundness Exams

There are typically two types of breeding soundness examinations. One includes two ejaculates collected one hour apart from sexually rested stallions. The second ejaculate should have approximately 50 percent of the spermatozoa as the first ejaculate. If the second ejaculate does not contain half the spermatozoa, then one or more of the following should be suspected: a) one ejaculate is incomplete; b) the stallion has abnormally low sperm reserves; c) the stallion's sperm reserves have been depleted; d) the stallion is very young and immature or suffering from age-related testicular degeneration; or e) the stallion is abnormally accumulating large numbers of spermatozoa in the extragonadal sperm reserves.

A more complete evaluation includes daily collection for 10 to 14 days. The first several days' collections are used to stabilize the sperm reserves of the stallion and the last three ejaculates can be used to estimate average daily sperm output for that stallion. This latter evaluation is more appropriate for pre-purchase evaluations and for giving an accurate estimate of the number of mares that the stallion can handle.

The requirements for a breeding soundness examination include an artificial vagina that elicits a favorable response and maintains the temperature of the semen, a tease mare that can be used to assess the stallion's sex drive, and a phantom or live mare that is properly restrained for mounting by the stallion. In addition, the proper equipment for counting and evaluating the quality of the semen is essential.

Breeding Soundness Exam Procedures

The stallion should be brought into the breeding shed and presented to a mare in estrus positioned behind a padded rail. Generally, the stallion should obtain an erection in a matter of a few minutes although some novice stallions can take a lot longer and might, in fact, not obtain an erection on the first session. These young stallions should be handled with extreme care and provided with whatever stimulus is necessary to obtain an erection. Once erect, the stallion's penis is washed with warm water. At the time of washing, the penis is examined for any abnormalities. Teaching the horse to stand to be washed should be done with great patience, and the washing procedure should be stimulatory to the stallion. If the stallion attempts to withdraw the penis, one should stop the washing procedure, tease the stallion again, and repeat the process. If care is taken when the stallion is first being trained to be washed, then normal behavior can be established throughout the life of the stallion. One should examine the penis

AT A GLANCE

◆ Every stallion should undergo a breeding soundness exam.

◆ A novice stallion should be handled carefully during the exam.

◆ Sperm quality is assessed based on the percentage of spermatozoa that is progressively motile and morphologically normal.

◆ In a normal stallion, the sex drive usually determines the number of mares to which the stallion can be bred.

carefully during the washing process, particularly the glans and urethral process for any signs of abrasions or sores. Once the stallion is washed, he is either presented to a live, hobbled mare or a phantom mare. Typically, the stallion should ejaculate after only one or two mounts, depending upon the time of year in which the breeding soundness exam is performed.

There are three ways to discern whether ejaculation has occurred normally. Typically, the stallion will flag his tail during the ejaculatory process. However, it is also helpful to place the flat part of the hand on the base of the penis and feel the jets of semen being propelled through the urethra. Thirdly, once the stallion comes off the mare, squeeze the end of the glans. A white, frothy secretion indicates the presence of semen; a thin, watery

All new stallions should be examined

An artificial vagina

secretion could indicate pre-sperm.

The stallion should be taught to come off of the mare and stand quietly so that cultures can be taken for possible isolation of bacteria. Cultures generally are taken from the prepuce, urethra, and semen of each ejaculate. The potential pathogenic bacteria generally associated with uterine infection include *Beta hemolytic streptococcus*, *Klebsiella pneumoniae*, *Pseudomonas aeruginosa*, and *E. coli*. The presence of non-pathogenic bacteria, such as bacillus and staph, is quite typical in a stallion's ejaculate. These generally are normal bacterial flora that are part of the reproductive tract. Isolation of one of the pathogens in several of the cultures certainly would be of concern because these bacteria are capable of inducing uterine infection in mares after breeding or insemination. Fortunately, very few stallions are ever actively infected with bacteria and are merely carriers. Thus, in an artificial insemination program, the easiest way of eliminating the bacteria is to treat the semen with extender containing antibiotics. Unfortunately, with natural mating, elimination of bacteria from the stallion is quite difficult and generally requires antibiotic treatment of the stallion.

Once the semen is collected, it should be taken into a clean laboratory

Presenting a stallion to an estrous mare

and evaluated. The parameters measured include: volume of gel; gel-free and total seminal volume; concentration of spermatozoa per milliliter; total sperm in the ejaculate; percentage of progressively motile spermatozoa; percentage of morphologically normal spermatozoa; and testis size. The artifi-

A stallion mounts a mare, and semen is collected for evaluation

cial vagina should contain an in-line filter, which allows separation of the gel from the gel-free fraction. The filter can be removed from the collection bottle and the gel portion poured into a cylinder and measured. The gel-free fraction can be poured into a specimen cup or graduate cylinder and its volume determined. The volume of gel is not terribly important and varies tremendously from stallion to stallion and with season. Stallions teased heavily prior to collection will produce more gel, and gel volume also is greatest during the middle of the breeding season.

The number of spermatozoa per milliliter of gel-free semen can be determined by several instruments. These include Spectronic 20 sperm counter (Bausch & Lomb), Densimeter (Animal Reproduction Systems), Spermicue (MiniTube Corp.), and HRI (Hamilton Thorne). An alternative to the automated system of

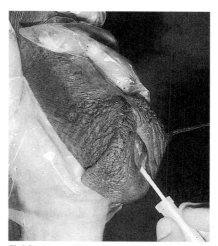

Taking a culture from the penis

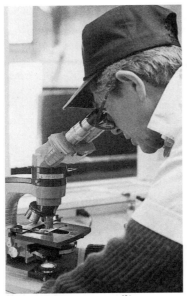

Assessing sperm quality

counting sperm is the use of a hema-cytometer, in which the number of spermatozoa are counted on a slide. Regardless of the method, the number of spermatozoa/ml must be obtained and multiplied by the volume of gel-free semen to determine the total sperm in the ejaculate.

Quality of the spermatozoa is assessed by evaluating the percentage of spermatozoa that are progressively motile and the percentage of spermatozoa that are morphologically normal. Sperm should be diluted to approximately 20 to 25 million spermatozoa/ml in a skim milk extender for proper assessment of spermatozoal motility. Proper visualization of the sperm requires a phase-contrast microscope with a heated stage set at 37 degrees Celsius. The percentage of spermatozoa moving in a straight line is estimated. Notice also should be given to the total number of spermatozoa that are moving and to the velocity of the sperm. A sample of raw semen should be used to compare with that of the extended semen. Typically, in undiluted semen samples, one observes head-to-head agglutination (or clumping) of spermatozoa, which results in a swirling motion of a clump of spermatozoa. Thus, it is difficult to estimate percentage of progressively motile spermatozoa in undiluted samples.

One also should examine the ejaculate of semen for the presence of any abnormal cells such as immature germ cells, white blood cells, or red blood cells. Certainly, the presence of any of these abnormal cells indicates a problem. The two most important seminal characteristics of an ejaculate appear to be total sperm number in the ejaculate and percentage of spermatozoa that are progressively motile.

Another parameter of great importance is the percentage of morphologically normal spermatozoa. This is generally assessed by mixing the semen with a stain on a clean microscope slide and by examining the spermatozoa under 1,000-times magnification. The percentage of morphologically normal spermatozoa should be at least 50 percent of the ejaculate, and the percentage of progressively motile spermatozoa in a normal ejaculate should be in the range of 50 percent to 80 percent.

Pickett et al. (1988) reported on breeding soundness examinations of 1,044 stallions between 1968 and 1987. The data were used to compare seminal characteristics and total scrotal width of stallions that "passed" a seminal evaluation to those that "failed." Additional data were obtained on seminal characteristics of stallions by breed, age, and month of the year. Overall, for stallions that passed, the average gel-free volume in an ejaculate was 45 ml, concentration 305 million/ml, total sperm/ejaculate 11 billion, and the percentage of progressively motile and morphologically normal spermatozoa was 53 percent and 51 percent, respectively.

The study indicated that daily sperm output appeared to increase sharply to five years of age and then remained essentially constant to 12 years of age. A total of 73 of the 1,044 stallions failed their seminal evaluation exclusively because a majority of culture sites were positive for either *Klebsiella*, *Pseudomonas*, or *Beta hemolytic streptococcus*. Of the 530 stallions that passed the biological portion of the breeding soundness examination, 154 (29 percent) had at least one culture positive for a potential pathogenic organism. However, the frequency of isolation or the growth level was insuf-

Sperm counters

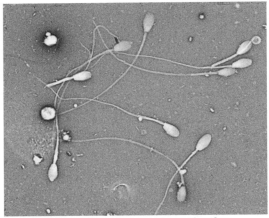

Sperm stained for morphologic evaluation

ficient to warrant failing these stallions. *Klebsiella pneumoniae* was the most commonly isolated organism (68 stallions or 12.8 percent of the stallions). The presence of potential pathogens in the semen did not adversely affect the seminal characteristics or total scrotal width.

One of the most important parts of the breeding soundness examination is palpation and measurement of the stallion's testes. Each individual testis should be evaluated separately by placing the thumb on the lateral part of the testicle and the fingers on the medial portion. The testicle then should be slid between the hands and felt for any evidence of roughness, lobulation, or change in consistency, such as extreme softness or firmness. The tail of the epididymis also can be felt at the caudal portion of the testicle; its size is related

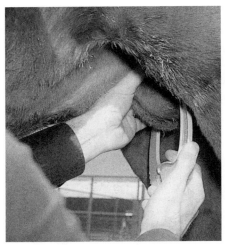

Calipers used to measure the scrotum

somewhat to the sperm reserves of the stallion. If the tail of the epididymis is not located at the caudal portion of the testicle, then the testicle is probably rotated within the scrotum.

Total scrotal width, assessed by using calipers, is the best measurement for predicting sperm output of the stallion. The testicle also can be measured by using ultrasonography. A cross-sectional area through the widest portion of the testis can be determined, as well as the length. By using the formula 4/3 πAC, where A is the cross-sectional area and C is the length divided by 2, testicular volume can be obtained. Once testicular volume is obtained, this can be placed into a formula to calculate the expected daily sperm output.

Determining the Optimum Number

Numerous factors must be considered when devising strategies to determine the maximum number of mares to which a stallion can be bred in a given year. There is no simple equation to calculate this number accurately. The components include the reproductive history of the stallion, age, testis size, semen quality, sex drive, and the breeding method. Certainly, more mares can be bred with artificial insemination than with natural mating. Furthermore, a knowledge of the previous reproductive performance of the stallion helps to predict further capabilities. Generally, if a stallion has normal-sized testes, the single limiting factor is sex drive. The type of mares presented to the stallion also can be quite important. For example, if a large number of barren mares are presented to the stallion, then perhaps more frequent breedings are needed to obtain pregnancies. Furthermore, if a large number of foaling mares are booked to the stallion, then these mares generally foal later in the season and might impose additional stress on the stallion by having a large number of mares to be bred late in the season. The most advantageous situation is to have an equal distribution of maiden, barren, and lactating mares.

It is important to obtain the stallion's previous breeding performance and any history of illness, injury, or medication. A general physical exam should be conducted to determine the horse's overall condition and particularly to determine lameness in the hind legs or back problems. The unwillingness to mount or the inability to complete the breeding process is sometimes associated with pain in the hocks or stifle or possibly the back.

References

Pickett, BW; Voss, JL; Bowen, RA; Squires, EL; and McKinnon, AO. 1988. Seminal characteristics and total scrotal width (TSW) of normal and abnormal stallions. Proc. 33rd Ann. Conv. AAEP. pp 487-519.

Love, CC; Garcia, MC; Riera, FR; and Kenney, RM. 1991. Evaluation of measures taken by ultrasonography and calipers to estimate testicular volume and predict daily sperm output in the stallion. *J. Reprod. Fertility*, Suppl. 44: 99-105.

CHAPTER **33**

Training the Stallion To Breed

Puberty in the stallion has been defined as the ability to produce an ejaculate containing at least 50 million spermatozoa of which 10 percent are motile. This has been shown to occur at approximately 15 to 24 months, depending upon the season of the year when colts were born. Those colts born early in the year might, in fact, achieve puberty in the following spring or summer whereas those born later in the season may be closer to two years of

age at the time of puberty. Certainly colts and fillies should not be housed together after one year of age because there is a chance of the young colts impregnating the young fillies.

Training the young stallion to breed is extremely critical. Stallions should be allowed to show aggressiveness but should not be allowed to endanger any of the personnel. Typically, the young stallion is quite naive to the

Stallion handlers should be experienced

breeding process. Many young horses will mount without an erection and might even mount the front of the mare instead of the rear. This requires an experienced mare holder to assist in positioning the stallion properly on top of the mare.

Young horses should not be disciplined harshly for making mistakes during the breeding process. Generally, once a stallion has experienced ejaculation during collection or breeding, he will gain confidence, and after a few matings will complete the ejaculatory process with few mistakes. Once a stallion has learned the proper way to mount, enter the mare, and ejaculate, then the stallion handler can begin to discipline the stallion if needed. Often, personnel who handle stallions are afraid of the stallions and overcompensate with excessive discipline. The stallion is generally capable of identifying fearful handlers and might become even more aggressive. Thus, it is best for only experienced and confident stallion handlers to train a young horse.

Safety in the Breeding Shed

Safety to the stallion and to the personnel is the most critical feature whether the stallion breeds naturally or has semen collected for artificial insemination. Being kicked by a mare during the breeding process is one of the major causes of low libido and abnormal sexual behavior. If the stallion is to mount a live mare, the mare should be properly restrained. In the Thoroughbred industry, where natural mating is most common, the types of restraint include a chain shank, a nose twitch, and boots on the hind feet of the mare. In addition, it is quite common for the front leg of the mare to be elevated during the mounting process. Once the stallion is on the mare and she is standing quietly, her front leg is lowered. Maiden mares experiencing their first breeding are often mounted by a tease stallion to discern the degree of receptivity. Once a mare is shown to be in good standing estrus, the breeding stallion is allowed to mount.

Another type of restraint is a scotch hobble, in which a soft cotton rope is placed around the mare's neck and the left leg is pulled forward such that the mare cannot kick during breeding.

Twitching the mare

For semen collection and artificial insemination, generally the stallion is mounted on a docile "jump" mare. This mare has been selected for her willingness to be mounted during estrus. Hock hobbles are the preferred restraint used on the jump mare. A rope pulley extending from the front legs to each of the hind legs allows the mare to move but prevents the mare from kicking the stallion. The ability to lead the mare while she is wearing hobbles is an advantage when breeding stallions that have low sex drives. The additional excitement of following a mare stimulates an erection and produces a desire by the stallion to mount.

Having properly trained personnel in the breeding shed is extremely important for safety and accomplishing the breeding process. Typically, in a natural-mating program there are one or two personnel who handle the mare, a stallion handler, and an additional person who assists the stallion in entering the mare. With artificial insemination, a mare handler, stallion handler, and collector are needed. Obviously, if the stallion is

Elevating the mare's front leg

mounted on a phantom mare, then this eliminates the need for a mare handler, and the collection process can be accomplished with only two people.

Proper Positioning

The proper positioning of the mare and stallion is extremely important. In pasture breeding, it is quite common to test the mare's readiness by having the stallion approach her side and head before moving to the rear for mounting. With hand-mating, the stallion handler should allow the stallion to approach the mare from the side at about a 45- to 90-degree angle or approach the mare directly from the rear. It is often dangerous if the stallion handler allows the stallion to go directly to the mare's head. One common mistake is for the stallion handler to have the stallion parallel with the mare, then pull the stallion toward him to separate the mare and stallion. This generally results in the stallion kicking at the mare, which could injure the mare and/or mare handler. The stallion should always be backed away from the mare and then presented to the rear of the mare and allowed to mount.

In semen collection for artificial insemination, the semen collector should orchestrate the collection process. If a jump mare is being used, the stallion handler should approach the mare from the rear, and upon being told by the collector that the stallion has an erection, the stallion should be allowed to mount. The collector then deflects the stallion's penis into the artificial vagina and collects semen.

For those stallions with low libido, allowing the stallion to approach the mare's side or front is sometimes stimulating.

An artificial vagina used to collect semen

Other types of stimulation can include leading the mare slowly or placing another mare alongside the jump mare. If the stallion requires more than two mounts before ejaculation, then changes need to be made. This might include changes in the temperature and pressure of the artificial vagina or providing the stallion with another

Approaching the mare's front can stimulate a stallion with low libido

mare in estrus. Those stallions that readily obtain an erection and mount the phantom mare are certainly most desirable.

Handling the Stallion

The majority of stallions on large commercial breeding farms are handled with great care and skill. In contrast, stallions on smaller farms handled by personnel not used to dealing with stallions often are mishandled. One typical mistake is allowing someone who shows obvious fear to handle the stallion. This either results in the stallion endangering the handler and personnel or, in some cases, over-correction and rough treatment of the stallion. The stallion should be handled with a 20-foot leather lead-shank that has a short chain. The chain portion should be long enough to thread down one side of the halter and be connected to the ring on the opposite side. Place the chain in the stallion's mouth over the tongue. A slight tug on the stallion's shank will cause the stallion to pay immediate attention and respect the stallion handler. Certainly, one should not be overly aggressive with this method of restraint because it is possible to damage the stallion's mouth or tongue. Other handlers prefer to place the chain underneath the stallion's chin. This has the

A muzzle to prevent biting

unfortunate disadvantage of causing the stallion to jerk and raise his head. The third option is to place the chain over the stallion's nose, which many breeders seem to prefer. However, if the stallion needs to be reprimanded severely during the breeding process, this could cause some damage to the bridge of the stallion's nose.

The stallion handler should allow the stallion to be aggressive and not discourage the stallion from bellowing or obtaining an erection. However, in no case should the stallion be allowed to endanger the handler or personnel. The correct position for the stallion handler is standing beside the stallion with contact between the handler's right elbow and the stallion's shoulder. The handler should not be in front of the stallion as this puts the handler in the position of being jumped on if the stallion bolts. If the stallion rears, then use of a long stud shank will prevent the stallion from breaking away. Once the stallion lands, the handler can gather the stallion and regroup. One common mistake is for the handler to pull on the stallion when he is in the air, which in most cases causes the stallion to rear higher and might, in fact, cause the stallion to fall over.

The best approach is to allow the stallion to obtain an erection prior to being presented to the mare. If, however, the stallion requires more sexual stimulus than just proximity to the mare, the stallion should be presented to the mare's buttock or flank area. If the stallion comes alongside the mare, the handler should be sure to back the stallion away from the mare prior to allowing the stallion to mount. Another common mistake is for the handler to pull the stallion away from the mare in a way that places the stallion's hind end against the mare. In most cases the stallion will kick at the mare if he is in such a position. This certainly is dangerous and could cause harm to the mare or to the mare handler.

Stallions that have developed the bad habit of biting should be muzzled during the breeding process. The preferred type of muzzle is a leather one that snaps onto the halter. This is much more preferable than continual jerking of the stallion's head to prevent him from biting at the mare. With the use of a muzzle, the stallion still is able to sniff and touch but not bite the mare or the stallion handler.

AT A GLANCE

◆ A stallion kicked during breeding can develop low libido or abnormal sexual behavior.

◆ In the Thoroughbred industry mares often are restrained in some manner during breeding.

◆ Proper positioning of the stallion and mare is extremely important.

◆ Some stallions require extra stimuli before they will breed.

◆ A mare should be washed and her tailed wrapped before breeding to prevent contamination to the stallion.

In some extreme cases, it is necessary to keep the stallion handler out of the stallion's view. This is particularly true of stallions with abnormal sexual behavior or perhaps very young stallions who are disturbed easily by the movement of the stallion handler or collector. This is best accomplished by placing blinkers on the stallion's head. These keep the stallion's vision directly in front toward the mare and not toward the handler or collector.

Patience in proper training of the stallion will result in normal sexual behavior throughout the stallion's life.

Training To a Phantom

Proper training of a stallion to mount a phantom mare is quite important. The ideal situation is for the stallion to be presented to a tease mare, obtain an erection, maintain the erection during the washing process, then immediately mount the phantom upon presentation. If stallions are taught the process of mounting a phantom mare and have been properly handled, these stallions will continue to mount a phantom mare and have semen collected throughout their reproductive life.

Studies conducted at Colorado State University determined what percentage of stallions would mount the phantom. These stallions were mature stallions that had previously experienced semen collection with an artificial vagina. The three treatment groups were: 1) presented to the phantom without any stimulus from a mare; 2) presented to a tease mare, and once an erection was obtained, presented to the phantom; and 3) presented to the tease mare, and upon obtaining an erection, the tease mare was placed parallel to the phantom mare. Five of 10 stallions in group one, four of 10 stallions in group two, and eight of 10 stallions in group three mounted the phantom and ejaculated the first time.

Training to the phantom should be done during the time that the stallion has the highest sex drive, which is generally in the middle of the breeding season. Although many breeders would like to train their stallions to the phantom prior to the breeding season, this is the time of year when sexual behavior is lowest.

We would suggest that a stallion be presented to a tease mare, and upon obtaining an erection, be presented to the phantom. If after several sessions the stallion has failed to mount the phantom, then the tease mare should be positioned parallel to the phantom as an added stimulus. It is important that the stallion be positioned at an approximately 45-degree angle to the phantom and allowed to reach over the phantom and tease the mare. This generally results in the stallion becoming quite aggressive and, eventually, mounting the phantom. Generally, the stallion rears and must be directed on the phantom. If the stallion is positioned too far to the rear of the phantom, he will more than likely mount the tease mare

Breeding to a phantom

and not the phantom. In many cases, once the stallion learns to mount the phantom and ejaculate on a regular basis, the tease mare positioned beside the phantom can be eliminated. However, if stallions are experiencing difficulty in mounting the phantom or difficulty in ejaculating once mounted on a phantom, then occasionally positioning the tease mare beside the phantom can help.

Breeders commonly ask if something should be put on the phantom to make the stallion mount. The answer is nothing. Placing estrus mare urine on the phantom increases sniffing and flehmen but does not encourage mounting.

Preparation of the Mare

Preparation of the mare for natural breeding or semen collection is important to prevent contaminating the stallion. For either natural mating or semen collection, the tail of the mare should be wrapped so that no tail hairs are visible. This can be accomplished using gauze, leg wraps, velcro wraps, or tube socks. The material should be taped so that the wrap will not come off during breeding. The vulva and buttocks area then should be washed with clean water or water containing a disinfectant such as an iodine solution. This can be accomplished using cotton or paper towels. Any area where the stallion might touch the mare should be cleaned thoroughly. It is important to work from the lips of the vulva toward the outside of the buttocks. It is helpful if a string is tied to the mare's tail so that once the stallion is mounted, the tail can be pulled away from the vulva area.

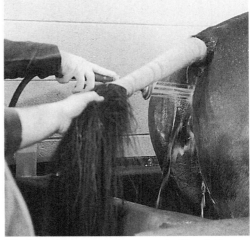

Washing the mare after wrapping her tail

Preparation of the Stallion

For natural mating, the stallion is generally washed before and after breeding. Excessive use of antiseptics or antibacterials should be avoided since overuse of these compounds results in destruction of the natural bacterial flora of the stallion's penis. Once this occurs, then opportunistic bacteria invade the stallion's penis. Warm water usually is sufficient for washing the stallion prior to and after breeding. In an artificial insemination program, the stallion is only washed before the collection process.

Stallion Management

G eneral considerations for good stallion management are
maintenance of the stallion in excellent health and a stress-
free environment that promotes normal sexual behavior
and sperm production. The size and construction of housing for the
stallion is generally a matter of personal preference. However, stallions should not be maintained in complete isolation but should be
able to see mares and other stallions. The type of housing used for
stallions in Central Kentucky would appear to be ideal. The majority of these stallions are maintained in a barn containing several
stallions, but each stallion has its own paddock separated from
adjacent paddocks by double fencing. This allows a stallion to have

considerable exercise
and interaction with
other stallions.

Exercise

The requirements for
exercise vary consider-
ably with the individual
stallion. Some stallions,
given the opportunity, **Exercise requirements differ for individual**
will exercise freely to **stallions**

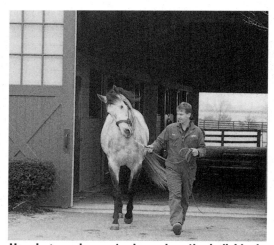
Housing requirements depend on the individual

the point of weight loss. Lazy, more complacent stallions might have to be force-exercised by lunging or hot walking. Exercise maintains a stallion in good body condition so that he does not become too fat. Excess fat on a stallion will insulate the testicles and could affect semen quality. However, the major reason for exercise is to prevent boredom and maintain a good mental attitude and sex drive. Signs of boredom can include stall weaving, cribbing, and aggressive behavior. Some less-aggressive stallions can be maintained in a barn that also houses mares. At Colorado State University, stallions are housed in 12 by 12-foot stalls and alternate being turned out in 12 by 36-foot runs. Many farms invest significant money to ensure the safety and comfort of the stallion, as well as to provide attractive surroundings for promotion of their stallion.

Nutrition

The nutritional requirements of the stallion vary, depending upon his size, condition, work load, and temperament. During the breeding season, the work load for a stallion is greater than that of a performance horse, and, therefore, the stallion should be fed as an animal under heavy work conditions. This would include a good quality roughage at 2 percent to 3 percent of body weight, as well as 0.5 percent to 1 percent of a grain ration. An alternative would include adequate pasture supplemented by a good-quality hay, grain, and salt-and-mineral mix. During the non-breeding season, the stallion generally can be given maintenance ration. Typically, breeding stallions are overfed, which can affect their sex drives and seminal quality. The need for vitamin supplementation has not been documented for the stallion. In fact, supplementation of vitamins A and E had no effect on sperm production. Stallions also should be placed on a routine vaccination and deworming schedule. It is important that the stallion be given proper hoof and dental care as well.

The Older Stallion

It is difficult to define exactly when a stallion should be placed in the category of "older" as behavioral and testicular changes occur at various times in individual stallions. Some stallions show significant changes by 12 years of age whereas other stallions remain unchanged even at 20. A thorough breeding soundness examination should be performed on stallions each year, particularly as they get older, to determine if significant changes have occurred. This information will allow proper management of a stallion during his mature years. This might include a change in breeding frequency or number of mares that are booked to the stallion. The goal is to maximize the stallion's performance each year.

One common problem in the older stallion is the

Older stallions have special requirements

inability to maintain good body condition. This might require the assistance of an equine nutritionist, who could evaluate and perhaps fortify the stallion's diet so the stallion is more likely to maintain weight. It also might result in a change of housing so that the stallion does not exercise as vigorously. Another problem detected in mature stallions is soreness in the legs and back that might impact their ability to breed mares. If a stallion is used in an artificial insemination program, this can be corrected by adjusting the height of the phantom mare so that the stallion is comfortable when mounted on the phantom. Horses with severe laminitis or hock problems might require a phantom lowered to where the stallion's front legs are only off the ground a few inches. Another possibility is giving the stallion a pain killer prior to breeding.

Loss of libido in older stallions is not uncommon. This is typically true of stallions that have become sexually satiated toward the latter part of the breeding season. This could require a decrease in the stallion's book or a shortened breeding season. A stallion also might require more stimulus, such as several mares of various sizes and colors in estrus. There is always a great desire to enhance a stallion's sexual behavior with hormone therapy.

As discussed previously, it is extremely important to analyze the stallion's hormonal profile prior to injection of additional hormones. Furthermore, consultation with a veterinarian is extremely important. With proper management, it is possible to extend the reproductive life of the mature stallion and allow him to perform to his maximum.

When To Castrate

Obviously, the decision whether to castrate a stallion is an extremely important one. Generally, only a very small percentage of male horses should remain stallions if breeders want to improve a particular breed's genetics. Thus, very careful selection should take place in deciding which of the young colts to maintain as stallions.

Other considerations are the economics of maintaining a stallion.

Once stallions experience puberty, they generally become quite aggressive and might need to be maintained in separate facilities. Certainly, they will need to be separated from mares. Some breeders who are not interested in showing or racing may decide to maintain their colts as a group in a pasture or paddock until the animals are several years old. The breeder always takes a chance that one of these young colts will become injured when it spars with its mates.

Once the breeder has decided that the young stallion is not of sufficient quality to be used as a breeding animal, then castration should be done immediately. Some breeders prefer to castrate their colts as weanlings whereas others are more apt to castrate their colts as yearlings. The advantage of allowing the colt to reach 12 to 18 months is to allow further time for evaluation of the young stallion to determine whether he is truly a stallion prospect. In addition, it is sometimes easier to castrate a stallion as a yearling because his testicles are bigger and have descended into the scrotum. Stallions that display extreme aggressiveness during showing or racing competition also could warrant castration. In addition, some racehorses that have large testicles experience pain during training and racing, possibly affecting performance.

The recuperation period after castration depends somewhat upon the horse's age. Obviously, the younger the colt is castrated, the less traumatic the process and the quicker the recovery. However, generally it requires seven to 10 days for recovery from castration. It is important to provide the horse with exercise during this recovery period to minimize swelling to the scrotum. In addition, it is important to monitor the health

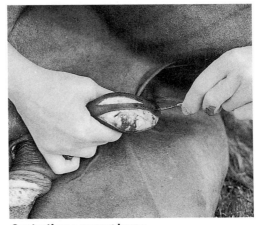

Castrating a young horse

and attitude of the castrated horse during this recuperation period.

One commonly asked question is, "Why do some geldings retain stallion-like behavior after castration?" This is often blamed on the veterinarian leaving a portion of the testicle within the scrotum. The term "proud cut" refers to a gelding in which part of the tail of the epididymis, or any portion of the epididymis, is left in the horse after the testicles have been removed. Contrary to some claims, the tail of the epididymis does not produce testosterone nor cause stallion-like behavior after castration. A gelding continuing to have stallion-like characteristics after castration is probably the result of learned behavior and is not hormonally controlled. Generally, the older the stallion at castration, the more likely it is that the horse will retain some stallion-like characteristics after castration. These stallion-like characteristics will more than likely subside a few months after castration. However, it is possible for a gelding to continue to have certain types of stallion characteristics even several years after castration, particularly if he was castrated late in life and if he was a very aggressive stallion prior to castration.

Breeders should wait at least 30 days before turning a recently gelding out with a group of mares. The Colorado State University conducted a study in which stallions were castrated and then continued to be collected with an artificial vagina for several weeks after castration. Within a week after castration, the ejaculates contained only fluid from the accessory sex glands, which contained an extremely low number of spermatozoa, all of which were dead. It is unlikely that, even as early as a week after castration, a gelding would be able to impregnate a mare. However, it is probably safest to wait at least 30 days, and, hopefully, by that time the sex drive of the gelding will decrease to the point he will not be interested in mounting and mating a mare.

Facilities for Breeding

The type of facility used for breeding depends upon the type of breeding (natural mating or artificial insemination) and the number of mares to be bred. The use of a clean pasture with good footing might be adequate for hand-mating of a stallion to a relatively small number of mares. In most cases, however, a breeding shed that is covered, is well-lighted, and has good footing is desirable. A typical breeding area should be at least 400 square feet (20 feet by 20 feet) and preferably as much as 40 feet by 40 feet. The primary consideration should always be safety of the animal and personnel. The doors into the breeding shed should be at least 10-feet wide and 14-feet high, with a 14-foot ceiling. The flooring of the breeding shed is a matter of personal preference but might include such elaborate material as rubber bricks or shredded rubber, tanbark, or Fibar. If inexpensive materials such as wood shavings, sawdust, pea gravel, or sand are used, then the area should be dampened to minimize dust. The breeding shed also should include a raised area so that animals of disproportionate size can be mated. Furthermore, the area of the breeding shed should include a padded tease rail for stimulation of the stallion, an area for washing the stallion's penis, and an area for breeding. One should consider a flow pattern that would minimize any injury to the personnel.

For artificial insemination, the breeding shed should include a phantom that is situated to allow placement of a mare parallel to the phantom. This is sometimes needed to encourage the stallion to mount the phantom. A head should be placed on the phantom for two reasons: 1) to prevent the stallion from going over the front of the phantom, and 2) to provide a possible stimulus to the stallion. If possible, a window from the breeding shed to the labo-

A well-constructed breeding shed

ratory is desirable. This also can include a way to pass the semen sample into the laboratory without tracking in dirt. Some breeding sheds also include an observation area for visitors. Stallions slow to obtain erections and mount mares sometimes are stimulated by being housed in a small, safe enclosure within the breeding shed so that they can observe other stallions breeding.

For artificial inseminations, mares should be placed in stocks, and these stocks should be close to the laboratory. The most common mistake in constructing stocks is making them too long or too wide. Breeding stocks are best made out of pipe and should be six-feet long and approximately 30-inches wide. The flooring in the breeding shed should be a non-skid surface that can be disinfected. It is best to have a place beside or in front of the mares where the foals can be held while the mare is being inseminated.

The laboratory for semen evaluation should be a dedicated facility that is clean and dust free. Space should be available for storage of the artificial vaginas and liners and room for preparation of the artificial vagina. In addition, the lab should have enough counter space to hold a sperm counter, microscope, and possibly incubators. The equipment should be arranged in such a way that the artificial vagina would be brought into the laboratory, the collection bottle removed, and a clean specimen cup or graduate cylinder taken from the incubator for measurement of gel-free volume. The samples then should be evaluated for motility using a phase-contrast microscope and some form of counting device to determine the number of sperm per milliliter. If possible, windows in the laboratory should face the palpation shed so that one can communicate with the staff. A slide-through window allows the semen sample to be passed from the laboratory into the insemination room.

Sexual Behavior of the Stallion

Normal Sexual Behavior

Not until one has had the agony of handling a stallion with abnormal sexual behavior does that person truly appreciate a stallion with normal sexual behavior. Breeders and veterinarians who have stood for hours waiting for a stallion to obtain an erection and ejaculate can certainly appreciate a stallion with good sexual behavior. Normal sexual behavior includes obtaining an erection within two to three minutes of being exposed to a mare in estrus. This stallion is then able to maintain that erection, and when presented to the mare, mount, and ejaculate after only one or two mounts. Stallions that have normal sexual behavior can be hand-mated to one to three mares per day or ejaculate into an artificial vagina every other day throughout the entire breeding season.

Masturbation

Many breeders are concerned when they see a stallion with an erection moving his penis up toward the body wall and down. This is commonly referred to as masturbation. The reason breeders become concerned with this behavior is that they think the stallion will become sexually satiated and, therefore, his sex drive will decrease and/or a stallion will ejaculate and sperm numbers will be lower the next time the stallion is asked to breed or ejaculate into an

It is normal for stallions to masturbate

artificial vagina. Sue McDonnell, a professor at the University of Pennsylvania, has observed both domesticated and free-running stallions and noted that masturbation occurs with equal frequency in free-running and confined stallions at the rate of once every one to three hours in undisturbed animals. However, ejaculation is very seldom observed. The incidence of spontaneous erection or masturbation does not appear to be associated with confinement nor does it affect fertility.

Many breeders and veterinarians become disturbed with this behavior and attempt to inhibit the behavior by putting a stallion ring on the stallion's penis, which prevents erection, and/or strapping a brush on the stallion's belly to discourage movement of the penis against the belly of the stallion. Both of these techniques are extremely detrimental to the stallion's well being. Many stallions have been rendered infertile through the use of a stallion ring and/or brush on the belly.

In most cases, this behavior should not cause alarm. It should be considered normal for a sexually mature stallion.

Frequency of Breeding

One of the most commonly asked question is: How many mares can a stallion breed? If the stallion has normal testis size, the most important factor determining the number of mares a stallion can breed is his sexual behavior. Stallions in a pasture mating system have been known to mate several times a day. In a study by Bristol (1982), researchers demonstrated that the criterion for a stallion breeding a mare in pasture is the mare's willingness to stand. In this study, a mare often was bred several days before ovulation. Thus, the misconception that a stallion is smart enough to breed a mare once only at the time of ovulation is not substanti-ated. The frequency at which stallions breed in a pasture is considerably high-er than that of those that are hand-mated. The exact reason for this is unknown but could be due to a variety of mares in estrus at a given time and the lack of any manmade restraint. Apparently the restraint we impose when hand-mating or artificially col-lecting semen alters sexual behavior. Because of the increased frequency of breeding during pasture mating, most stallions are housed with no more than 50 mares.

AT A GLANCE

- ◆ A normal stallion will obtain an erection within two to three minutes of exposure to a mare in estrus.
- ◆ A normal stallion can be hand-mated to one to three mares a day or ejaculate into an artificial vagina every other day throughout the breeding season.
- ◆ Masturbation is normal in domesticated and free-running stallions.
- ◆ Mismanagement is the most common cause of abnormal sexual behavior.

The Thoroughbred is the largest horse breed not allowing artificial insemination. All of the mares in this breed are hand-mated by nat-ural breeding. A stallion with normal-sized testicles and good sexual behavior can be used once or twice a day and, in many cases, three times a day during the peak of the breeding season. It is important to space the breed-ings throughout the day such that some mares are bred in the morning and some in the after-noon; if three mat-ings are required per day, the last matings are done in the evening. The typical number of mares mated to a Thoroughbred stal-lion would be

Frequency of breeding depends on the individual stallion

approximately 40 to 50 although some of the popular Thoroughbred stallions are breeding 100 or more mares in one breeding season, and those stallions that service mares in both the Northern Hemisphere and Southern Hemisphere may breed 200 or more mares each year by natural mating.

Artificial Insemination

The majority of breeds allow artificial insemination, which has many advantages for the stallion. With artificial insemination, a stallion can be collected once every other day, and on the average 10 to 15 mares can be bred with each collection. The other important

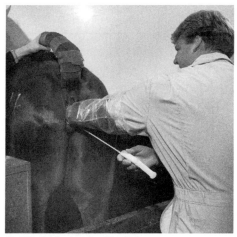

advantage of artificial insemination is that the stallion can be mounted on a phantom mare, thus preventing any chance of the stallion being kicked during the mating process. Additionally, the semen can be added to an extender containing antibiotics and, thus, minimize any chance of infecting the mare with bacteria that might be contained in the semen. With

Artificial insemination of a mare

artificial insemination, the number of mares that can be bred within a given year is increased, with a book of 100 to 200 mares in a breeding season being quite feasible.

Common Behavioral Problems

One of the most common causes of infertility in stallions is abnormal sexual behavior. The most common cause of abnormal sexual behavior is mismanagement. Therefore, it is extremely important to train a stallion properly to ensure that he develops normal behavior. Ideally, stallions should not be used for breeding until at least three years of age. This has nothing to do with lack of testicular tissue or sperm numbers but rather with development of good sexual behavior. Those stallions used at two years of age are more likely to develop such bad habits as mounting without an erection, failure to obtain an erection, and excessive biting of the mare. Many breeders are anxious to obtain offspring from their

Stallions should not be isolated

young stallions and, thus, attempt to breed a few mares when the stallions are two years old. If this is to occur, then the breeder should be very aware of any indications of abnormal behavior. Certainly, a two-year-old stallion should not be used for more than five or 10 mares, regardless of his apparent maturity and sexual behavior.

Other management practices that could lead to abnormal sexual behavior in older stallions include overuse, particularly in the fall and winter, unnecessary roughness, housing stallions in complete isolation, lack of exercise, and, most importantly, being kicked during the breeding process. Stallions certainly should not be allowed to endanger any of the personnel, but excessive roughness during the breeding process can discourage the stallion and induce poor sexual behavior. Stallions should be housed where they can see other horses. Housing a stallion in complete isolation can result in poor libido. Stallions that experience difficulty in obtaining an erection should be exposed to a variety of mares in estrus and given the opportunity to select the mare that is stimulatory. Furthermore, these stallions should have a blood sample taken and have a variety of hormones measured to determine if the lack of sex drive is due to a hormonal dysfunction. Stallions that experience difficulty in mounting and entering the mare might be suffering from physical pain in the hocks, stifle, or back area. A veterinarian should examine these stallions to determine if there is any abnormality resulting in this mounting difficulty. Another possible reason for a stallion failing to enter a mare is his fear of being kicked. Generally, stallions that have been kicked are psychologically impotent. Retraining this type of stallion is difficult and generally requires mounting the stallion on a phantom and collecting semen or mounting the stallion on a mare in estrus that he has selected. This approach improves the stallion's confidence and, in most cases, will restore his ability to mount, enter, and ejaculate. One of the most common types of abnormal behavior is mounting, entering, and thrusting but dismounting prior to ejaculation. Again, these stallions generally have been kicked during the breeding process and associate the act of ejaculation with being kicked. Once again, these stallions must be retrained to gain confidence before they will establish normal sexual behavior.

References

Bristol, F. 1982. Breeding behavior of a stallion at pasture with 20 mares in synchronized oestrus. *J. Reprod. Fertility*, Suppl. 32: 71-77.

What Affects Reproductive Performance?

Season

One major factor affecting reproductive performance of the stallion is season. Although the stallion does not show dramatic seasonal changes as the mare does, there are some very distinct hormonal, behavioral, and physiological changes that occur during the fall and winter. The stallion, like the mare, is considered a long-day breeder, and peak sperm output occurs from April to June, corresponding with the mare's physiologic (natural) breeding season. Alterations in hormone levels cause the seasonal changes in the stallion. During the fall and winter when the day length decreases, GnRH secretion from the hypothalamus and LH and FSH secretion from the pituitary are suppressed. This suppression of the hypothalamus and pituitary results in lowered levels of testosterone from the testes. The result is lowered numbers of spermatozoa during the fall and winter.

Sperm production declines in fall and winter

The number of Sertoli

cells in the testes is also influenced by season. Sertoli cell numbers in testes of adult stallions are greater during the breeding season than during the nonbreeding season. Approximately half the sperm numbers are obtained in an ejaculate collected during January as compared with an ejaculate collected during the peak of the breeding season (April to May). In addition, the volume of the ejaculate is reduced by approximately 50 percent in the fall and winter, but the semen quality, based on progressive motility, does not change throughout the year. This maintenance of consistent semen quality throughout the year is contingent upon the stallion voiding the excess spermatozoa in the urine. Those stallions that accumulate an excessive number of spermatozoa in the storage areas could have poor spermatozoal motility in the initial ejaculates after several days or weeks of sexual rest.

Season also has a dramatic effect on sexual behavior. The number of mounts required per ejaculation and the time required for a stallion to obtain an erection, mount the mare, and ejaculate is more than doubled in the fall and winter compared with summer. Although stallions produce sperm throughout the year, continued attempts to breed stallions year round might adversely affect sexual behavior.

Artificial photoperiod has been used to hasten the onset of peak sperm production. Stallions placed under 16 hours of light beginning December 1 will have maximum sperm production in February and March, as opposed to the usual peak production of sperm in May and June. This is only an advantage if one wants to breed most of the mares early in the year and

A stallion under lights

shorten the breeding season

because sperm output of stallions exposed to artificial light declines earlier in the breeding season than it does for stallions under natural photoperiod.

Breeding the same stallion in both the Northern Hemisphere and Southern Hemisphere has increased with some of the more popular Thoroughbred stallions. These stallions are asked to work year round and are exposed mostly to days of long photoperiod. Studies have shown that exposure of a stallion to 16 hours of light for an entire year still results in seasonal changes in sexual behavior and seminal characteristics.

AT A GLANCE

◆ Peak sperm output occurs from April to June; sperm production declines during the fall and winter.

◆ Stallions do not become sexually mature until age five or six.

◆ It is not advisable to breed two-year-old colts.

◆ Sperm numbers in the ejaculate correlate directly to testicle size.

◆ Anabolic steroids can decrease testis size, sperm output, and semen quality.

Age

The number of sperm the stallion is capable of producing is also influenced by the stallion's age. Too often a young horse is over-used and an older stallion is under-used. A stallion's age, because of its effect on testis development and function, is one of the most important factors affecting sperm production and output and, thus, number of mares that can be bred. Number of sperm available for ejaculation depends upon sperm reserves in the tail of the epididymis, deferent ducts, and ampullae. Sperm reserves of sexually rested stallions increase with advancing age. Approximately twice the number of spermatozoa are present in the body of the epididymis from 10- to 16-year-old stallions than from two- to four-year-olds.

Seminal characteristics were compared among stallions ages 2, 3, 4, and 6 and 9 to 16. Semen volume and sperm numbers were lower in ejaculates obtained from two- to three-year-old stallions than those from 4 to 6 and 9 to 16. Most of the seminal characteristics were similar between stallions 4 to 6 and 9 to 16. It would appear that stallions do not sexually mature until approximately five to six

Age influences sperm production

years of age. The number of sperm produced in a horse of any age is related to testicular size, which in stallions appears to increase steadily until approximately 12 years of age. Although many two-year-old stallions have sufficient sperm to breed several mares, we recommend that the stallion not be used as a two-year-old due to the possibility of acquiring abnormal sexual behavior. Even a three-year-old stallion should have the number of mares he breeds monitored carefully. It is best to evaluate the stallion's breeding potential each year prior to the breeding season to predict how many mares he can handle successfully. This is particularly true once stallions are 14 to 16 years of age.

Testicular Size and Consistency

Sperm numbers in the ejaculate correlate directly to the size of the stallion's testicles. Approximately 55 percent of the variation in sperm production can be accounted for by testicle size. Stallion managers and veterinarians should measure the stallion's testicles at least once a year and, preferably, once a month during the breeding season. There are two methods of measuring stallion testicles: a set of calipers (Animal Reproduction Systems, Chino, California) or ultrasonographically measuring the stallion's testicles and using a formula published by Love et al. (1991) that calculates the volume of testicular tissue. This equation can be used to predict the number of spermatozoa the stallion is capable of producing. A stallion's testicular size does not change due to ejaculation frequency but does change due to season. Mean scrotal width decreases from 109 mm in July to 90 mm in November.

Not only should the testicles be measured but their consistency or tone should be assessed. Both testicles should be positioned in the scrotum in a horizontal position. Each testicle should be positioned between the thumb and fingers by push-

Measuring a stallion's testicles

ing the opposite testicle upward. Evidence of abnormal conditions should be detected, such as soft, mushy testes; excessively hard testes; ventral ribbing; rotation of testes in the scrotum; and lobulation and constriction bands. Testicular abnormalities that are of concern can include a soft, mushy-feeling testicle. This could possibly indicate that the testicles have degenerated or that the stallion received drugs such as anabolic steroids or testosterone. In contrast, very firm, rough-feeling testicles also are undesirable. These characteristics also could indicate testicular degeneration.

Stallions that have only one descended testicle are called cryptorchid stallions and the number of sperm they can produce is reduced. Although the descended testicle can compensate by growing, the one testicle will never increase to a size that approximates the testicles of a normally developed stallion. In addition, stallions with only one testicle descended are more likely to develop aggressiveness and other forms of abnormal sexual behavior. If the

Top sire A.P. Indy was born a cryptorchid

testes and epididymis are both within the abdomen, the horse is termed a complete abdominal cryptorchid. Retained testes do not produce spermatozoa because of the elevated temperature within the body cavity.

Testicular descent into the scrotum is a very complex process. Therefore, causes of abnormal descent can be varied and difficult to document. Mechanical causes for abnormal testicular descent in stallions include overstretching of the gubernaculum cord, insufficient abdominal pressure, inadequate growth of the gubernaculum and related structures, inadequate dilation of the vaginal ring and inguinal canal for passage of the testes, and displacement of the testes into the pelvic cavity. Several studies have suggested a genetic basis for cryptorchidism in the horse. However, definitive studies to determine the genetic basis for cryptorchidism in the stallion have not been conducted. Many breeds discourage the use of a cryptorchid stallion because of the possible inheritance of this developmental problem. For horses with one retained testis and one scrotal testis, a search for and removal of the retained testis should proceed castration of the descended testis.

Frequency of Ejaculation

Frequency of ejaculation is one of the most important factors affecting sperm output. As the frequency of ejaculation for artificial insemination or natural service increases, the number of spermatozoa per ejaculate decreases, providing frequency equals or exceeds one ejaculate every other day. If the stallion has an extremely high sex drive and can ejaculate several times per day, fertility could decline because he ejaculates insufficient numbers of sperm, particularly if used early in the breeding season.

A series of studies conducted to determine how often stallions could be used in a natural service program and an artificial insemination program demonstrated that the total number of sperm per ejaculate was the same whether stallions were collected six times per week or three times per week. In addition, the total sperm collected on a weekly basis was the same for stallions collected three versus six times per week. Based on these data, it was determined that collection frequency exceeding every other day will not result in more sperm per week. Thus, the most efficient collection schedule for a stallion in an artificial insemination program is once every other day (Pickett et al., 1989).

For a natural mating program, the number of mares that can be bred in a given day depends on the stallion's sexual behavior and testis size. Assuming the stallion has been bred at least once a day for 10 days, the number of spermatozoa in the ejaculate after this 10-day period is essentially what the stallion is capable of producing (daily sperm production). We know that approximately 100-500 million progressively motile spermatozoa are needed for maximum reproductive efficiency. Therefore, if the number of sperm in the stallion's ejaculate is several billion, then, more than likely, the limiting factor as to the number of mares the stallion can breed is based on his willingness to breed. Generally, stallions can be used once or twice a day in a natural breeding program and, possibly, three times per day for a limited period. Any time the stallion is given one or two days of sexual rest, sperm numbers will accumulate in his sperm reserve.

Hormone Injections

Anabolic steroids are testosterone-like hormones often given to young stallions in an attempt to increase muscle mass and size. Because all anabolic steroids have some testosterone-like properties, they have the ability to decrease LH secretion from the pituitary. This ultimately results in decreased stimulation of the testes by LH and a decrease in testosterone. Continued treatment of a stallion with anabolic steroids results in a decrease in testis size, sperm output, and semen quality. Anabolic steroid administration is particularly detrimental to young males prior to puberty (weanlings and yearlings). It is likely that if sufficient anabolic steroids are given to young horses prior to puberty, development of the testes will be impaired for life. In contrast, administering anabolic steroids to older stallions will

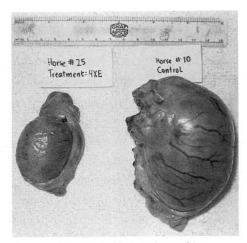

Horse #25
Treatment: 4XE

Horse #10
Control

A normal testis (right) and one from a stallion that received 2 mg of Equipoise per pound of body weight once every three weeks for 15 weeks

cause temporary changes in testis size, sperm output, and semen quality, but after cessation of treatment, testicular size, sperm output, and semen quality will improve in three to five months. Many times, stallions that have been shown or raced heavily have very poor testicular consistency and semen quality during their first breeding season but might improve in subsequent years. Needless to say, administration of anabolic steroids is not recommended for stallions at any age.

Testosterone injections have been advocated for stallions with low sex drive. However, studies have demonstrated that injection of testosterone into stallions also can have a negative effect on LH secretion. Once LH levels fall, testosterone produced by the testicles also is decreased. This, again, results in low levels of testosterone at the level of the testicle and decreased sperm production and semen quality. Furthermore, there is no strong evidence that injecting testosterone into a stallion will improve his sexual behavior. More appropriately, a stallion with poor sexual behavior should have blood drawn and hormonal levels measured. If, in fact, testosterone is lower than normal, then the gonadotropin-releasing hormone (GnRH) should be given. This hormone is more appropriate because it simulates normal hormonal events in a stallion. Upon injecting GnRH, the pituitary is stimulated to produce LH, which subsequently stimulates the testes to produce testosterone. A veterinarian should be consulted in determining the regimen for treating a stallion with GnRH. Typically, several pulses of GnRH are released in the stallion, under natural conditions, each day. Therefore, to simulate the natural secretion of GnRH, this hormone should be given several times per day.

Stallions used for racing or showing are often very aggressive and difficult to manage when around other stallions or mares. Thus, veterinarians are often asked: How can one suppress sexual behavior in the stallion temporarily during the training, racing, or showing events? Regu-Mate® is an orally active synthetic progesterone compound used to suppress estrous behavior in the mare. The mechanism in the mare is through suppression of LH levels. Regu-Mate® has been shown to suppress sexual behavior in the stallion. Administration of Regu-Mate® at twice the recommended dose for mares (approximately 20 ml/day) resulted in decreased sperm output, semen quality, and testis size after approximately 45 days of continued administration. Decreased LH secretion, however, was detected within a few days after the initiation of Regu-Mate® treatment. Other studies also have demonstrated an effect of Regu-Mate® on seminal

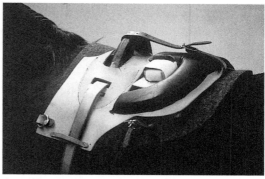

A stallion outfitted with a GnRH pump

characteristics. Breeders have stated that Regu-Mate® takes "the edge off the stallion," allowing stallions to be more manageable during training, racing, or showing.

The mechanism for decreased testis size, sperm output, and semen quality in stallions receiving Regu-Mate® appears to be the same as that of anabolic steroids and testosterone, i.e., the suppression in LH secretion. Breeders should be concerned with using Regu-Mate® on extremely young, prepubertal stallions as there is a possibility of suppressing development of the reproductive system. Treatment of older stallions appears to have only a temporary effect on these testicular and seminal characteristics, and these characteristics improve several months after treatment stops. Certainly, one should not attempt to administer Regu-Mate® and use the stallion as a breeding stallion at the same time.

References

Pickett, BW; Squires, EL; and McKinnon, AO. 1987. Procedures for collection, evaluation, and utilization of stallion semen for artificial insemination. *Colorado State Univ. Animal Reprod. Lab Bull.* No. 03.

Pickett, BW; Amann, RP; McKinnon, AO; Squires, EL; and Voss, JL. 1989. Management of the stallion for maximum reproductive efficiency, II. *Colorado State Univ. Animal Reprod. Lab Bull.* No. 05.

Love, CC, Garcia, MC, Riera, FR, and Kenney, RM. 1991. Evaluation of measures taken by ultrasonography and calipers to estimate testicular volume and predict daily sperm output in the stallion. *J. Reprod. Fertility.* Suppl. 44: 99.

Squires, EL; Badzinski, SL; Amann, RP; McCue, PM; and Nett, TM. 1997. Effects of altrenogest on total scrotal width, seminal characteristics, concentrations of LH and testosterone, and sexual behavior of stallions. *Theriogenology.* 48: 313-328.

Cooled and Frozen Semen

The acceptance of artificial insemination (AI) by the majority of breed registries dramatically affected the horse industry. However, the recent acceptance of cooled, transported semen by most breeds and the acceptance of frozen-thawed semen by some breeds will influence horse breeding even more in coming years. The ability to preserve semen in a cooled or frozen state provides more opportunity and flexibility for horse breeding.

The major advantage of cooled semen is eliminating the cost and stress of shipping a mare or a mare and foal to a breeding farm and reducing cash outlay for mare care. Leaving the mare at home also reduces the possibility of disease transmission through exposure of the mare or foal to a new environment.

The disadvantages of cooled semen are the costs to the mare owner of collecting, packaging, and shipping the semen container and the increased veterinary costs for mare examination and hormonal control of the mare's cycle. Also, some semen does not survive cooling and shipping.

Handling Cooled Semen

For proper handling of cooled semen, a laboratory equipped with clean equipment and supplies should be available. Initial handling and evaluation of semen is the same, whether the semen will be used immediately or whether it will be cooled. It is essential that the number of spermatozoa per milliliter be determined, as well as the percentage of spermatozoa that are progressively motile. Ideally, each shipment will contain 1 billion progressively motile spermatozoa. There are several factors to consider when packaging a dose of semen for shipment. The two most important factors are concentration of the spermatozoa per milliliter and the dilution of extender with semen. Samples that are too concentrated or too diluted result in poor viability and reduced fertility. A rule of thumb is to estimate the motility of the sample and determine the volume of semen needed to provide 1 billion progressively motile spermatozoa. Add this volume of raw semen to enough extender to provide

at least a 3:1 dilution (3 parts extender to 1 part semen) and/or dilute to a concentration of approximately 25 million motile spermatozoa per milliliter. Taking a volume of raw semen containing 1 billion motile spermatozoa and adding enough extender to provide a final volume of 40 ml, produces a concentration of 25 million motile spermatozoa/ml. However, if a dilution of 3:1 is not obtained, then more extender will have to be added.

The Equitainer, used to transport cooled semen

The semen packaging system that has been tested most extensively and one that is highly recommended is the Equitainer manufactured by Hamilton Thorne. This is a passive cooling unit that allows semen to be cooled at a slow rate from 37 degrees Celsius to 5 degrees Celsius. For shipment of semen, an extender composed of nonfat dried milk solids, glucose, and antibiotics should be used.

The extender, E-Z Mixin CST (Animal Reproduction Laboratories, Chino, Calif.), containing the antibiotic amikacin, is designed specifically for shipping equine semen. The E-Z Mixin CST should be added to the semen and the extended semen poured into a baby-bottle liner or a whirlpack bag. The excess air should be expressed out of the baby-bottle liner by twisting the top. The sealed bag of extended semen

AT A GLANCE

◆ Cooled and frozen semen provide more opportunity and flexibility for horse breeding.

◆ Advantages include eliminated shipping costs for the mare and reduced exposure to disease.

◆ Disadvantages include the cost of collecting and shipping semen and lower conception rates when using frozen semen.

containing 1 billion progressively motile spermatozoa then is placed into the specimen cup. The extended semen should be wrapped in one or two ballast bags to provide the appropriate total liquid volume of 120 to 170 milliliters. The specimen cup containing semen and ballast bags then is placed inside the isothermalizer, which is placed inside the Equitainer on top of the coolant cans. The coolant cans have been in a deep freeze for at least 24 hours prior to being placed in the Equitainer. The extended semen in the Equitainer will be cooled to 5 degrees Celsius during transit. An information sheet should be placed on top of the semen, which contains the stallion's name, date, time of seminal collection, date of seminal collection, volume of raw semen, volume of extender, type of extender used, and number of spermatozoa shipped per dose. The Equitainer is then shipped by commercial airlines or courier service.

Factors that affect the fertility of cooled semen include storage time, cooling rates, storage temperature, dilution, antibiotics, and timing of insemination. If properly diluted, semen from most stallions can be stored for 24 hours and for some stallions, 48 hours. Semen that is cooled too rapidly from 37 degrees Celsius to 5 degrees Celsius results in cold shock. Semen must be cooled very slowly (less than or equal to 3 degrees Celsius per minute) between the temperatures of 20 degrees Celsius and about 8 degrees Celsius. This is the temperature range of sperm's susceptibility to cold shock. Studies have shown that storage of semen is better at 5 degrees Celsius than at 0 degrees Celsius. Based on numerous studies, if semen is to be used within 12 hours of collection, it can be stored at either 20 degrees Celsius or 5 degrees Celsius. However, for storage longer than 12 hours, semen must be cooled slowly to 5 degrees Celsius. Storage at 4 to 5 degrees Celsius is better for maintenance of equine spermatozoa than at 0 degrees Celsius or 2 degrees Celsius.

Little information is available on the proper timing of insemination of cooled semen to maximize fertility. However, it is quite likely that timing of insemination of cooled semen is more critical than that of fresh semen. It is recommended that mares be inseminated with cooled semen within 24 hours prior to ovulation or within six hours after ovulation.

Frozen Semen

There are several advantages to using frozen semen over fresh or cooled semen:

1) Semen can be stored indefinitely in a liquid nitrogen container.

2) The breeding season can continue even when the stallion is at a performance event, ill, or recovering from an injury.

3) Differences in the breeding season between the Northern Hemisphere and Southern Hemisphere would not pose a problem.

4) The semen would only have to be shipped once to the breeding farm and would be available throughout the breeding season.

The major disadvantage with the use of frozen semen is the considerable technology and skill required for processing, packaging, freezing, and inseminating. The most serious disadvantage of frozen semen is the reduced pregnancy rates obtained with semen from most stallions. It is likely that as the technology improves, the use of frozen semen will increase and that of cooled semen will decrease. However, new and improved techniques are needed for minimizing the damage to semen during the freezing and thawing processes.

The major steps in freezing stallion spermatozoa include dilution, centrifugation to remove seminal plasma and concentration of the spermatozoa, resuspension in a freezing extender containing a cryoprotectant, cooling to -120 degrees Celsius, and storage in liquid nitrogen at -196 degrees Celsius. Success in cryopreservation of spermatozoa depends on a complex series of interactions among extenders, cryoprotectants, and cooling and warming rates.

The major components that damage spermatozoa during the freezing and thawing process include ice crystal formation and the toxic effects of the extender components. The goal is to dehydrate the spermatozoa successfully during the cooling process using salts, sugars, and cryoprotectants such as glycerol without exposing the spermatozoa to these components for too long. Most equine semen is packaged in 0.5 ml straws or 4 or 5 ml straws prior to cooling over liquid nitrogen vapor. Once frozen, the semen is maintained in liquid

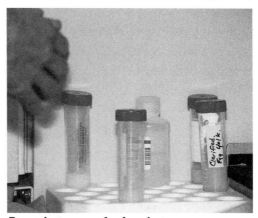

Preparing semen for freezing

nitrogen at a temperature of -196 degrees Celsius. At this temperature the semen can be maintained in a viable state indefinitely.

The major factor affecting the fertility of frozen-thawed equine spermatozoa appears to be the individual stallion. For unknown reasons, some stallions have spermatozoa that withstand the freezing and thawing process better than others. In general, if semen of 100 different stallions were frozen, 25 would have frozen-thawed semen that provides a pregnancy rate of approximately 40 percent to 60 percent per cycle, 50 would have frozen-thawed spermatozoa that provide a pregnancy rate of 25 percent to 40 percent per cycle, and 25 would have extremely low fertility with frozen-thawed spermatozoa (less than 25 percent per cycle).

Tremendous effort is going into developing techniques for freezing and thawing equine spermatozoa. It is likely that tremendous progress will be made in the next decade in developing these technologies. Development of procedures for assessing damage to the spermatozoon after freezing and thawing is an important prerequisite to the development of techniques for freezing equine spermatozoa. Unfortunately, spermatozoal motility of frozen-thawed equine spermatozoa is not a good indicator of fertility. Therefore, other laboratory tests are needed to assess the viability of frozen-thawed equine spermatozoa. These tests could be used to identify spermatozoa that have been severely damaged during the freezing and thawing process, thus preventing the breeder from using damaged spermatozoa. Numerous laboratory tests are expected to be developed to evaluate the various techniques for freezing and thawing equine spermatozoa.

Glossary

Abdomen — Area between the chest and pelvis containing the viscera.

Abortion — Expulsion of a fetus between 50 and 300 days of gestation.

Abortion storm — Loss of fetuses from multiple mares during a narrow time frame on a single farm or geographic area.

Accessory sex glands — Seminal vesicles, prostate, and bulbo urethral glands of the stallion.

Adrenal corticosteroids — Hormones produced by the adrenal cortex (e.g., cortisol), frequently in response to stress.

Agalactia — Failure to produce milk postpartum.

Allantoic cavity — Fluid-filled placental cavity between the allanto-chorion and the amnionic placental membranes.

Allantoic fluid — Fluid that fills the allantoic cavity and acts as a protective cushion around the fetus.

Altrenogest — Synthetic progesterone (Regu-Mate®).

Amnion — White placental membrane surrounding the fetus.

Amnionic cavity — Fluid-filled, placental space or cavity between the developing foal and the amnionic membrane.

Anemic — Blood condition in which the concentration of hemoglobin (and frequently the concentration of red blood cells as well) is below normal levels.

Angel slippers — Membranous pads that cover the unborn foal's hooves and protect the soft tissues of the mare's reproductive tract from the foal's hoof edges during development and delivery.

Angular limb deformity — A limb deformity characterized by a deviation in the frontal plane.

Anthelminitics — Compounds that expel and/or kill intestinal parasites.

Artificial insemination — Replacing the normal copulatory act between two animals by manually collecting semen from the stallion and then placing it (usually transvaginally) directly into the mare's uterus.

Barren mare — A mare that failed to establish a viable pregnancy the previous breeding season and that is now not pregnant.

Breeding season — The natural equine breeding season occurs during the spring and summer when day length is long. In response to increasing day length mares begin to cycle. Mares are referred to as seasonally polyestrus, long-day breeders.

Caesarean section — Surgical delivery of a foal across the uterine and abdominal walls.

Caslick's — Procedure in which the edges of the vulvar lips are surgically cut, then sewn together from the top of the vulva to part way down its length so that the vulvar lips will heal together to form a protective barrier between the outside air and contaminates and the interior structures of the mare's reproductive tract.

Cervix — A narrow tubo muscular structure in mares that connects the vaginal and uterine lumens. It is composed of an external vaginal opening (external os), a straight tubular body, and an internal uterine opening (internal os). During diestrus and pregnancy the cervix is tightly closed to prevent outside contamination and invading organisms from entering the uterine lumen.

Clitoris — Female organ homologous with the male's penis, located just within the ventral commissure of the mare's vulva.

Clubfoot — Acquired hyperflexion of the coffin joint.

Conception — Successful fertilization of the mare's oocyte with a stallion's spermatozoa to form an entirely new individual.

Chorion — Red, velvety placental membrane that directly attaches to the mare's uterus via thousands of interlocking/ interdigitating microvilli to facilitate nutrient, waste, and oxygen exchange between the fetal and maternal blood circulations.

Colic — Abdominal pain.

Colitis — Inflammation of the colon, frequently resulting in diarrhea.

Colostrum — First milk produced by the mare at foaling, which is rich in protective antibodies that the foal needs to ingest as soon as possible during the first 24 hours of its life to receive the humoral immunity that will protect it for the first few months until its own immune system reaches competency.

Conjunctivitis — Inflammation and frequent swelling of the mucous membrane tissues lining the inner surface of the eyelids.

Congenital effect — A defect or abnormality that develops in utero.

Contracted tendons — Usually manifested as a flexural deformity in the newborn, and sometimes fast-growing foals, in which the limb bones elongate faster than the flexor tendons, resulting in a relative contracture of the limb in a flexed position.

Corpus luteum — Ovarian structure that forms post ovulation from the cells that previously lined the ovulated follicle. The corpus luteum produces progesterone.

Cryptorchid — A stallion with an undescended testis.

Cycling — A mare undergoing the normal transitions through the estrous cycle (proestrus-estrus-metestrus-diestrus) that is ovulating in association with her estrus periods.

Diestrus — Period of the mare's estrous cycle that is characterized by a corpus luteum on the ovary, lack of receptivity to the stallion, and production of the hormone progesterone.

Double ovulation — Two ovulations that occur within the same estrus period.

Dummy foal — A foal suffering from hypoxic ischemic encephalopathy, previously known as neonatal maladjustment syndrome. Affected foals can have a poor suckling reflex, be disoriented, and even have seizures. Frequently these foals also are septicemic due to failure of passive transfer. Dummy foals are believed to have been oxygen deprived during birth.

Dysmature — Foal born small, thin, and premature in appearance, but after a longer than average gestational length (i.e., more than 350 days).

Dystocia — Difficult delivery of a foal.

Early embryonic loss — Failure of an equine embryo to continue to develop and survive past the first 30-plus days of gestation.

Edema — Swelling of any body part due to collection of fluid in the intercellular spaces of the tissues.

Embryo — An organism in the earliest stage of development.

Endometritis — Inflammation of the lining of the uterus, frequently due to either an infection or a chemical irritant.

Endotoxin — A toxin produced and retained by bacterial cells and released only by destruction or death of the cells.

Enema — Infusion of fluid into the rectum for cleansing or other therapeutic purposes.

Enteritis — Inflammation of the intestines.

Entropion — An abnormality seen in newborn foals where the lower eyelid and eyelashes are inverted and touching the eye's surface.

Epididymis — An oblong organ attached to each testis. Its function is to aid in maturation and storage of spermatozoa.

Equine chorionic gonadotropin — Hormone produced by the equine placenta's endometrial cups between days 40 and 90-plus of gestation.

Equine Viral Arteritis — Viral disease of horses causing respiratory disease, conjunctivitis, abortion, and limb and fascial edema.

Estrus — Period of the estrous cycle during which the mare is receptive to being bred and has an ovulatory follicle(s) present on the ovary that is producing large amounts of estrogen. Also referred to as "heat."

Failure of passive transfer — Failure of the newborn foal to ingest adequate amounts of good quality colostrum within the first 24 hours of life, resulting in the foal's being extremely susceptible to infection due to a lack of circulating antibodies.

Fertilization — The union of a spermatazoa with an oocyte.

Fetal diarrhea — Term referring to the presence of meconium (first feces) in the amnionic fluid surrounding the foal within the amnion at birth, accepted as a sign of fetal stress.

Fetal membranes — The placenta.

Fetus — The unborn, developing individual. In horses, this term refers to the developing foal from day 40 of gestation until term.

Flehman — Characteristic exaggerated lip curling demonstrated by horses (stallions and geldings especially) typically after sniffing urine or a mare's genitalia, but also might be seen in horses in pain.

Flexural deformity — A syndrome of flexor tendon disorders characterized by hyper flexion and inability to extend a joint or area of the leg.

Foal heat — The first postpartum estrus that typically begins three to 10 days post-foaling with the first post-partum ovulation occurring typically seven to 14 days post foaling.

Follicle — Ovarian structure containing an oocyte. Mares generally ovulate follicles that are between 35 mm and 55 mm in diameter. The follicle produces estrogen and is the dominant ovarian structure during estrus.

Fraternal twins — Twins that arise from two different pairings of oocytes and sperm cells.

Gestation — The period of time between conception and birth.

Gravid — Pregnant.

Gut closure — Cessation of the neonatal intestine's ability to absorb immunoglobulins (antibodies) from ingested colostrum across the intestinal wall and into the foal's bloodstream. Gut closure occurs at an increasing rate starting at birth and is complete when the foal is approximately 24 hours old.

Heat — Estrus. Period of receptivity to being bred by a stallion.

Histotroph — Essential uterine milk produced by the endometrial glands; thought to nourish the developing conceptus and fetus until the placenta is fully established.

Hormone — Glandular chemical secretion produced by one organ or part of the body and carried in the bloodstream to a target organ to stimulate or retard its function.

Horsing — Mare demonstrating behavioral signs of estrus.

Hymen — Membranous fold that (when present) partly or completely closes the vaginal orifice in a virgin animal.

Identical twins — Twins that result from an abnormal cleavage of one individual zygote arising from the pairing of a single oocyte and spermatazoa so that two separate individuals arise from what was initially a single cell.

Immune compromise — Suppression of the function of the immune system.

Immunoglobulin — A protein molecule functioning as a specific antibody.

Immunoglobulin G (IgG) — The most abundant class of immunoglobulins, they provide immunity to bacteria, viruses, parasites, and fungi that have a blood-borne dissemination.

Impaction — A blockage of the intestinal lumen with ingesta, parasites, or foreign material (sand, cloth, etc.).

Interestrus interval — Time between heat periods in a mare.

Jaundice — Yellow pigmentation of the skin and/or the sclera and mucous membranes caused by high levels of biliruben in the blood. Also referred to as icterus.

Joint ill — A condition, usually seen in young foals, where one or more joints becomes infected, swollen, and inflamed after being seeded with a blood-born organism (usually bacterial).

Lactation — The production of milk.

Laminitis — Inflammation of the sensitive lamina of the equine foot. Causes acute and chronic lameness, and if severe enough can result in separation of the hoof wall from the underlying structures of the foot. In extreme conditions the coffin bone of the foot can rotate down through the sole of the foot or the entire hoof wall can become detached and the horse's foot sinks completely out of its supportive attachments. Also referred to as founder.

Libido — Sexual desire.

Live cover — Natural mating, whether at pasture or in hand, of a stallion and a mare.

Maiden mare — Mare that has never had a foal; also can refer to a mare that has never been bred.

Mammary gland — Glandular tissue that produces milk.

Mastitis — Inflammation (usually due to infection) of the mammary gland.

Masturbation — Self manipulation of the penis with or without the occurrence of ejaculation.

Maternal recognition of pregnancy — Point during pregnancy when the embryo signals the mother that it is present, thereby blocking production of prostaglandin by the uterus, which would otherwise terminate the pregnancy and return the mare to estrus. In the mare this occurs on approximately day 14 post-ovulation.

Meconium — The dark-colored feces produced in the intestines during fetal life and present in the rectum and colon at birth.

Meconium impaction — A large accumulation of meconium within the foal's rectum or small colon that the foal has difficulty passing.

Milk let down — Process by which the mare is stimulated by the presence of her foal and its suckling action to release oxytocin, which in turn acts on smooth muscle cells within the mammary gland, causing them to contract and squeeze milk out of the glandular tissue and on down into the duct system so that it can be suckled from the teat and ingested by the foal.

Multiparous — Having born two or more offspring in separate pregnancies.

Naso-gastric tube — Tube placed into the horse's nostrils, through the pharynx, into the esophagus, and down into the stomach. Used to administer large volumes of oral medications and intestinal lubricants directly into a horse's stomach. It is also used as a means of providing an escape route for built-up ingest and gas from the stomach in colicking horses. Horses cannot normally vomit, and severe gas buildup and ingesta can result in a gastric rupture.

Neonate — Newborn.

Nurse mare — Mare used as a foster mother to adopt a foal and nurse and rear it when its own mother cannot do so.

Oocyte — Cell in the ovary, derived from primordial germ cells, that becomes the haploid progenitor female cell that when fertilized by a male's spermatazoa will go on to form a new individual.

Open mare — Mare that is not pregnant because she was not bred the previous breeding season.

Ovaries — Paired female gonads, contain the oocytes and produce estrogen (ovarian follicle) and progesterone (ovarian corpus luteum).

Ovulation — The rupture of the ovulatory follicle through the ovarian ovulation follicle and the release of the oocyte.

Palpation — Examination by touch or pressure of the hand over an organ or body area, as a diagnostic aid. In mares the reproductive tract is examined by palpating it through the mare's rectal wall.

Parturition — Giving birth.

Patent urachus — Failure of the umbilical urachus to close completely after birth, resulting in urine being dribbled directly from the bladder through the umbilical cord remnant. The presence of a patent urachus also provides bacteria ready access to the foal's bladder and bloodstream.

Pathogen — Microorganism or substance capable of causing disease.

Pathogenic bacteria — Bacteria capable of causing uterine infection in mares.

Pathology — Study of disease; term also used to refer to the mechanisms and or results of the development of a disease condition.

Peritonitis — Inflammation of the peritoneal (abdominal) cavity and lining usually as a result of chemical irritation or infection.

Photoperiod — Period of time each day that an animal is exposed to either natural or artificial light.

Pitting edema — Edematous swelling (usually under the skin) that holds an indentation mark if pressed with a fingertip.

Placenta — Membranes of fetal origin that provide a point of attachment and exchange of nutrients, oxygen, and waste products between the maternal and fetal bloodstreams in the pregnant uterus. The placenta also functions as an endocrine organ and produces several hormones that help regulate pregnancy.

Placentitis — Inflammation of the placenta usually due to a fungal or bacterial organism.

Pneumonia — Inflammation of the lungs caused by viruses, bacteria, or chemical agents and foreign bodies.

Pneumovagina — Air-filled vaginal cavity usually as a direct result of aspiration of air through the vulvar lips in mares predisposed to this condition due to poor vulvar and or perineal conformation.

Postpartum — After birth.

Premature — A foal born before day 320 (gestational age) with immature physical characteristics, such as low birth weight, weakness, short and silky hair coat, etc.

Progestagens — Hormones produced by the equine placenta that have similar effects as progesterone and are responsible for maintaining the equine pregnancy after approximately days 120 to 150 of the gestation.

Progesterone — Ovarian steroid produced by the corpus luteum that stimulates changes in the uterus to support and maintain a developing pregnancy, maintains the uterus in a quiescent state, and keeps the cervix tightly closed. High levels of progesterone produced during pregnancy and diestrus normally cause the mare to reject the advances of a teaser.

Progressive motility — Percentage of spermatozoa traveling in a straight line.

Prolactin — Hormone produced by the pituitary gland that promotes and maintains lactation and is also believed to be responsible for stimulating maternal behavior.

Prostaglandin — Hormone produced by a number of tissues and liberated during a number of pathologic conditions, causes uterine contractions and destruction of a mature corpus luteum.

Puberty — Period in which the stallion first becomes capable of sexual reproduction.

Pyometra — Rare condition in the mare in which there is a large accumulation of pus in the uterus. Abnormalities in the mare's cervix after trauma or otherwise that do not permit drainage of fluid and debris from the uterine lumen are believed to predispose a mare to this condition.

Red-bag delivery — Premature placental separation during foaling in which the allantochorion fails to rupture and the chorionic surface begins to detach from the uterus. There is no "breaking of the waters," and the red chorion appears at the vulva rather than the white amnion. Premature separation of the placenta threatens to disrupt the foal's oxygen supply prior to its delivery, and it is vital that the allantochorion be ruptured manually to deter any further separation and that the foal be delivered as quickly as possible.

Retained placenta — A term used to describe any placenta that has not been expelled in its entirety within three hours of the delivery of the foal.

Rhinopneumonitis — Herpesvirus infection with EHV I or IV resulting in upper-respiratory symptoms in affected horses. Also used to refer to EHV I in terms of causing equine abortions.

Semen — Stallion's ejaculate comprising sperm cells originating from the testicles and seminal plasma originating from the accessory sex glands.

Septicemia — Systemic disease caused by the presence of pathogenic organisms in the body, sometimes used to refer to infections where pathogenic organisms and their toxins have gained access to the bloodstream.

Shedder — Infected individual who is releasing an infectious agent into the environment.

Short cycle — The premature termination of the diestrus period and the hastened return of the mare to estrus.

Singleton pregnancy — Pregnancy during which the mare is carrying only one viable embryo or fetus.

Sperm reserves — Reservoir of sperm stored in the tail of the epidymis, ductus deferens, and ampullae.

Spermatozoa — Specialized male haploid progenitor cell derived from primordial germ cells and produced in the male's testicles. Combines with an oocyte during fertilization to form a new individual.

Spermatozoal concentration — Number of spermatozoa per milliliter of semen.

Strangulating intestinal colic — Pathological intestinal lesion in which the blood supply of a portion of the intestinal tract has been cut off due to the intestine twisting back on itself along its mesentery, a lipoma wrapping itself around the intestine, thrombosis of the mesenteric blood supply secondary to a larval migration, etc.

Tail head — The root of the tail where the tail emerges from the base of the spine.

Tease — Process of exposing a mare to a male to see whether she is receptive to being bred.

Teaser — A male horse (stallion or gelding with good libido) that is used to stimulate a mare to see if she is receptive to being bred.

Theriogenology — Study of reproduction.

Thirty-day heat — Term used to refer to the first estrus period following the foal heat, which usually occurs approximately 30 days after the mare has foaled.

Titer — Measured level of antibodies in the blood against a given antigen.

Torsion — Act of turning or twisting of a structure around its long axis.

Trimester — One third of the length of gestation.

Twin reduction — Term that loosely applies to any one of a number of techniques by which one member of a twin pregnancy is destroyed, leaving a single viable embryo or fetus to carry to term.

Twitch — A restraint device applied to the upper lip of a horse.

Ultrasound — Process by which sound waves are generated by a crystal and pass into tissues where they are reflected back in different intensities depending upon the density of the reflecting tissue or medium. A transducer receives the reflected sound waves and converts the various intensities into an image that can be used to interpret the structure of the tissues being examined.

Umbilical cord — Structure connecting the placenta with the fetus.

Unilateral twins — Twin embryos that fixate and implant side by side in the same uterine horn.

Urachus — Tube structure that allows excretion of urine from the foal's bladder to the allantoic cavity while the foal is in utero.

Urine pooling — Condition in which urine runs forward into the vagina during urination and collects in the floor of the cranial vagina adjacent to and sometimes submerging the cervix. The presence of the urine results in a chronic vaginitis, cervicitis, and endometritis due to the chemical irritation of the urine. Urine pooling can occur secondary to a poor, sloping vaginal and pelvic conformations, injury, and or relaxation and stretching of the vaginal structures during estrus, late pregnancy, and/or post foaling.

Uterine involution — Postpartum process during which the uterus returns to its pre-pregnant size and shape and the endometrial lining recovers and regenerates to be able to support a new pregnancy. A very rapid process in the normal mare.

Uterine lavage — The act of flushing the uterine lumen with fluid to retrieve an embryo or flush out accumulated fluid and inflammatory debris.

Uterus — Muscular and glandular organ of pregnancy; in the mare it is a T-shaped organ made up of two uterine horns (left and right) that form the crossbar of the "T" and a uterine body that forms the base of the "T."

Uveitis — Inflammation of the inner structures of the eye (in the horse also referred to as periodic opthalmia or moon blindness).

Vaginal speculum — Instrument used to view the interior of the vaginal lumen and the external cervical os.

Valgus — An angular deformity resulting in deviation of the leg laterally (toward the outside).

Varus — An angular deformity resulting in deviation of the leg medially (toward the inside).

Venereal — Related to or resulting from sexual intercourse.

Vulva — The external female genitalia, the opening to the female urogenital tract bordered by the vulvar lips or labia.

Waxing — Accumulation of a waxy secretion on the mare's teat endings typically when she is within 24 hours of foaling.

White blood cells — Cells in the blood stream that are part of the body's immunologic defense, neutrophil white blood cells will leave the blood stream and migrate to areas of cellular damage and infection as part of the cellular defense mechanisms.

White muscle disease — Muscle cell deterioration and death due to body deficiencies in selenium and or vitamin E; can result in weakness and even death of the neonate if the cardiac muscle is severely affected.

Winking — Act by which the mare everts and briefly visibly exteriorizes her clitoris. Mares commonly will do this after urinating and the behavior is exaggerated and also seen in direct response to stimulation by a teaser when a mare is in estrus or heat.

Wry Muzzle — Congenital deformity in which a foal's muzzle is twisted to one side. In severe cases the misshapen head can cause a dystocia.

Yolk sac — Highly vascular umbilical vesicle enveloping the nutritive yolk of an early embryo.

Zygote — The initial, single, diploid-fertilized cell formed by the union of the oocyte and spermatozoa.

Index

Photo Credits

BROODMARE CARE

Christine M. Schweizer, DVM, 19, 23, 26, 48, 62, 74, 85; 188; Anne M. Eberhardt, 20, 30, 40, 50, 60, 159, 161; 164; 166; 167; 174; 185; 187; 193, 217; 219; 221; 225; Barbara D. Livingston, 227; Arnd Bronkhorst, 92; Paula da Silva, 109; *The Horse* magazine, 129; *The Blood-Horse* magazine, 144; Barry Ball, 150, 213; Robert Hillman, 190; Skip Dickstein, 195; Christina S. Cable, DVM, 210.

FOAL CARE

Anne M. Eberhardt, 232, 242-43, 250-51, 254, 259, 262, 264, 273, 277, 300; John Wyatt, 236; *The Blood-Horse* magazine, 239, 269, 281; Bonnie Nance, 248; Barbara D. Livingston, 280, 282.

STALLION CARE

Anne M. Eberhardt, 315, 316, 317, 318, 325, 331, 334, 342, 343, 361; E.L. Squires, 316, 319, 320, 326, 328, 348, 351, 354, 355; Barbara D. Livingston, 323, 325, 333, 335, 345, 347, 350, 351; *The Horse* magazine, 330; Kendra Bond, 337; Suzie Picou Oldham, 339; U.S. Trotting Association, 344; Jonathan F. Pycock, 358.

Photo wells: Christine M. Schweizer, DVM; Robert Hillman, DVM; Barry Ball; Barrie Britt, DVM; Katherine Houpt, DVM; Anne M. Eberhardt; Michael A. Ball, DVM; Barbara D. Livingston; Cristina S. Cable, DVM; E.L. Squires.

Illustrations: Robin Peterson, Colorado State University (Stallion Care).
Cover photographs: Suzie Picou Oldham, Anne M. Eberhardt.

About the Authors

Christina S. Cable, DVM, Diplomate ACVS, operates a specialty equine practice, Early Winter Equine, in Lansing, New York, with her husband, veterinarian Michael A. Ball. Cable received her undergraduate degree in biology and her veterinary medicine degree from the University of Georgia. She completed post-doctoral work at The New York State College of Veterinary Medicine at Cornell University, where she developed a special interest in foals, worked as a veterinary surgeon, and taught lameness and surgery.

Christine M. Schweizer, DVM, Diplomate ACT, is on the faculty of the New York State College of Veterinary Medicine at Cornell, where she is a lecturer and clinician in the small and large animal clinics. Schweizer received her bachelor's degree in animal science from Cornell University and her degree in veterinary medicine from the New York State College of Veterinary Medicine at Cornell. After graduating, she completed a residency program at Cornell in theriogenology (reproductive medicine). She spent part of her residency at Hagyard-Davidson-McGee equine hospital (now Hagyard Equine Medical Institute) in Lexington, Kentucky.

E.L. Squires, PhD, is a professor in the department of biomedical sciences at Colorado State University. He has a master's degree in reproductive physiology from West Virginia University and a PhD in endocrinology/reproductive physiology from the University of Wisconsin. Squires is supervisor of the equine reproduction laboratory, and his clinical duties include reproductive evaluation of mares and stallions, commercial embryo transfer, and freezing stallion semen. A pioneer in the field of embryo transfer, Squires directs the Preservation of Equine Genetics, a program focused on developing assisted reproductive techniques for old mares and stallions.